W9-AOZ-083

Minority Students
in East Asia

Routledge Series in Schools and Schooling in Asia

SERIES EDITOR: KERRY J. KENNEDY

1. Minority Students in East Asia
Government Policies, School Practices
and Teacher Responses
Edited by JoAnn Phillion, Ming Tak
Hue and Yuxiang Wang

Minority Students in East Asia

Government Policies, School Practices, and Teacher Responses

Edited by JoAnn Phillion, Ming Tak Hue, and Yuxiang Wang

Routledge
Taylor & Francis Group
New York   London

First published 2011
by Routledge
711 Third Avenue, New York, NY 10017

Simultaneously published in the UK
by Routledge
2 Park Square, Milton Park, Abingdon, Oxon OX14 4RN

Routledge is an imprint of the Taylor & Francis Group, an informa business

© 2011 Taylor & Francis

The right of JoAnn Phillion, Ming Tak Hue and Yuxiang Wang to be identified as the authors of the editorial material, and of the authors for their individual chapters, has been asserted in accordance with sections 77 and 78 of the Copyright, Designs and Patents Act 1988.

Typeset in Sabon by IBT Global.
Printed and bound in the United States of America on acid-free paper by IBT Global.

Library of Congress Cataloging-in-Publication Data
   Minority students in East Asia : government policies, school practices, and teacher responses / [edited by] JoAnn Phillion, Ming Tak Hue, Yuxiang Wang.
   p. cm. — (Routledge series on schools and schooling in Asia)
   Includes bibliographical references and index.
   1. Children of minorities—Education—East Asia.   2. Children of immigrants—Education—East Asia.   3. Multicultural education—East Asia.   4. Education and state—East Asia.   5. Ethnicity—East Asia.   I. Phillion, JoAnn.   II. Hue, Ming-tak.   III. Wang, Yuxiang.
   LC3737.E18M56 2011
   370.117095—dc22
   2010052029

ISBN13: 978-0-415-88839-4 (hbk)
ISBN13: 978-0-203-81331-7 (ebk)

Contents

PART II
Minority Students in Hong Kong

PART III
Minority Students in Japan, South Korea, and Taiwan

Figures

Tables

Series Editor's Note

The "Asian century" provides opportunities and challenges for the people of Asia as well as those in the West. The success of many of Asia's young people in schooling often leads educators in the West to try and emulate Asian school practices. Yet these practices are culturally embedded. One of the key issues to be taken on by this series, therefore, is to provide Western policymakers and academics with insights into these culturally embedded practices in order to assist better understanding of them outside of specific cultural contexts.

There is vast diversity as well as many disparities within Asia. This is a fundamental issue, which is addressed in this series by making these diversities and disparities the subject of investigation. The "tiger" economies initially grabbed most of the media attention on Asian development, and more recently China has become the center of attention. Yet there are also very poor countries in the region, and their education systems seem unable to be transformed to meet new challenges. Pakistan is a case in point. Thus the whole of Asia will be seen as important for this series in order to address questions relevant not only to developed countries but also to developing countries. In other words, the series will take a "whole of Asia" approach.

Asia can no longer be considered in isolation. It is as subject to the forces of globalization, migration, and transnational movements as other regions of the world. Yet the diversity of cultures, religions, and social practices in Asia means that responses to these forces are not predictable. This series, therefore, is interested in identifying the ways tradition and modernity interact to produce distinctive contexts for schools and schooling in an area of the world that impacts across the globe.

Against this background, I am pleased to welcome this book to the *Routledge Series on Schools and Schooling in Asia*.

Kerry J. Kennedy
Series Editor
Routledge Series on Schools and Schooling in Asia

1 Introduction
Minority Students in East Asia

JoAnn Phillion and Yuxiang Wang

OVERVIEW OF THE BOOK

In *Minority Students in East Asia: Government Policies, School Practices, and Teacher Responses,* edited by JoAnn Phillion, Ming Tak Hue, and Yuxiang Wang, the chapter authors discuss their research on the experiences of minority students in schools from the elementary grades to higher education in mainland China, Hong Kong, Japan, South Korea, and Taiwan. The educational issues of minority students are often neglected in the literature and in practice, and this issue is emerging as a worldwide phenomenon. Due to the focus on economy and trade, social and educational conditions that have resulted from globalization, particularly issues pertaining to the education, language, and other human rights of minority groups, receive less attention. Moreover, in many parts of East Asia, countries traditionally view themselves as single-ethnicity countries and do not have a strong agenda on minority rights. Although there are specific provisions in the law for the preservation of minority rights, these are often ignored or only partially implemented in practice.

The purpose of the book is to highlight key educational conditions for specific minority populations in specific regions in East Asia. The books addresses the following themes: government policies on the protection of the language and educational rights of minorities, school practices and teacher perspectives on minorities, identity construction in terms of language and culture, national versus ethnic identity, teacher education issues, and parental educational concerns, among others. As the authors come from a variety of backgrounds, they also bring in unique theoretical orientations to understand minority educational issues. This is a key strength of the volume.

To investigate a wide selection of topics and to develop an eclectic array of perspectives, the editors drew on a diverse array of scholars with expertise in the geographic regions of East Asia where they engage in research and in the particular topics they investigate. The authors range from being well-established experts in their respective research fields (e.g., Kerry Kennedy on multiculturalism in Hong Kong and Celeste Yuen on students from mainland China in Hong Kong schools) to emerging scholars working on novel issues in their newly developing fields (e.g., Jungmin Lee on children of international marriages and children of migrant workers in South Korea and Tae Umino on the language learning of minorities in Japan). These authors were chosen to meet a key goal of this book: to provide a contextualized understanding of the educational issues of minority students by discussing their experiences.

The authors begin the chapters with a brief statement of their personal engagement with their project. They document specific educational issues faced by minorities by discussing government policies pertaining to the education of minority students in terms of retaining their native language, learning of new languages, cultural adaptation, psychological adjustment, and preparation for higher education, among other concerns. The disparity between government policies and the experiences of students in schools and educational outcomes is described based on the research conducted by the authors and extensive reviews of relevant literature. The methods of research and analysis are briefly discussed. Issues such as loss of first language, low teacher expectations, neglect of culture in the curriculum, early drop-out rates due to grade placement and retention in grade, and low attendance in higher education are discussed. The findings are interpreted in a variety of ways depending on the theoretical foundation used by the author: for example, some link their discussion to theories on multicultural education, compare these to the educational landscape of minorities in the US or elsewhere, and give critiques using post-colonial theory, critical pedagogy theories, and globalization or other theories. The authors also provide recommendations or suggestions where appropriate.

There are different definitions of "minority students" in this book; the exact definition depends on the context and population under investigation. For the specific purposes of this book, in mainland China, the term refers to people from one of the 55 different minority groups; in Hong Kong, it refers to immigrants from mainland China and elsewhere; in South Korea, it refers to those from families with one or both parents who are not Korean or overseas workers from other countries; in Japan, it refers to immigrants; and in Taiwan, it refers to those from indigenous families. Linking the discussions on specific minority students are overarching concerns about social justice, equality, and equal educational opportunities. These concerns are expressed in questions that relate the chapters: What are the school experiences of minority students in these countries? Have their language and cultural rights, quality education, and equal education been protected by government policies? Are there any gaps between government policies and practices? How do teachers respond to the needs of these students?

Officially, many countries in East Asia deal with minority issues by claiming to adhere to some form of what can be called multiculturalism and by embracing multicultural education. China, a country featured in this book, claims that it is a multicultural and multiethnic nation where different peoples from different ethnic groups can live together harmoniously. China's constitution (1982) stipulates that the language, cultural, and ethnic rights of minority groups should be protected. Although policymakers and educators have made efforts to provide culturally relevant materials such as Tibetan Cultural Readers (Wan, Nima, & Luo, 1999) to Tibetan students, provide multicultural education courses to pre-service and in-service teachers in northwestern China, and conduct comparative studies on multicultural education in China and in Western countries, researchers and educators have not reached a consensus on whether the majority Han population needs multicultural education (Bahry, Darkhor, & Luo, 2009). Multicultural education also raises concerns about stability and unity, China's national priorities (as multicultural education challenges nationalism), national identity, Han privilege, and Han hegemony over the minority groups in China.

In Hong Kong, the language, culture, and education rights of minority students are guaranteed by law. However, school administrators and teachers have limited skills and knowledge in providing culturally relevant teaching methods to minority students in Hong Kong. Japan also claims to be a multiethnic and multicultural country because immigrants continue to move to Japan, but teaching these immigrants in school is a challenge to the teachers. Many teachers incorrectly believe that multicultural education is a panacea for all "problems of discrimination" (Murphy-Shigematsu, 2003). However, Murphy-Shigematsu found that teachers do not know how to integrate what immigrants bring to class or how to foster pride in their ethnic and cultural identity.

In Taiwan, although the Act of Aboriginal Education was approved in 1998, "nationally standardized school curricula and textbooks merely reinforced national Chinese identity and Chinese themes of patriotism while excluding the voices and experiences of different social, cultural, and ethnic groups in Taiwan" (Su, 2007, p. 206). In South Korea, to guarantee the equal education rights of undocumented children, the South Korean government created laws and established guidelines to promote multicultural education in schools. While the rights of minority students are guaranteed as human rights, teachers and administrators do not know how to assist undocumented students and how to implement multicultural education in class.

Countries and regions in East Asia have developed policies to protect the rights of minority students. However, researchers and practitioners have discovered gaps between government policies and practices. Minority students lose their home language and ethnic identity (Wang & Zhou, 2003); their drop-out rates are higher than those of mainstream students (Postiglione, 1999); and the reproduction of mainstream ideology through school curriculum and the exclusion of minority beliefs, culture, and knowledge from school textbooks have made minority people feel that state school education is not relevant to their daily life. As such, minority students become uninterested in the school curriculum and class instruction (Qian, 2007; Su, 2007) and drop out of school.

Researchers have documented a growing need to examine government policy, determine the gaps between government policy and practice, and critically explore the factors that create these gaps. There is also a need to listen to teachers' views about minority students; their interpretation of the language, culture, and identity of minority students; and their teaching of minority students. The goal of the book is to address this growing need by examining the experiences of minority students in school from the perspectives of government policies, school practices, and teacher responses.

CONTENTS OF THE BOOK

The book consists of three parts, aside from the introduction and the conclusion. Part I, entitled "Minority Students in Mainland China," includes five chapters that examine the educational experience of Hui, Tibetan, and Mongolian minority students; the teaching methods of their teachers; and the gaps between policy and practice. Part II, entitled "Minority Students in Hong Kong," consists of five chapters that focus on policy analysis and the prospects for multiculturalism in Hong Kong, the school experiences of mainland Chinese students and cross-border Chinese students in Hong Kong schools, and the possibility of providing culturally responsive teaching and counseling to minority students. In Part III, entitled "Minority Students in Japan, South Korea, and Taiwan," researchers and teacher educators discuss the minority policy and practice and the experiences of minority students, focusing on their language, culture, and identity issues.

In Chapter 2, entitled "Language, Culture, and Identity: Experiences of Hui Students in Eastern China," Yuxiang Wang explores the experiences of Hui students in school in eastern China; how their teachers interpret their beliefs, culture, and knowledge and construct their identity; and the influence of their school experiences on their identity. Based on the findings from his research, Wang calls for multicultural education to be provided to in-service teachers, pre-service teachers, policymakers, curriculum designers, and school administrators so that all stakeholders can learn to respect and value minority culture and knowledge and to integrate them into school textbooks, school curricula, and class instruction. To compare his findings in China with those in the US, Wang examines the discriminatory language policies and practices that led to the academic failure of minority students in the US, the role of native language in the cognitive development and long-term academic achievement of minority students, and the influence of their cultural differences and learning in school. This review discusses the findings on the cultural recognition and identity construction of two Hui girls in eastern China.

In Chapter 3, entitled "Why Are Hui Minority Girls Dropping Out of School in China?" Ying Sun, Wei Yu, and Yuhua Ye examine the reasons why Hui girls in Gansu Province drop out of school. The findings of the study indicate that poverty is the major reason why Hui girls drop out and often end up as manual laborers. The second reason is the lack of consistency between the school curriculum and Hui culture and family expectations, causing Hui girls to lose interest in schoolwork. The third reason is the early marriage of Hui girls. This chapter echoes Wang's chapter in that the authors also call for multicultural education and the inclusion of Hui beliefs, culture, and knowledge in school curriculum and class instruction. The authors focus on the unbalanced economic development in China, the national school curriculum, the social environment that discriminates against girls, and the views of Hui parents regarding the education of their daughters.

In Chapter 4, entitled "Multiculturalism in China: Conflicting Discourses in Universities," Zhenzhou Zhao discusses ethnic minority college students in China. Preferential policies that set lower admission requirements for minorities make higher education a controversial terrain. The study is based on fieldwork at three institutions of higher education attended by minority students. The author explores how universities build multicultural environments for students from diverse backgrounds and compares the institutional framework, including university policy and structure, with daily life discourse on campus. The purpose of the study is to examine the effectiveness of institutional strategies for supporting ethnic border-crossing in the university and to discover the reasons for the inconsistency between the institutional discourse and the daily life discourse. Gaps between state discourses and school and college practice demonstrate that the purpose of state education and higher education is to reproduce mainstream culture and build state identity. Based on her findings and a review of relevant literature, Zhao calls for respect and value for minority culture and knowledge in universities in China

In Chapter 5, entitled "School Life and Ethnic Identity: A Case of Tibetan Student Narrative," Zhiyong Zhu presents the diaries of Tibetan students attending middle school in a Han-dominated region in eastern China and shows how mainstream Han ideology is reproduced through mainstream Han curriculum and class instruction, how national identity is assigned to them, and how they construct their own identity. Zhu reviews the dynamic nature of the ethnic identity of Tibetan intellectuals and the historical development and cultural significance of modern school-based Tibetan-language education in Songpan County in Sichuan Province. The author also discusses a proposal to integrate Tibetan and Chinese culture into the school curricula.

In Chapter 6, entitled "Constructing Tibetan Students' National and Ethnic Identities in Tibetan School Education," Zhiyan Teng explores the influence of state policy and school curriculum on the construction of the national and ethnic identities of Tibetan students. Teng reviews the different views on ethnic minority and national identities and scholarly arguments about the possibility of integrating the minority identity within the Chinese nation. The author also examines the language rights of the minority, stipulated in the Constitution and Compulsory Education Law, and bilingual education practice in China. The findings indicate tension in the identity construction of Tibetan students between the national identity imposed on them and the ethnic identity they assert through the representation of Tibetan culture in the school curriculum. The study also discusses the ways in which Tibetan students construct their national and ethnic identities in school.

In Chapter 7, entitled "Critical Perspective on New Arrival Children from Mainland China in Hong Kong: Government Policies, School Practices, and Teacher Responses," Stella Chong explores the migration of new arrival children (NAC) to Hong Kong and the effects of that migration on democratic education in Hong Kong. The responses of schools and their administrators and teachers are critically examined to determine how they consider the linguistic and cultural backgrounds of NAC students and how they provide quality education for these students. The goal of Chong's work is to effect change on future policies, school practices, and teacher education in Hong Kong. She reviews literature on the experiences of NAC in Hong Kong schools, particularly on how they belong, their academic achievement, and their self-esteem. Using critical pedagogy as a framework, Chong discusses the factors facilitating the adjustment of NAC to Hong Kong society. She points out the similarities and differences of issues between these students and minority students in the West.

In Chapter 8, entitled "Culturally Relevant Counseling Practices for New Immigrant Students," Betty C. Eng discusses the counseling needs of Chinese immigrant students in Hong Kong. She proposes culturally relevant counseling and emphasizes the importance of cultural awareness in reconstructing counseling theories and practices. Eng reviews the literature on mental health issues of new immigrant students (NISs). According to Eng, although children from China are considered Chinese, they have special needs that are different from those of their Chinese counterparts in Hong Kong. Thus, tension and conflict arise between these two communities. Issues of identity, culture, language, and sense of belonging are the common concerns addressed through counseling. Eng also explores the multiple identities shaped by a "one country, two systems" policy, a Confucius heritage culture, and an indigenous storytelling.

In Chapter 9, entitled "Building a Culturally Responsive School: Cross-Cultural Experiences of Ethnic Minority Students in Hong Kong Schools," Ming Tak Hue examines the views of teachers on the cross-cultural experience of ethnic minority students. The study shows that the diverse learning needs of ethnic minority students and their classroom behavior are culturally different from those of the majority of Hong Kong Chinese students. The study further reveals that despite some negative experiences reported by teachers and students, they eventually adopt a "culturally relative" approach in addressing the diverse needs of ethnic minority students. Hue argues that, to manage classroom diversity effectively, it is necessary for the school not only to develop culturally responsive approaches—in making sense of the classroom environment and supporting the learning of students who have different ethnic backgrounds—but also to create a connected classroom ecology where the diverse learning needs of ethnic minority students and their well-being can be supported in classrooms, schools, at home, and in communities. Two implications for the promotion of culturally responsive approaches to teaching and learning and pastoral care are discussed. Hue also reviews the experiences of minority students in mainstream schools in the West, focusing on their diverse needs, their difficulties in learning the language, and the economic insecurity of their families, and how these factors prevent them from achieving academic success and personal growth.

In Chapter 10, entitled "The 'Long March' toward Multiculturalism in Hong Kong: Supporting Ethnic Minority Students in a Confucian State," Kerry Kennedy provides a theoretical framework and policy context on the experiences of minority students in Hong Kong schools. He argues that cultural diversity is a feature of many societies, and responses to it vary; many Western countries have adopted liberal multiculturalism because it highlights the importance of individuals, including their values, languages, and cultures. However, this is not a universal response. Individualism can be considered a threat to the state, and thus cultural diversity has to be carefully managed within a framework determined by the state. The worst-case scenario is where cultural diversity is regarded to be such a threat that the state, or the individuals within the state, seeks to eliminate it altogether. However, these different responses do not exhaust the possibilities for responding to ethnic diversity. Kennedy examines the response of Hong Kong to ethnic minority students. His examination provides an insight into the way cultural diversity is regarded and responded to in a context where Chinese and Western and modern and ancient values influence society. This unique context provides insight into both theory and practice relating to cultural diversity and offers an explanation for new policies and their inability to meet the expressed needs of community groups.

In Chapter 11, entitled "Cross-Boundary Students in Hong Kong Schools: Education Provisions and School Experiences," Celeste Y. M. Yuen examines the experiences of cross-boundary students (CBSs) in Hong Kong. CBSs are students who live in mainland China but go to school in Hong Kong. Yuen finds that most of these students adapt well to the schools that enroll a large number of CBSs in terms of language, social activities, and academic achievement. However, some teachers claim that there are few differences between CBSs and Hong Kong students and thus use the same curriculum, homework, and teaching approaches for both groups. Her findings also indicate that parental involvement plays an important role in the survival of CBSs in Hong Kong schools academically, emotionally, and socially. Yuen discusses her findings and includes a review of related literature on the mainstream curriculum and instruction provided to cross-boundary students by monoculturally trained teachers. A one-size-fits-all pedagogical practice and few culturally relevant teaching methods cause minority students to fail academically. Yuen also reviews other factors that cause this low academic achievement, such as the educational levels of parents, their occupations, social networks, and home income.

In Chapter 12, entitled "Language Learning Experiences of International Students in Japan: Facilitating Access to Communities of Practice," Tae Umino discusses how international students, based on their narratives, learn Japanese by communicating with native Japanese speakers in community services. She contends that community services provide opportunities for international students to participate in various and meaningful communication with native Japanese speakers, which, in turn, provide opportunities for them not only to improve their spoken Japanese but also increase their understanding of Japanese culture. Umino reviews the literature on the role of communities of practice (COPs) in how international students learn the Japanese language. She uses situated learning theory (Wenger, 1998) to help explain learning as participation in social practices. She contends that language learning is not about acquiring the grammatical rules of a language but about developing a relationship with others through which language appropriateness, forms of expression, and cultural knowledge are acquired. She also reviews the factors, such as disparate power relations, hindering the language proficiency of international students in COPs and in classrooms.

In Chapter 13, entitled "Migrant Workers and International Marriage Minorities in South Korea," Jungmin Lee explores the views of teachers on issues related to children from international marriages and children from migrant worker families. She finds that the assimilative approach of teachers and their idea that there should be the same treatment of Korean children and children from the minority make it impossible to provide culturally relevant teaching to children from international marriage families. Lee discusses the South Korean government policies that protect the educational rights of children of foreign migrants and the policy of the Educational Support Plan for Children from Multicultural Families, established by the Korean Ministry of Education and Human Resources Development in 2006. However, there are large gaps between what is stipulated by law and what is practiced by government officials and school teachers because of the misunderstanding of the needs of children of undocumented foreign workers and international marriages and the lack of multicultural training for teachers.

In Chapter 14, entitled "From Assimilation to the Assertion of Subjectivity: Critiques of the Indigenous Education Policies in Taiwan," Dorothy I-ru Chen examines the education policy of indigenous people in Taiwan.

She argues that the policy is mostly assimilation oriented and serves mainstream ideology, politics, and economy. She proposes the voice of indigenous people to be included in the process of policy formation and the assertion of subjectivity in indigenous culture to be a key element in the education policy for indigenous people. Chen reviews Banks' (1994) category of two ideologies toward race and ethnicity in the world: an assimilation ideology and a cultural pluralism ideology. Banks proposed a multicultural ideology that promotes respect for, and the value of, minority culture and knowledge in school curriculum and instruction. Chen also reviews the historical development of indigenous policy and education in Taiwan. Although indigenous policy, laws, and the constitution stipulate the rights of indigenous people, gaps are reported in educational practices. Teachers are not familiar with indigenous culture and knowledge and how to integrate them into their teaching methods to meet the needs of indigenous students.

Finally, in "Conclusion: Where Does Multicultural Eduction in Asian Countries Lead?" Tak Cheung Chan summarizes the lessons from a review of the studies in earlier chapters and the implications of, and for, multicultural education. Chan discusses the major concerns of multicultural education in East Asia as expressed by the book contributors. He provides a synthesis of the major themes that emerge from the research discussed in the chapters. He also discusses the lessons learned about government policy and instructional strategy.

A CRITICAL NEED FOR MULTICULTURAL EDUCATION: POSSIBILITIES FOR SCHOOL PRACTICES AND TEACHER EDUCATION

In the remainder of this chapter, we focus on the need for multicultural education in East Asia. To do this, we build on previous studies (Phillion, Wang, & Lee, 2009) and the work done by the contributors to this book. Through an examination of official minority policies and school practices and teacher responses in various areas of East Asia, the contributors to this book and other researchers have documented that the discrepancy between the intention of government policies and the experiences of students in schools and their educational outcomes is significant. Officially, there is a claim that minority cultures and languages are respected and preserved, and that language rights and political rights are guaranteed. However, in practice, researchers have found large gaps. Unequally distributed wealth and social and educational resources, as well as inadequate teacher and administrator preparation, contribute to the insurmountable challenges for the educational attainment and resulting life chances of minority students. Although each area has different issues and concerns and different policies and practices, this discrepancy has a negative overall effect on minority students: home language and culture loss, identity confusion or loss, high drop-out rates, and little chance of higher education.

The research and reviews of existing literature of the chapter authors show a growing need to address these issues. One way to do this is to apply multicultural education theories to teacher education and administrator education programs as well as to practice in schools. Although it is not a panacea, applying the established theories of multicultural education derived from the US and other countries to the East Asian context will be beneficial in addressing the issues on educational inequity for minority students. As Gay (1992) contends, the major goals of multicultural education apply to all settings, although practices should be appropriately contextualized. With this in mind, as some chapter authors suggest, initial steps could be implemented using established theories. At the same time, as other chapter authors suggest, steps in developing a ground-up approach suitable for each specific area could be applied. Aside from the need for multicultural education and for specific contextually grounded practices, there is a need for research that systematically and deeply engages these issues.

With this premise, we believe that many well-developed and well-researched multicultural education principles can be infused in teacher education, administrator education, school policies, and teacher practices to meet the needs of minority students in East Asia. As a starting point, to build on the research conducted by the chapter authors, Banks' (2006) five dimensions of multicultural education can be used as a guideline for policymakers, school administrators, and teachers to address East Asian issues as regards minority students: (1) content integration (include minority perspectives as well as minority knowledge and languages in the curriculum and textbooks); (2) knowledge construction process (infuse a systematic critique of the sources of knowledge and perspectives used in teaching and learning); (3) equity pedagogy (modify teaching to include strategies that can promote diverse student success); (4) prejudice reduction (utilize multicultural textbooks, teaching strategies, and cooperative learning to enable positive inter-group interactions and positive racial attitudes among students); and (5) an empowering school culture and social structure (restructure schools to enable minority students to experience educational equality and cultural empowerment). These principles can provide an overall framework to develop multicultural education plans in East Asia.

Specifically, as some chapter authors indicate, there is a need for practices such as a culturally relevant pedagogy (Ladson-Billings, 1994), which brings the experiences of minority students into the curriculum and focuses on their specific learning styles. There is also a need for culturally responsive teaching (Gay, 2000) that is culturally compatible and congruent with the home cultures and languages of minority students. These two approaches have been well researched, have been successfully applied in a variety of minority students in the US and elsewhere, and can be adapted to the East Asian context. These strategies can be used to develop the instructional basis for teacher education programs for pre-service and in-service teachers, as well as administrators working with minority students.

The work of Nieto (Nieto & Bode, 2008) is also a useful guide for policymakers and practitioners willing to develop multicultural education in their districts, schools, and classrooms. Nieto considers multicultural education as "a process of comprehensive school reform and basic education for all students" (Nieto, 1992, p. 208). She views multicultural education as a process that challenges and rejects all forms of discrimination, such as racism in schools and society, and accepts and affirms the pluralism that students, their communities, and teachers represent, such as ethnicity, race, language, religion, socioeconomic status, and gender. She argues that the process of multicultural education should permeate the curriculum and instructional strategies, such as textbooks and policies used in schools, as well as interactions among teachers, students, and parents.

Nieto's (Nieto & Bode, 2008) comprehensive view of multicultural education, Banks' (2007) key dimensions of multicultural education, and Ladson-Billings (1994) and Gay's (2000) teaching and instructional strategies for diverse students provide the outline for a multicultural education policy and plan for East Asia. Multicultural education, which has long been established in the US and elsewhere, is well researched, has a proven record of effecting change, and is of growing interest in mainland China, Hong Kong, Japan, Taiwan, South Korea and other areas in East Asia, holds promise as a solution to urgent problems regarding educational equity for minority students.

REFERENCES

Bahry, S., Darkhor, P., & Luo, J. (2009). Educational diversity in China: Responding to globalizing and localizing forces. In G. A. Wiggan & C. B. Hutchison (Eds.), *Global issues in education: Pedagogy, policy, practices, and the minority experience* (pp. 103–129). Lanham, MD: Rowman & Littlefield Education.

Banks, J. A. (1994). *Multiethnic education: Theory and practice*. Allyn & Bacon.

Banks, J. A. (2006). Democracy, diversity, and social justice: Educating citizens for the public interest in a global age. In G. Ladson-Billings & W. F. Tale (Eds.), *Education research in the public interest* (pp. 141–157). New York: Teachers College Press.

Banks, J. A. (2007). Approaches to multicultural curriculum reform. In J. A. Banks & C. A. M. Banks (Eds.), *Multicultural education: Issues and perspectives* (6th ed., pp. 247–269). Hoboken, NJ: John Wiley & Sons.

Compulsory Education Law of the People's Republic of China. (1986). Retrieved July 5, 2010, from http://www.edu.cn/20050114/3126820.shtml

Gay, G. (1992). The state of multicultural education in the United States. In K. A. Moodley (Ed.), *Beyond multicultural education: International perspectives* (pp. 41–65). Calgary, Alberta: Detselig Enterprises.

Gay, G. (2000). *Culturally responsive teaching: Theory, research, and practice*. New York: Teachers College Press.

Ladson-Billings, G. (1994). *The dreamkeepers: Successful teachers of African American children*. San Francisco: Jossey-Bass.

Murphy-Shigematsu, S. (2003). Challenges for multicultural education in Japan. *New Horizons for Learning*. Retrieved June 15, 2010, from http://www.newhorizons.org/strategies/multicultural/murphy-shigematsu.htm

Nieto, S. (1992). *Affirming diversity: The sociopolitical context of multicultural education*. New York: Longman.

Nieto, S., & Bode, P. (2008). *Affirming diversity: The sociopolitical context of multicultural education* (5th ed.). Boston: Allyn & Bacon.

Phillion, J., Wang, Y., & Lee, J. (2009). Minority students in Asia: Government policies, school practices, and teacher responses. In G. A. Wiggan & C. B. Hutchison (Eds.), *Global issues in education: Pedagogy, policy, practice, and the minority experience* (pp. 239–258). Lanham, MD: Rowman & Littlefield Education.

Postiglione, G. A. (1999). Introduction: State schooling and ethnicity in China. In G. A. Postiglione (Ed.), *China's national minority education: Culture, schooling, and development* (pp. 3–19). New York: Falmer Press.

Qian, M. (2007). Discontinuity and reconstruction: The hidden curriculum in schoolroom instruction in minority-nationality areas. *Chinese Education and Society*, 40(2), 60–76.

Regional Autonomy for Ethnic Minorities in China. (1984). Retrieved July 5, 2010, from http://www.china-un.ch/eng/bjzl/t187368.htm

Su, Y. (2007). Ideological representations of Taiwan's history: An analysis of elementary social studies textbooks, 1978–1995. *Curriculum Inquiry*, 37(3), 205–237.

Wan, M., Nima, B., & Luo, J. (1999). *Tibetan cultural readers: Graders 4–6*. Lanzhou, Gansu: Canadian International Development Agency & Gansu People's Publishing House.

Wang, C., & Zhou, Q. (2003). Minority education in China: From State's preferential policies to dislocated Tibetan schools. *Educational Studies*, 29(1), 85–104.

Wenger, E. (1998). *Communities of practice: Learning, meaning, and identity*. Cambridge, UK: Cambridge University Press.

Part I
Minority Students in Mainland China

2 Language, Culture, and Identity

Experiences of Hui Students in Eastern China

Yuxiang Wang

There are 56 nationalities in China. The Han Chinese comprise 90% of China's 1.3 billion people; the other 55 nationalities are minorities, representing approximately 130 million people (Information Office, State Council of People's Republic of China, 2000). The Han Chinese control most institutions and government agencies (Veeck, Pannell, Smith, & Huang, 2007). Almost half of China's territory is occupied by minority nationalities, and they inhabit the inner border regions where there are either deserts or mountains (Veeck et al., 2007). Tibetans and Uygurs constitute the majority in Tibet Autonomous Region and Xinjiang Uygurs Autonomous Region in western China, respectively. In China, 53 nationalities have their own spoken languages; Manchus and Hui speak Mandarin Chinese (Veeck et al., 2007). There are about 120 mother tongues in minority regions, but only 30 minority languages have written scripts; 20 languages have fewer than 1,000 speakers (Sun, 2004).

Among the 55 minority groups in China, there are 10 Islamic minority groups: Hui, Uygurs, Tartars, Uzbeks, Kazaks, Tajiks, Kirgiz, Salar, Dongxiang, and Bonan (Lynn, 2004). Most of these groups live in northwestern China: Xinjiang, Gansu, Ningxia, Qinghai, and Shaanxi. The Hui people, who comprise half of China's Muslim population, are scattered in 90% of China's cities and townships (Israeli, 2002; Lynn, 2004).

The researcher grew up in eastern China, and the Hui people were the first minority people that he encountered. Hui men wear small white hats and Hui women have scarves wrapped around their heads. They do not eat pork. A novel, *Musilin de zangli* (Muslim Funeral; Huo, 1988), written by a Muslim novelist and broadcast over Chinese radio in the late 1980s, presented the researcher with vivid and romantic pictures of Hui people's life and work, their successes and failures, and their worries and happiness. He learned about their culture, religion, life, and work. They are different from the Han people. The researcher had two female colleagues who were faculty members at Anhui University, China; one was Manchu, the other was Hui. He worked with them for six years. He also shared a university dorm with a Korean for three years while he was doing his graduate study in China.

Through his research projects on minority languages, government policies and practices, and elementary textbooks in China (Y. Wang & Phillion, 2009), the researcher found a large gap between government policies and practices. Numerous studies have been conducted on the Hui people in western China where large Hui populations reside. However, few studies have been conducted on the Hui people in eastern China; these people, who live among the Han people, are scattered in 90% of the cities and townships. Although the Hui people have lost their home language and use Mandarin Chinese, they still believe in Islam; hence, it is necessary to explore how the culture of Hui students is recognized in schools and how this recognition affects their identity construction.

Through a narrative inquiry on the school experiences of Hui students, this chapter investigates how the culture of Hui students is recognized in schools, how teachers construct the identity of Hui students, and how this recognition affects the identity construction of Hui students.

MINORITY POLICY AND PRACTICE IN CHINA

Officially, the language and cultural rights of minority students are protected under the People's Republic of China (PRC) Constitution (1982) and the PRC Regional Autonomy Law for Minority Nationalities (1984). The PRC Constitution (1982) stipulates the equality of ethnic groups in China:

> All ethnic groups in the People's Republic of China are equal. The state protects the lawful rights and interests of the minority nationalities and upholds and develops the relationship of equality, unity, and mutual assistance among all of China's nationalities. Discrimination against and oppression of any nationality are prohibited; any acts that undermine the unity of the nationalities or instigate their secession are prohibited.

Furthermore, the PRC Regional Autonomy Law for Minority Nationalities (1984) sets the language of instruction in schools:

> In schools which mainly recruit students of minority nationalities, textbooks in languages of minority nationalities concerned should be used where conditions exist. Languages for instruction should also be the languages of the minority nationalities concerned. Primary school students of higher grades and secondary school students should learn [the] Chinese language. Putonghua [Mandarin Chinese], which is commonly used throughout the country, should be popularized among them. (cited in Hu & Seifman, 1987, p. 178)

However, there is a wide gap between what is legally mandated and what is being practiced. Gladney (2004) found that Hui and Han students in

Beijing use the same curriculum, except that pork is not served to Hui students at lunchtime. Nima (2001), a Tibetan scholar, found that Mandarin Chinese has permeated Tibetan life—from government documents to telegrams, from instructions in electrical appliances to technical concepts used in work environments, and from businesses to schools. This massive use of Mandarin Chinese has produced devastating effects on Tibetan language learning, maintenance, and use. In their study of elementary school textbooks in China, Y. Wang and Phillion (2010) found that minority culture and knowledge are under-represented and misrepresented to a large extent. Qian (2007) found that the ignorance of schools and teachers on the culture of minority students, as shown in classroom teaching and school curricula, cause minority students to drop out early and to fail academically.

LITERATURE REVIEW

This section examines the literature on minority language, culture, and identity at the international level, especially in the US. In China, there is limited research on the language and cultural rights of minority students, as well as on their identity construction in schools. This section compares and contrasts the international literature with the setup in China to discuss similar situations that minority students experience internationally and to argue for the inclusion of multiculturalism in the education of Hui students in eastern China.

Home Language and Academic Learning

Research shows that assimilation and discriminative language policies lead to the academic failure of minority students (Sleeter, 2005; Soto, 1997; Valenzuela, 1999), as well as to resistance from minority students and their parents (Soto, 1997; Valenzuela, 1999; Y. Wang & Phillion, 2007). The high drop-out rate of minority students originates from their resistance to assimilatory and English-only policies and practices; what they learn in school is different from their culture and knowledge, and their home language is often denigrated or forbidden in schools (Gay, 2000; Ladson-Billings, 1994). In the US, English-only policies and assimilation practices in schools subjugate minority students; these policies and practices make ethnic minorities doubt not only the value of their language and culture in the learning process, but also their ability for academic success (Nieto, 2002; Valenzuela, 1999).

The home language of minority students plays an important role in their cognitive development and academic achievement (Cummins, 1996; Nieto, 2002; Wong-Fillmore, 1991). Wong-Fillmore (1991) found that preschool students who are in English-only classes lose their first language, and they become unable to communicate with their parents and grandparents in their home language. Students who cannot retain their mother language lose the chance to develop their cognitive abilities through communication with their parents in their home language. Cummins (1996) demonstrated that children must develop their cognitive abilities by learning subjects in their home language before they start learning these subjects in a second language. Cummins recommended five to seven years of home language instruction in reading, writing, math, and social studies, along with communicative English as a Second Language (ESL), to promote the cognitive development of students. Based on a literature review on the role of home language in ESL learning and in the academic success of students in school, Nieto (2002) concluded that "rather than an impediment to academic achievement, bilingualism can actually promote learning" (p. 88). Therefore, it is evident that the home language of students helps in the development of their cognitive abilities and in their academic achievement.

Bilingual Education

The debate on bilingual education in the US demonstrates the emphasis on political correctness in school practices. Sleeter (1997) studied multicultural teaching in standards-based classrooms and claimed that "even though good bilingual education promotes educational achievement and English acquisition, it also supports bilingualism, which many monolingual Americans regard as anti-English and anti-American (a view which itself reflects historic amnesia)" (p. xii). Gort (2005) studied the early bilingual and biliteracy development of English- and Spanish-dominant learners in two-way bilingual programs, and argued that "bilingual education continues to be controversial not because it has not proven itself worthy as a pedagogical practice, but because it represents emancipatory and liberating education for traditionally subordinated groups whose voices have been silenced for too long" (p. 34).

Bilingual educational policies in minority regions in China emphasize fluency in both minority languages and Mandarin Chinese. In 1984, for instance, Qinghai Province proposed the use of minority languages and Mandarin Chinese for ethnic secondary and elementary schools. Minority students were encouraged to learn their spoken and written languages and, from these languages, to learn Mandarin Chinese (Dai & Dong, 2001). Many minority textbooks were published in different minority languages. Local newsletters and even the Bible were published in minority languages, and minority folklore and literature in minority languages were also made available (Schein, 2000). Guangxi Zhuang Autonomous Region and Tibet Autonomous Region have adopted the principle of using their minority languages for basic education. Learning Mandarin Chinese is also necessary for the goal of fluency in both languages (i.e., Mandarin Chinese and one's minority language) after secondary school graduation (Dai & Dong, 2001).

However, some local minority officials, staff members, minority peasants, and workers in Tibet prefer to send their children to schools where the medium of instruction is Chinese (C. Wang & Zhou, 2003). They do not want their children to attend schools where the medium of instruction is Tibetan (Ma, 2007). This phenomenon demonstrates the effects of Mandarin Chinese in Tibet—fluency in Mandarin Chinese is positively related with employment, promotion to high school, and even promotion to college. Bilik (1998) argued that bilingual education in Inner Mongolia serves as a means for Inner Mongolians to better master the official language (i.e., Mandarin Chinese) and to realize socioeconomic mobility. Consequently, the Mongolian language is used only for family communication.

Cultural Differences and Student Performance

Home–school cultural differences put minority students at a disadvantage in terms of their values, behavior, and performance in mainstream classrooms (Ladson-Billings, 1994; Qian, 2007). Minority students expect that what they bring to classrooms will be acknowledged and respected. Mainstream middle-class culture, however, declares what should be done and what should not, what is popular and what is not, and what is appropriate and what is not. These cultural conventions silence and marginalize minority students (Ladson-Billings, 1994; Nieto & Bode, 2008). Hence, minority students become resistant and unwilling to follow class rules; they refuse to study, and they even drop out of school. According to Erickson (2007), "marginalization is alienating, and one response to alienation is resistance—the very thing that makes teaching and learning more difficult for students and their teachers" (p. 51). By examining what makes Native American students quiet in class, Philips (1983) found that students in the Warm Springs Reservation perform poorly if individualized performance and competition are required. On the other hand, the students perform well if cooperation and group work—rather than public performance— are required because cooperation is encouraged in Native American culture. Therefore, it is important for teachers and schools to understand and appreciate what minority students bring to class. Most importantly, teachers should integrate what students bring to class into the school curriculum and class instruction (Erickson, 2007; Nieto, 2002).

In a study involving Yugurs, Salas, and Baoans, three of the 55 minority groups in China, Qian (2007) proved the relationship between school failure among minority students and the exclusion of the culture and knowledge of minority students from the school curriculum. Qian found that students are required to learn Mandarin Chinese and mainstream culture and knowledge, although student populations are culturally diverse. Qian also found that most of these students drop out of school before they finish high school. Qian argued that the school curriculum, which excludes the culture, knowledge, and religions of minority students, makes these students feel that school education is not relevant to their lives and that their culture and knowledge are not worth learning.

Gay (2000) proposed the adoption of culturally responsive teaching to improve the school performance of under-achieving students of color. She concluded that minority students will perform better if evaluation measures other than standardized tests are used, and if their cultures are integrated into classroom teaching and learning. Ladson-Billings (2007) used culturally relevant teaching to "maintain their [minority students'] cultural integrity while succeeding academically" (p. 231) so that successful African American students would not be isolated and mocked by their peers. She suggested that three criteria must be met to achieve culturally relevant teaching: "the ability to develop students academically, a willingness to nurture and support cultural competence, and the development of a sociopolitical or critical consciousness" (p. 238). Sociopolitical and critical consciousness enables teachers to know why the culture of minority students is denigrated and taken away through schooling.

Identity and Learning of Minority Students

Identity demonstrates who one is, which cultural group one belongs to, and with whom one shares the same ancestry and history. Identity is acquired when one is born, and it is developed through language learning, and cultural immersion and construction; it is reinforced through family and community environments (Hall, 1992). Based on life stages, socioeconomic and sociopolitical status, and other factors, identity is ever changing. Dominant groups who disregard the identity of minority groups do not provide opportunities for minority students to learn their home language and culture; they cut the relationship between minority students and their families and communities (Spring, 2007). In addition, they downgrade minority knowledge, language, and culture through knowledge reconstruction and through misrepresentation in public media, textbooks, and literature (Apple, 2004; Sleeter, 2005).

The cultural identities of students influence their experiences and learning in schools (Nieto & Bode, 2008; Qian, 2007). Their cultural identities demonstrate where they were raised, under what home language and culture, and in what communities. Their identities influence how they respond to class and school culture, which, in turn, influences teachers' expectations of students (Nieto, 2002; Nieto & Bode, 2008; Qian, 2007). However, the cultural identity of students is often ignored by mainstream teachers who emphasize individual differences as the sole factor that determines student intelligence. Standardized tests or IQ tests are used to measure student intelligence; these tests are of course partial and incomprehensive (Gay, 2000; Sleeter, 2005) because the home language and culture of minority students are not taken into consideration in the design of these tests. Public schooling is a process of reproducing middle-class ideology, and it reflects "the traditional image of the intelligent, academically prepared young person" (Nieto, 2002, p. 17); hence, minority students will inevitably be misunderstood and misinterpreted as at-risk students and academic failures. Teachers should examine whether they are taking the identity of minority students into consideration, and whether they are integrating their language, culture, and knowledge into the school curriculum and practice. Teachers should also respect the identity and life experiences of minority students.

METHODOLOGY

This study concentrated on how the culture of Hui students is represented in the school curriculum and class instruction, how their identity is constructed by their teachers, and how Hui students construct their identity in school. Few studies have focused on the experiences of Hui students in eastern China; hence, this research contributes to the international study on the recognition of Muslim culture and belief in schools and on the impact of this recognition to the identity construction of Muslim students. A case study on two Hui girls, Lingling[1] and Bai Lan, in Dongsheng Elementary School in eastern China was conducted. To better understand their school experiences, the girls and their teachers were interviewed. They were also observed in their classes. Based on the case findings, this chapter discusses the need for multicultural education in China so that the culture and knowledge of Hui students may be valued and respected. Culturally relevant teaching (Ladson-Billings, 1994) or culturally responsive teaching (Gay, 2000) for Hui students in China and for all minority students is also discussed.

This chapter seeks to answer the following research questions:

1. What are the experiences of Hui students in schools in eastern China?
2. How do teachers view the culture and identity of Hui students in eastern China?
3. How is the culture of Hui students recognized in schools, and what is the impact of this recognition on their identity construction?

Narrative Inquiry

The narrative inquiry approach (Clandinin & Connelly, 2000; He, 2003; Phillion, 2002) focuses on the stories and experiences of participants, makes meaning out of their stories and experiences, and understands participants through their stories and experiences. Phillion (2002) summarized the three qualities of the approach: context of participants' experience, immersion in participants' experience, and development of a good relationship for better understanding of participants' experiences. These qualities emphasize the importance of positioning the researcher as an inquirer and the participants as collaborative inquirers (Phillion & He, 2008). This creates an equitable environment for the researcher and the participants to negotiate the meaning of participants' experiences.

Although this study is not as in-depth as most narrative inquiries are, Phillion's three qualities of the narrative inquiry approach guided the exploration of the two Hui students' experiences within a sociopolitical and historical context. The approach helped the researcher "live" the experiences of Hui students through class observations and interviews with Hui students and their teachers.

FINDINGS AND DISCUSSION

Teachers' Reponses to Hui Culture and Hui Students' Construction of Their Identity

Lingling's Teacher, Mr. Ma's Responses

Mr. Ma, Lingling's teacher, graduated from a two-year college. He teaches moral education and social science to students in six Grade 4 classes. Each class has one-hour lessons in moral education and social studies per week. He has been a teacher at Dongsheng Elementary School for five years.

Mr. Ma admits that he knows little about Hui culture, except for these people's belief in Islam and their abstention from eating pork. He reads related books or retrieves information from the Internet when he needs to discuss other cultures or religions. He also encourages students to read and search for information on different cultures or religions. During his school and college education, he received little education on other cultures. He does not see Lingling as a Hui student because Lingling grew up in Dongsheng, a Han-dominated town. Besides, he sees no differences between Lingling and Han students. Therefore, he does not take measures to help Hui students learn their culture and construct their identity based on Islamic culture and knowledge. He does not utilize any culturally responsive teaching methodology to provide distinct academic help to Hui students. According to him, Lingling has no problems in her learning and school performance. Mr. Ma claims that the culture and knowledge contents of textbooks are appropriate for Hui students because they have to compete with Han students in tests, especially in the National College Entrance Examination. Therefore, Hui students have to learn the same knowledge that Han students learn.

Bai Lan's Teacher, Mr. Wan's Responses

Mr. Wan graduated from a normal school, and he earned the equivalent of a two-year associate's degree through independent study and examination.

He teaches Mandarin Chinese in Class 1, Grade 6 (two hours a day, five days a week). He has been with Dongsheng Elementary School for more than eight years. He claims that he does not see any differences between Bai Lan and Han students, and he treats all students equally in his class. He believes that Bai Lan's strong leadership and good academic achievement demonstrates that Bai Lan is a great student in his class and in the school in general.

Mr. Wan believes that proficiency in Mandarin Chinese is a basic and indispensable skill for students to continue their education. In teaching Mandarin Chinese, he emphasizes reading, writing, recitation, and class discussion. He believes that proficiency in the language provides opportunities for students to learn from famous writers, to emulate classic and well-written articles, and to start their own writing. He cites a well-known saying to support his view: "After you read fluently 300 poems written in the Tang Dynasty, you can read poems with emotion even if you cannot write poems." Mr. Wan's Mandarin Chinese class was observed six times. Mr. Wan is passionate in his teaching. Students are energetic. They read aloud and discuss in groups and in unison; they raise questions and pose answers.

Mr. Wan believes that the Hui culture and belief are not important. What matters is Bai Lan must compete with Han students in the National College Entrance Examination. If she does not master mainstream knowledge and ideology, it will be impossible for her to go to college and receive higher education, which means few opportunities for social mobility.

Hui Students' Construction of Their Identity

We Are the Same

Lingling and Bai Lan construct their identity based on the mainstream culture, knowledge, and ideology found in the school curriculum, as well as based on their teachers' construction of their identity. Although Lingling and Bai Lan claim that they are Hui, they explain that they are not different from Han girls. They both assert that they are all the same. Bai Lan claims that she agrees with what she learns in moral education class: "56 nationalities are a family." She continues to explain that it is good that people love each other like family members. Bai Lan accepts the mainstream hegemonic ideology that "56 nationalities are a family," which obscures cultural, racial, and religious differences between the Han people and minority groups. The hegemonic ideology imposes the national identity (i.e., Chinese) on Bai Lan. The contradiction between Bai Lan's and Lingling's claims that they are Hui and they are comfortable with their national identity (i.e., Chinese) demonstrates that they are confused about their identities.

Identity shows who a person is, which cultural group a person belongs to, and with whom a person shares the same ancestry and history. Hall (1992) used the term *cultural identity* to refer to a shared culture, shared history, and ancestry. Hall commented that "our cultural identities reflect the common historical references and shared cultural codes which provide us, as 'one people,' with stable, unchanging, and continuous frames of reference and meaning" (p. 223). The school curriculum alienates Lingling and Bai Lan from their history, knowledge, and culture; hence, it becomes difficult for them to maintain their culture and identity. They try to emulate Han students in both appearance and ideology. School education is assimilating them into the mainstream ideology. The mainstream Han-controlled educational system does not provide opportunities for Hui students to learn their home knowledge and culture (Qian, 2007), and it downgrades minority knowledge and culture through knowledge reconstruction and through misrepresentation in public media, textbooks, and literature (Gladney, 2004; Schein, 2000). Furthermore, the mainstream Han group takes away the identities of minority groups to emphasize that the only choice for Hui students is to become Chinese. Hui students sacrifice a great deal in becoming Chinese. The Hui people lose their home language as they shift from being Muslims in China to Chinese Muslims. The Hui people continue to lose their culture and identity (Gladney, 2004; Lynn, 2004; Mackerras, 1998).

The cultural identities of Lingling and Bai Lan influence their experiences and academic performance in school. Their cultural identity demonstrates where they are raised, under what home language and culture, and in what communities (Hall, 1992). The cultural identities of students influence how they respond to the class and school culture, which, in turn, influence teachers' expectations of them. Mr. Ma and Mr. Wan, however, often ignore Lingling's and Bai Lan's cultural identities. They only see similarities among Lingling, Bai Lan, and Han students. Mr. Ma and Mr. Wan are constructing the identity of Lingling and Bai Lan through their understanding of them. They are using Chinese identity to interpret Hui students. Similar findings were found among US mainstream white teachers who argue that they only see students, not color. "Color blindness" (Ladson-Billings, 1994, p. 31) is an excuse to blur sociopolitical and educational differences between minority students and mainstream white students—without providing culturally relevant teaching (Ladson-Billings, 1994) to help minority students learn and construct their own identities (Nieto, 2002). The misinterpretation of the identity of Hui students may cause teachers to misunderstand them and to eventually hurt them. Nieto (2002) interviewed Linda, who identified herself as black and white American. However, her teacher frequently mistakes her to be Latina or Chinese without asking her who she is. Although she was accepted by a highly regarded university and awarded a four-year scholarship, she dropped out of the university after half a year. She told the interviewer, "I felt like a pea on a big pile of rice" (Nieto, 2002, p. 12). The tension created by issues regarding her identity made Linda give up higher education.

Purpose of Schooling

Teachers emphasize the recitation of stories or paragraphs in school text-books, which is believed to be beneficial in the effective transmission of knowledge (Interviews, 2008). Lingling, Bai Lan, and other students are regarded as receptacles of knowledge, and teachers are regarded as owners of knowledge. The task of the teacher is to transmit the required knowledge to students. Students do not need to reflect on knowledge, and critical thinking is not encouraged. This is what Freire (1970) called the "banking concept of education," which is the easiest way of imposing mainstream ideology and values. The purpose of such an education is not to cultivate critical thinking skills among students but to reproduce mainstream ideology, culture, and identity (Apple, 2004; Freire, 1970). Giroux (1997) used the phrase "prepackaged curriculum materials" (p. 88) to criticize the emphasis on teachers as transmitters of knowledge.

Mr. Wan, in his Chinese class, uses individual reading, group reading, and recitation as assignments. His emphasis on recitation in learning Chinese demonstrates that he positions himself as a knowledge transmitter. Teachers, administrators, and parents expect students to remember knowledge in textbooks and to earn high scores in tests (Interviews, 2008). Lingling and Bai Lan write notes in class. They review notes and finish homework at home to earn high scores and to attend better high schools (Field notes, 2008; Interviews, 2008). Furthermore, according to their study of elementary school textbooks in China, Y. Wang and Phillion (2010) found that minority knowledge and culture in elementary school textbooks are under-represented. The lack of Hui culture and knowledge in elementary school textbooks in China afford Lingling and Bai Lan little opportunity to experience and learn Hui culture (Interviews, 2008). In addition, Mr. Ma and Mr. Wan both admit that they have little knowledge of Hui culture, and they provide little culturally relevant teaching to Lingling and Bai Lan (Interviews, Mr. Ma and Mr. Wan, 2008). Therefore, Lingling and Bai Lan have minimal opportunities to gain access to Hui knowledge and culture in their formal schooling. In effect, formal education becomes a process of taking away Lingling's and Bai Lan's culture and identity.

Qian (2007) investigated three culturally diverse minority regions in China and found that schools do not provide multicultural curricula to meet the needs of different groups. Instead, schools choose to impose the mainstream knowledge and culture on students from different minority groups. Qian argued that cultural differences between the homes and schools of minority students contribute to the academic failure of these students. La Belle and Ward (1994) argued that minority students are disadvantaged in schools because of conflicts between mainstream ideologies and the home cultures of these students.

The mainstream Han group excludes and even downgrades Hui culture and knowledge through culture and knowledge selection, construction, and strict censorship from the Chinese Communist Party. Schooling, therefore, is a process of taking away the culture and knowledge of Hui students, creating social stratification, and maintaining the status quo (Giroux, 1983; Spring, 2007). Similar findings were reported in the US. According to Ladson-Billings (1994), high drop-out rates among African American students demonstrate that little African American culture and knowledge are included in school curricula, and minimal culturally responsive teaching is provided. The performance of African American students is misinterpreted by white teachers. Valenzuela (1999) used the term "subtractive schooling" to describe how the language, culture, and identity of Mexican American students are taken away through public school education. Carger (1996) examined a Mexican American boy and his school experiences, and revealed the factors that caused him to fail in school: little culturally responsive teaching, lower expectations from white teachers as compared to other students, and little quality education.

Mr. Ma and Mr. Wan do not talk about Hui culture in their classes, and they do not engage in culturally responsive teaching to help Hui students. They offer the excuse that Hui students are good students, both academically and socially (Interviews, 2008). Both Mr. Ma and Mr. Wan state that they do not see any differences between Hui students and Han students (Interviews, 2008). They believe that there is no culture in the curriculum at all (Interviews, 2008). They do not talk about culture, and they do not teach culture. Mr. Ma and Mr. Wan expect students to follow mainstream rules and regulations in their classes, to respect the teacher, to work hard on assignments, and to earn high scores in standardized tests (Field notes, 2008). As Bourdieu argued, "the school and other social institutions legitimize and reinforce through specific sets of practices and discourses class-based systems of behavior and dispositions that reproduce the existing dominant society" (as cited in Giroux, 1983, p. 39).

Mr. Ma's moral education class discusses respect for ancestors as a virtue, and students are asked to share how they respect their ancestors. Lingling also shares her story of respecting her ancestors. The Hui people do not practice fealty to their ancestors, and Mr. Ma supposes that Hui students should also learn fealty. These people believe in Allah, the only God, a belief that differs radically from the Confucian ideology of being filial to ancestors (Israeli, 2002; Lynn, 2004). This classroom practice demonstrates how the Han culture is imposed on Lingling and other Hui students in the class. Similar findings have also been reported in the US. Gay (2000) and Nieto (2002) found that mainstream teachers take the culture of minority students for granted. They do not teach it explicitly. However, every day, minority students experience the mainstream culture; they test and challenge it. Boykin (1994) believed that a culture of European and middle-class origin is ingrained in schooling practices in the US; this culture is regarded as normal and therefore everyone is expected to learn it. The minority culture, on the other hand, is regarded as backward, unscientific, and problematic, and therefore not worth learning (Sleeter, 2005).

IMPLICATIONS

Contributions to the Research Literature on Minority Students in China

This study contributes to the scant research literature on Hui students in eastern China. It helps readers understand the experiences of Hui students in Dongsheng Elementary School in eastern China, how the culture and beliefs of Hui students are recognized in schools, and how the identities of Hui students are constructed by Han teachers and mainstream schooling. It also helps readers realize the assimilative nature of schooling in China. Teachers treat Hui students as they treat Han students, and they do not take the culture and identity of Hui students into consideration. Teachers construct the identity of Hui students as Han or Chinese rather than Hui. This study also provides an example of the gap between the national policy of respect for minority language, culture, and identity, and the assimilative practice against minority language, culture, and identity. Han teachers, administrators, and policymakers, therefore, have the responsibility to respect and value what Hui students bring to class and school. They likewise have the responsibility to represent the culture and knowledge of Hui students from the perspective of the Hui people—for Hui students to become proud of their culture and belief, knowledge, and identity. This study also reveals that Hui students are struggling with their identities. Hui students in Dongsheng Elementary School need not lose their identities simply because they are spatially far from the northwestern regions where most Hui people reside, they are living in a Han-dominated region, and they are attending a public school. It is the researcher's hope that this study will compel teachers and school administrators to think about this issue and to consider ways of helping minority students construct their ethnic identities.

By comparing the issues that Hui students are experiencing and those that other minority students—especially Tibetan students—are facing, this study also focuses on other minority students in China. On the one hand, the favorable responses of Tibetan parents to the practice of sending their children to Tibetan schools or classes in mainstream Han regions in China demonstrates that Tibetan students and their parents consent to the assimilative practice promoted by mainstream Han groups (C. Wang & Zhou, 2003; Zhu, 2007). On the other hand, the high drop-out rate and low literacy rate in Tibet demonstrate that Tibetan students and their parents are resistant to the public education provided by the Communist Party of

China. The Tibetan culture and knowledge that Tibetan students bring to school are under-represented, wrongly represented (Nima, 2001; Zhu, 2007), and not valued or respected. Tibetan parents can identify little in public education that is of value related to their lives (Zhu, 2007).

Implications for Teacher Education in China

This study has pivotal implications for teacher education in China. The two teachers in Dongsheng Elementary School and teachers in the studies of Liu (2007), Qian (2007), and Zhu (2007) demonstrate that school teachers in China know little about the knowledge and culture of minority students. Teachers are not ready to teach culturally and linguistically diverse students. The high drop-out rates and much higher illiteracy rates among minority students than among Han students (Qian, 2007) demonstrate the resistance of minority students and their parents to the imposition of Han culture and knowledge, as well as to the denigration of minority culture and knowledge (Zhu, 2007). Whether teachers value and respect minority culture and knowledge, and integrate the culture of students into the school curricula, determines the class participation and academic achievement of minority students (Banks, 2007; Ladson-Billings, 1994; Nieto & Bode, 2008; Qian, 2007). Therefore, multicultural education must be a required course for all pre-service teachers in China. Pre-service teachers may start from a self-examination of their views about race, ethnicity, class, gender, language, culture, and knowledge. Thereafter, they may focus on the importance of minority languages, culture, and knowledge in the academic achievement and identity construction of minority students. In addition, pre-service teachers should learn to value and respect minority culture, language, and knowledge; broaden their worldviews through readings, discussions, and personal reflections; and increase their understanding of the necessity to eliminate social oppression and discrimination.

Multicultural education must be included in teacher training programs in China. The attitudes of teachers toward diverse cultures and ethnicities, as well as toward democracy, determine whether they can deliver culturally relevant teaching to students (Gay, 2000; Ladson-Billings, 1994). Therefore, teachers need to be exposed to cultural diversity in teacher education programs (Sleeter, 2005), which will increase their cultural sensitivity and lead to an understanding of, and respect for, other cultures. Moreover, the shift from dominant culture–centered ideologies to critical, multicultural ways of thinking (hooks, 2000) determines the success of multicultural education. Mainstream Han teachers must move out of their comfort zones and examine—from the perspectives of minority students rather than from the mainstream ideology of denigrating minority groups—why minority students are experiencing educational inequality, poverty, and limited access to educational resources (Qian, 2007).

NOTES

1. Participants' names and school names are pseudonyms.

REFERENCES

Apple, M. W. (2004). *Ideology and curriculum* (3rd ed.). New York: Routledge Falmer.
Banks, J. A. (2007). Multicultural education: Characteristics and goals. In J. A. Banks & C. A. M. Banks (Eds.), *Multicultural education: Issues and perspectives* (6th ed., pp. 3–30). Hoboken, NJ: John Wiley & Sons.
Bilik, N. (1998). Language education, intellectuals, and symbolic representation: Being an urban Mongolian in a new configuration of social evolution. In W. Safran (Ed.), *Nationalism and ethnoregional identities in China* (pp. 47–67). Portland, OR: Frank Cass.
Boykin, A. W. (1994). Afrocultural expression and its implications for schooling. In E. R. Hollins, U. E. King, & W. C. Hayman (Eds.), *Teaching diverse populations: Formulating a knowledge base* (pp. 243–256). Albany: State University of New York Press.
Carger, C. (1996). *Of borders and dreams: A Mexican-American experience of urban education.* New York: Teachers College Press.
Clandinin, D. J., & Connelly, F. M. (2000). *Narrative inquiry: Experience and story in qualitative research.* San Francisco: Jossey-Bass.
Constitution of the People's Republic of China. (1982). Retrieved February 20, 2009, from http://english.people.com.cn/constitution/constitution.html
Cummins, J. (1996). *Negotiating identities: Education for empowerment in a diverse society.* Ontario: California Association for Bilingual Education.
Dai, Q., & Dong, Y. (2001). The historical evolution of bilingual education for China's ethnic minorities. *Chinese Education & Society, 34*(2), 7–47.
Erickson, F. (2007). Culture in society and in educational practices. In J. A. Banks & C. A. M. Banks (Eds.), *Multicultural education: Issues and perspectives* (6th ed., pp. 33–61). Hoboken, NJ: John Wiley & Sons.
Freire, P. (1970). *Pedagogy of the oppressed.* New York: Continuum.
Gay, G. (2000). *Culturally responsive teaching: Theory, research, and practice.* New York: Teachers College Press.
Giroux, H. A. (1983). *Theory and resistance in education: A pedagogy for the opposition.* South Hadley, MA: Bergin & Garvey.
Giroux, H. A. (1997). *Channel surfing: Race talk and the destruction of today's youth.* New York: St. Martin's Press.
Gladney, D. C. (2004). *Dislocating China: Reflections on Muslims, minorities, and other subaltern subjects.* Chicago: University of Chicago Press.
Gort, M. (2005). Bilingual education: Good for US? In T. A. Osborn (Ed.), *Language and cultural diversity in U.S. schools: Democratic principles in action* (pp. 25–37). Westport, CT: Praeger.
Hall, S. (1992). The question of cultural identity. In S. Hall, D. Held, & T. McGraw (Eds.), *Modernity and its futures* (pp. 268–288). Cambridge, UK: Polity.
He, M. F. (2003). *A river forever flowing: Cross-cultural lives and identities in the multicultural landscape.* Greenwich, CT: Information Age.
hooks, b. (2000). *Where we stand: Class matters.* New York: Routledge.
Hu, S. H., & Seifman, E. (1987). *Education and socialist modernization: A documentary history of education in the People's Republic of China.* New York: AMS Press.

Huo, D. (1988). *Musilin de zangli* [Muslim funeral]. Beijing: Beijing October Literature and Arts Publishing House.

Information Office, State Council of People's Republic of China. (2000). *National minorities policy and its practice in China.* Retrieved March 12, 2009, from http://news.xinhuanet.com/employment/2002-11/18/content_633175.htm

Israeli, R. (2002). *Islam in China: Religion, ethnicity, culture, and politics.* Lanham, MD: Lexington Books.

La Belle, T. J., & Ward, C. R. (1994). *Multiculturalism and education: Diversity and its impact on schools and society.* Albany: State University of New York Press.

Ladson-Billings, G. (1994). *The dreamkeepers: Successful teachers of African American children.* San Francisco: Jossey-Bass.

Ladson-Billings, G. (2007). Culturally responsive teaching: Theory and practice. In J. A. Banks & C. A. M. Banks (Eds.), *Multicultural education: Issues and perspectives* (6th ed., pp. 221–245). Hoboken, NJ: John Wiley & Sons.

Liu, Y. (2007). Life, culture, and education in a border region. *Chinese Education and Society, 40*(1), 60–77.

Lynn, A. M. (2004). *Muslims in China.* Indianapolis, IN: University of Indianapolis Press.

Ma, R. (2007). Bilingual education for China's ethnic minorities. *Chinese Education and Society, 40*(2), 9–25.

Mackerras, C. (1998). Han-Muslim and intra-Muslim social relations in northwestern China. In W. Safran (Ed.), *Nationalism and ethnoregional identities in China* (pp. 28–46). Portland, OR: Frank Cass.

Nieto, S. (2002). *Language, culture, and teaching: Critical perspectives for a new century.* Mahwah, NJ: Erlbaum.

Nieto, S., & Bode, P. (2008). *Affirming diversity: The sociopolitical context of multicultural education* (5th ed.). Boston: Allyn & Bacon.

Nima, B. (2001). Problems related to bilingual education in Tibet. *Chinese Education & Society, 34*(2), 91–102.

Philips, S. U. (1983). *The invisible culture: Communication in classroom and community on the Warm Springs Indian Reservation.* Prospect Heights, IL: Waveland.

Phillion, J. (2002). Becoming a narrative inquirer in a multicultural landscape. *Journal of Curriculum Studies, 34*(5), 535–556.

Phillion, J., & He, M. F. (2008). Multicultural and cross-cultural narrative inquiry in educational research. *Thresholds in Education, 34*(1), 2–12.

Qian, M. (2007). Discontinuity and reconstruction: The hidden curriculum in schoolroom instruction in minority-nationality areas. *Chinese Education and Society, 40*(2), 60–76.

Schein, L. (2000). *Minority rules: The Miao and the feminine in China's cultural politics.* Durham, NC: Duke University Press.

Sleeter, C. E. (1997). Foreword. In L. Diaz Soto, *Language, culture, and power: Bilingual families and the struggle for quality education* (pp. ix–xiii). New York: State University of New York Press.

Sleeter, C. E. (2005). *Un-standardizing curriculum: Multicultural teaching in the standards-based classroom.* New York: Teachers College Press.

Soto, L. D. (1997). *Language, culture, and power: Bilingual families and the struggle for quality education.* New York: State University of New York Press.

Spring, J. (2007). *Deculturalization and the struggle for equality: A brief history of the education of dominated cultures in the United States* (5th ed.). New York: McGraw-Hill.

Sun, H. (2004). Theorizing over 40 years personal experiences with the creation and development of minority writing systems of China. In M. Zhou & H. Sun

(Eds.), *Language policy in the People's Republic of China: Theory and practice since 1949* (pp. 179–199). Boston: Kluwer Academic.

Valenzuela, A. (1999). *Subtracting schooling: U. S. Mexican youth and the politics of caring.* New York: State University of New York Press.

Veeck, G., Pannell, C. W., Smith, C. J., & Huang, Y. (2007). *China's geography: Globalization and the dynamics of political, economic, and social change.* Lanham, MD: Rowman & Littlefield.

Wang, C., & Zhou, Q. (2003). Minority education in China: From state's preferential policies to dislocated Tibetan schools. *Educational Studies, 29*(1), 85–104.

Wang, Y., & Phillion, J. (2007). Chinese American students fight for their rights. *Journal of Educational Foundations, 21*(1/2), 91–105.

Wang, Y., & Phillion, J. (2009). Minority language policy and practice in China: The need for multicultural education. *International Journal of Multicultural Education, 11*(1), 1–14.

Wang, Y., & Phillion, J. (2010). Whose knowledge is valued? A critical study of knowledge in elementary school textbooks in China. *Intercultural Education, 21*(6), 567–580.

Wong-Fillmore, L. (1991). When learning a second language means losing the first. *Early Children Research Quarterly, 6*, 323–346.

Zhu, Z. (2007). Ethnic identity construction in the schooling context: A case study of a Tibetan Neidi boarding school in China. *Chinese Education and Society, 40*(2), 38–59.

3 Why Are Hui Minority Girls Dropping Out of School in China?

Ying Sun, Wei Yu, and Yuhua Ye

INTRODUCTION

There are 55 minority groups in China (Y. Ma, 1984), each with its own history and culture. For many complex reasons, the culture of some minorities is continuously disappearing; some are even on the edge of extinction (Yang & Liu, 2006). The Hui minority is one of the strongest minority groups in the country; they are widespread in certain areas, especially in northwestern China. The Hui minority has been able to maintain and further develop their traditions, culture, and customs better than most minorities. Even so, the Hui minority is greatly affected by the Han. How can the Hui continue to coexist with the Han, and why are other minorities' conditions so different? The dropping out of Hui minority girls is an important issue in contemporary Chinese society (F. Ma, 1997). This phenomenon appears in the rural areas of China, especially in minority residential areas. We selected a Muslim residential area for our research, focusing on the drop-out incidence among Hui minority girls. One researcher, Ye Yuhua, is a student of Northeast Normal University. She is a Hui and is fluent in the Arabic language. In addition, she was born and raised in the Muslim residential area of Qinghai Province. She is knowledgeable in the research field and can communicate with the local people in Arabic. In contrast, the other researchers are strangers to this research field, but we were interested in participating in their world. This research can be viewed from two different viewpoints: as an outsider and as an insider. Although we play different roles, we have the same purpose. We want the voices of Hui minority girls heard in the US (i.e., the origin of multicultural education) and in China— this is the purpose of our study.

DESCRIPTION OF THE MINORITY POPULATION

The Hui population composed 9.82 million (7.58%) of the 129.53 million total population of China in 2000 (China Yearbook [CY], 2006). In 2006, the total population of Hui minority was over 10 million. This number is just lower than the Zhuang and Man minorities (CY, 2006). The Hui minority live in many places in China, such as the Ningxia Hui Autonomous Region; the provinces of Gansu, Qinghai, and Henan; and the Xinjiang Weiwuer Autonomous Region. The characteristic pattern of dwelling areas of the Hui minority is scattered in wide areas, but they are also concentrated as small community populations (Ma, Y. 2000). For example, Gansu Province in northwestern China is typically an area where the Hui minority lives. Nevertheless, although the Hui minority were born and lived in China, they are not classified as one of the old clans or tribes of ancient China. The Hui minority are descendants of Arab and Persian traders from 7th century AD (Lei, 2008). In the 13th century, many Muslims moved their communities to China from Central Asia. They intermarried with the Han, Weiwuer, Menggu, and other nationalities. After years of integrating with other nations, they eventually developed into a new nation, the Hui. Thus, the Hui minority can be viewed from many factors but primarily from the racial and ethnic aspects. Overall, the introduction and development of Islam played an important role in the formation of the Hui minority. Incidentally, the language of the Hui is based on the Han language, and although it retains some words from Arabic and Persian, it does not have a separate written language (Su, 2008, para. 2).

POLICY CONTEXT

The Law on Compulsory Education of the People's Republic of China has been in effect since 1986 (National People's Congress [NPC], 1986). This law was revised in 2006 and was implemented in September 2008 (NPC, 2006). According to the law, school-aged children and teenagers should receive national education. The state, society, and family must guarantee this right for school-aged children. The law has three features: it should be compulsory, free, and public (Cheng, 2006, para. 3). "Free" refers to no tuition and no fees and is also linked to public welfare. In rural areas, tuition and fees have been retracted since 2007. In cities, school-aged children have not needed to pay fees since the beginning of 2008 (Liu, 2008, para. 1). However, in practice, eliminating such fees implies significant financial problems for China. Presently, the government has established a financial mechanism to ensure funding for compulsory education. "Public" is an absolute concept in the law on compulsory education (Yuan & Tian, 2003). In the revised law, unified compulsory education is placed on a huge scale, incorporating the implementation of a unified standard on textbooks, teaching, funding, construction, and public fees for each student. These elements manifest in different forms in the revised law. For example, Article 4 in the amendment of the compulsory provision rules that school-aged children and teenagers have the right to education regardless of gender, nationality, ethnicity, wealth, or religion. However, although they are entitled the right to compulsory education, students must also fulfill the obligation of compulsory education. "Compulsory" means that education for the youth must be provided by the school, their parents, and the society. Anyone who violates the law will be punished. If parents do not send their school-aged children to school, they will be responsible. In addition, if schools do not receive school-aged children, they will be reprimanded; if they cannot provide the relevant conditions for students, they will be regulated by law (NPC, 2006). The Law on Compulsory Education is national in scope. Apart from the national law, some education policies exist at the local level. For example, there are some regulations on bilingual teaching in local areas (Dai & Dong, 1996).

THE RESEARCH STUDY

The methodology that guides our research is ethnography, an approach that allows researchers to make sense of the question, "What is the culture of this group of people?" (Patton, 2002, p. 132). According to Patton (2001), ethnography, the primary method of anthropology, is the earliest distinct tradition of qualitative inquiry. The notion of culture is central to ethnography. We use many methods to acquire and analyze data, including in-depth interviews, direct observation, and written documents. The interviews provide direct data to support every point presented in the chapter. Although the Hui minority girls drop out at similar ages, the reasons are varied. Through the in-depth interviews, the reasons can been observed and grasped clearly and directly. The thoughts of the interviewees are reflected by their replies. At the same time, observation is an essential way to obtain indirect data. For example, household circumstances can give much information about the family, such as approximate income, social status in the village, and other information. Indirect data can be described as the "introduction of interviewees" and are linked to direct data. After data acquisition, analysis—although difficult to accomplish—is important. Based on the original data, it is necessary to analyze the meanings of conversations. Furthermore, classifying the information in different ways is also necessary. Analyzing documents provides for additional processing beyond the level of interviews and observation.

BACKGROUND

A government official introduced us to Village C. Village C is located beside a highway, so transportation is convenient. There are more than 100 families and 900 people in the village. Most of the farmlands are overseen by the women and the elderly, whereas most men work outside the village to earn more money. Not one minority girl in the village has had access to university education.

Village L is located on top of a hill and about 20 miles from Town G. There are more than 1,000 individuals, and all are Hui. The officer of Town G introduced the situation briefly. The population has decreased because many people have moved to Geermu, a city in Gansu Province. Village L is far from Town G, and the road is difficult for walking. Here, it is not easy to implement activities like education, planned birth, and the restoration of farmlands to forests. When we arrived at Village L, there were many people working in one mosque. The officer of Village L explained that the villagers volunteered to reconstruct the mosque, and they plan to spend 1 million RMB to reconstruct it. We were surprised when we heard this news. Incidentally, Village L is one of the poorest villages near Town G. The officer of Village L told us that the villagers have donated about 500,000 RMB; the rest of the amount is collected through donations. We were also surprised with the elementary school operation. Nobody was concerned with elementary schooling, although the infrastructure looked quite old. All of the interviewees lived in families of more than five members. The men (e.g., fathers) always work outside the village to earn money, and the women (e.g., mothers) work in the farmlands and at home. Parents could not pay much attention to, or have time for, their children's lives and studies. Some interviewees attributed the dropping out of school to lack of physical labor in the household. Most parents are illiterate, and the highest educational attainment for parents is Grade 2 in middle school.

Research Procedure and the Obtained Reasons for Dropping Out

Yuhua Ye, a member of the Hui minority girls group, conducted all interviews. All of the nine interviewees dropped out of school because of emotional weariness caused by various factors. Six of them dropped out because of their own emotional weariness. Interviewees have lost confidence in school. They have low exam scores, and they are always punished by the public school teachers. Thus, they are now unwilling to go to school. In addition, the Hui minority girls are affected by religion. Owing to Islam, they are worried about the older girls in school. If the Hui minority girls stay in school for a long period, gossip might ensue (e.g., from the other villagers). In addition, staying in school delays marriage for Hui minority girls. The other three interviewees dropped out mainly because of family reasons. Due to the current employment situation, many parents could not support the schooling of their children. Parents also believe that girls cannot find jobs even if they graduate from universities. Owing to religious influences, accordingly, Hui minority girls stay at home and are encouraged to learn to do housework. Some girls drop out because of the lack of working labor at home. Therefore, they have to give up their school lives.

Some girls drop out because of the dire economy. Parents cannot financially support education for girls.

INTERVIEW STUDY QUESTIONS

The broad questions we explored in our research are the following:

When did you drop out of school?
Why did you drop out of school?
Have you regretted dropping out?
What is your current living situation?
What was the response of your family when they learned that you wanted to drop out?
Did your parents prevent you from dropping out?
What was the response of the school when they learned that you wanted to drop out?
Did your teacher prevent you from dropping out?
Are many of your peers dropping out?
Did peers affect your decision to drop out? What are the effects?
What is your understanding of "compulsory education"?

The preceding research questions do not exist separately, and they are linked by some inner relations. By using these questions, the researchers aimed to learn the subjective and objective reasons resulting in the dropping out of children from schools. Which factor is the most important one for dropping out—inner thought, school, family, peers, or others? Possibly, there are other complex reasons that lead to the dropout. Through these questions, the researchers could assess the interviewees' thoughts and ideas on dropping out of school, as well as their perceived relevant policies. In effect, the researchers can learn much information on the current situation on education for minority girls.

Some religious people of the Hui minority believe that girls become adults when they are 9 years old. Girls are restricted by religious beliefs in other ways; for example, they are forbidden to dance, sing, or take part in social activities. Incidentally, these restrictions violate school rules. The Hui minority girls are sneered upon in school when they are over 9 years old. Essentially, Hui minority girls are always restricted by the opinion of others. They cannot speak out aloud. They cannot raise their heads when they walk in front of other people. They are not allowed to expose their hair. What is the role of education in such a religiously strict environment?

RESEARCH CONTEXT

This research study focuses on Hui minority girls who are dropping out during the compulsory education period; hence, the interviewees are the children dropouts and their family members. The interviews lasted five days. The interviewer arrived at Town G on April 19, 2009, and started the interviews the following day. The interviewer arranged the interviews in the afternoon because farmers are used to working on their farmland in the early morning. There are nine interviewees for the research. The interviewees talked about the reasons for their having dropped out of school. The reasons obtained from the interviews can be categorized into several groups.

The Reasons from the Perspective of Hui Minority Girls

Many interviewees said that their main reason for dropping out came from their own inclination. They were unwilling to go to school. For example, Han Xiaomei says, "They (the parents) actually prevented me from dropping out, but I told them that I am unwilling to go to school. My mother said 'okay. If you are unwilling to go, you can work with me at home'" (Interview, April 20, 2009).

Ma Wenmei says, "I am unwilling to go to school. I feel it is not interesting to learn knowledge. I feel embarrassed that I get low scores among the many students" (Interview, April 23, 2009).

Zhang Xiaozhen says, "My father forced me to go to school at that time, but I was unwilling. Now, I regret dropping out when I am working in the fields. I do not know what I was thinking at that time. My parents are not at home, and my score was low, so I dropped out when the final examination was coming" (Interview, April 25, 2009).

The Reasons from the Perspective of the Families of the Hui Minority Girls

School is an important place for education, but it is not the only place where individuals can acquire education. The family has a huge effect on students. Some girls decide to drop out because of their families. There is a heavy burden in the family. Therefore, students have to give up school and work part time at home. Han Xiaomei says, "At that time, my family was preparing to build a house, but there were no other workers in my family, so I chose to drop out from school. It was hard to learn literature. My father and two brothers rarely go home because they have to work outside the village. My mother is the only other person who works at home. Therefore, I had to drop out in order to relieve the pressure for my mother" (Interview, April 20, 2009).

Han Xiaohua's mother talked briefly about the situation of her daughter. She says Han Xiaohua never goes to school. "There is much work to do in the house. I work in the fields, and her father works outside the village. Her brother goes to school. Hence, she has to do the housework at home and take care of her little sister. At that time, my family was poor. There was no extra money for her schooling" (Interview, April 21, 2009).

Some family members explicitly do not support the education of Hui girls, as it is believed that girls have few rights in the family. Eventually, the girls drop out as a result of family pressure.

Ma Wenhua says, "My mother wanted me to drop out when I was in primary school. I cried to my mother to abandon this thought. I could not drop out at that time. Then my two older sisters got married. My father works outside the village, and my mother works in the fields. There were no more workers in the family, so I had to drop out" (Interview, April 23, 2009).

Family reasons are highlighted as an objective condition. Nevertheless, Hui girls feel regretful after dropping out of school.

Ma Xiaoxiao says, "She [Ma Xiaofang] will regret dropping out when she is married. Now, I have to do much work in my mother-in-law's family. I have to bear much. She will regret her decision [for dropping out]" (Interview, April 25, 2009).

The Reasons from the Perspective of the Teachers

This study focuses on Hui minority girls dropping out of school. Hence, we conducted interviews with the family and with teachers. There was rarely a chance to talk with teachers directly, but it seemed that teachers are one of the factors affecting the school dropout of Hui minority girls. For example, Han Xiaoying's mother tells me:

My child is willing to go to school. Although her exam score is low, my family still encourages her to go to school. She got into a car accident when she was in Grade 2. [The school is located in front of a main street, and its door opens directly to the street.] There was nothing special anymore after the accident. Her right eye became weaker and weaker within one year. Now, because of her bad academic performance, the teacher did not allow her to sit on the first row. She was unwilling to wear glasses because it is ugly, especially for a Hui minority girl. One day, Han Xiaoying was brought home by her teacher. The teacher told Han Xiaoying's father that she should not go to school any more. If schooling went on, Han Xiaoying would lose her sight in her right eye. If that happens, Han Xiaoying would be a burden for the whole family. From then on, Han Xiaoying dropped out of school. (Interview, April 22, 2009)

Ma Xiaofang says,

There are more than 60 students in my class. My exam score is in the lower-middle range in class. The score was quite good when I was in primary school. I got praise from the teacher every day. After I went to middle school, I was beaten by the teacher, so I am unwilling to go to school any more. I just joined the courses in Chinese and Math in primary school, but many more courses are offered in middle school. It was a little difficult for me. My teacher did not offer any help. Hence, I dropped out from school. (Interview, April 25, 2009)

The Reasons from the Perspective of Peers

Although peers are not considered the most important reason for youth dropouts, they sometimes affect children's choices on schools. Ye Xiaohui says, "Classmates laugh at me because I am an orphan. They always laugh at me because I do not know who my genetic parents are, and to which ethnic group I belong to [Hui or Han]. Therefore, I feel too shy to go to school. Some classmates scold me. Teachers knew nothing about this situation because I did not tell them at that time" (Interview, April 20, 2009).

In addition, Hui minority girls can earn money after dropping out of school. After they have earned income, it seems that they get a higher status in the family. Han Xiaohua says, "I dig up Cordyceps [a kind of medicinal herb in Qinghai Province] with my father and brother. I earn more than 2000 RMB by digging. Is it a great ability? [laughing] Now my grandparent forbids us to go" (Interview, April 21, 2009).

As it is a small village, girls have many chances to communicate. After dropping out, girls acquire a better status in the family, and other schoolgirls admire them. In such cases, schoolgirls would opt to give up school in order to earn money.

LITERATURE REVIEW

In the age of globalization, both Chinese and international researchers are concerned and interested in the education of minority girls in China. Some conduct research on education equality, and some on multicultural education (Wang, 2008). No matter from which aspect, they analyze the reasons for the dropout from various perspectives. The main themes are as provided in the succeeding segments.

Economic Situation in the Family

With the development of society, living standards have been improved in China (Liu 2008, para. 1). However, the economy's situation is not as good in rural areas, especially in northwest rural areas (Yao & Ren, 2008). Thus, the economic situation in the family seems an important factor in the dropout rates. On the one hand, families cannot provide ample money to support the education of their children. The income of the family is just enough for daily subsistence, and additional money is limited. Thus, parents would opt that their children drop out of school in order to increase current income. On the other hand, children who belong to poor families have to bear the family burden. Some parents work outside of the village for higher income, and limited attention is paid to the children. The children might not focus well in school and may drop out eventually (T. Ma, 2008). Children also have to work for the family after class; thus, study time is limited. As a result, passing exam scores are not guaranteed. Due to low exam scores, they are forced to drop out. Although low exam scores seem an obvious reason for the school dropouts, the economic situation is the deeper reason. There are some relations between poverty and school education. Poverty and poor health also have a close relationship. Health problems lead to low academic ability. Meanwhile, low-level academic experience is a significant reason leading to poverty and poor health. Thus, a vicious circle is formed between rural education and the economy (Wang, 2008). In addition, girls seem more unfortunate in poor families compared with the boys. Girls are forced to drop out to provide physical labor in the household. Compared with the boys, girls' schooling is difficult and complicated (Wang, 2008; Zhang, 2002; Zhu & Wang, 2000).

The Parents' Perspective

Parents play an important role in why girls drop out of school. Parents have an ambivalent attitude toward their daughters dropping out of school. They do not support it because they are afraid of complaints from their children in the future. However, they are against it because in their hearts, they do not support education for girls, similar to the findings of Wang (2008). Parents in rural areas make every decision from the current aspect (Jin, Zeng, Shan, & Fu, 2007). With the development of society, the government makes policies to satisfy its constituents. Government advocates job hunting for students, rather than providing jobs from the government. With the reform, government no longer has to focus much on providing jobs for university graduates (Ministry of Education of the People's Republic of China [MOE], 1994). Thus, students who graduate from university will have the chance to choose their own jobs. Parents cannot understand the policy well. Thus, they would rather spend the money on finding a job rather than on schooling. In addition, it is a common belief that individuals who graduate from middle school display similarities with illiterate people. As the content of the curriculum is not practical, the knowledge seems useless. Those realities force the parents to give up on schooling for their children (Zhang, 2002).

One particular case involving a Hui minority girl is worth highlighting. Han Xiaohua says, "My grandfather is against schooling for girls because there was a Hui girl who eloped with a Han boy secretly. . . . My grandfather thinks that Hui minority girls become bad if they are in school for a long time." Thus, the family will not support the schooling for Hui minority girls.

School Curriculum

There are some shortcomings in the current education system, especially for minority students (Long, 2008). Schools pay more attention to exam scores rather than to the children (Chang & Li, 2007). Although the evaluation system has been revised by administrative departments in some schools, the result is rather insufficient. In order to achieve higher exam scores, the students' leisure time is taken up. Children have to face much homework and "boring" classes. Some curriculums are different from practice, which means the knowledge from school will be useless in the future. Seeing this reality, students start to lose interest in school and thereafter are unwilling to go to school (Wang, 2008). In addition, it is a common phenomenon that minority girls have lower exam scores than Han students. Some teachers have biases against students who get lower scores. They punish the students by beating them or through other ways. These actions make students unwilling to go to school (Zhu & Wang, 2000). We cannot deny the importance of a unified curriculum, but the unified curriculum will not fit every school and every student. The curriculum could be changed according to local conditions. If the curriculum is based on the local situation, it can become more effective for both schools and the students.

Children's Perspectives

The children's perceptions are important factors leading to their dropout. As the thoughts of children are subjective reasons, they can decide whether to drop out or not. The government, schools, and families create many conditions that affect the dropping out of minority students, but the thoughts of children themselves are also key factors. There are many factors among children that cause them to believe they should drop out (Zhu & Wang, 2000). First, low exam scores lead children to drop out. Compared with Han students, minority students have low exam scores. Sometimes, they cannot catch up with the curriculum. This is why they feel that they lose interest in going to school. If students lose interest, dropping out may be unavoidable. Second, the lack of right ideas advances the idea of youth dropouts. Some limitations exist on the social environments in rural minority areas. Thus, some students always feel confused about what they can do in the future. They lose the confidence and determination to overcome the difficulties in studying. Thus, they opt to drop out from school. Marriage is the most crucial factor among many Hui minority girls. They think that working hard in school is unnecessary. Third, the influence of peers accelerates the rate of dropouts. Due to certain reasons, there are no alternatives to the dropping out of children from rural minority areas. Children believe they may live a better life if they simply drop out early in life. This phenomenon affects other children's studying in school. Some students choose to drop out to earn income and provide for their current needs (Zhang, 2002).

The Social Environment

Society has the duty to prevent student dropout. However, the social environment provides reasons otherwise. Although the law forbids the hiring of teenagers under 18 years old, some employers willingly hire people who have just dropped out of school. As compulsory education is new in the society, they do not pay much attention to income but hope to accumulate experience in the society. Thus, children who drop out are public in the labor market. In addition, those teenagers do not have as much family burden as adults do. Hiring them is relatively easy for employers. This is the reason why school dropouts can find jobs easily (Zhang, 2002). Apart from income, there are other temptations for students. Teenagers are not mature enough; therefore, they may make decisions based on temptations from the society. The social environment is another important factor affecting student dropouts.

DISCUSSION

Indeed, the reasons that lead children to drop out are complex. Through this study, we found some reasons why Hui minority girls drop out from school. The reasons can be categorized into the following aspects.

First, it is necessary to pay attention to the dropout rate in Hui minority girls. The rates of enrollment and dropping out are two important factors when assessing compulsory education (Yu & Du, 2007). Indeed, it is necessary to raise the enrollment rate and reduce the dropout rate. However, most people pay more attention to enrollment than dropout rates (Wang, 2008). Some reasons can be ascribed to this phenomenon. Before the setting up of the People's Republic of China, the level of education was low in Qinghai Province. In fact, the enrollment rate was less than 10% in the entire Qinghai. Girls rarely have access to schools; the rate of illiteracy was 99% for girls. After the establishment of the People's Republic of China, education in the minority areas was developed to a certain degree. The government took action to create good conditions for girls. Indeed, education for girls is fruitful in some areas. However, some other problems should be addressed in the education of minority girls. Many are used to placing attention on how to enroll girls in schools and, as much as possible, for a long period (Ma, J., 2000). The history of lower enrollment of minority girls causes people to pay attention to the enrollment rate, but the situation of education is changing day by day. The enrollment rate is increasing gradually (Wang, 2008). Hence, the next step should be to reduce the dropout rate. The situation of interviewees shows the facts about this phenomenon. There are nine interviewees in the study, and eight of them dropped out in different grades. Evidently, dropping out from school is an important factor that can defeat compulsory education. We have to usher in a new period to reduce the dropout rate.

Second, poverty is an important external reason for the dropout of minority students. The revised law on compulsory education provides free education for students in the rural areas (NPC, 2006). Such is meant to reduce the economic burden in the family. Accordingly, minority students and their families need not suffer from any economic burdens in relation to youth education. However, the actual situation is not the same as the policy itself. On the one hand, families have to pay extra fees in this new situation. For example, with the reduction of school-aged children in China, some schools were merged while others closed. Children have to go to other schools that are far from their homes. Families then have to pay for traveling fees. If the school is far enough, the families have to pay for lodging fees. These fees are not small. Hence, sending children to school is still a heavy economic burden for the families. On the other hand, parents in poor families do not support the schooling for children even if they pay nothing. Children are part of the labor force in the family, and they can earn money if they drop out of school. In the interviews, some students were proud of dropping out in order to earn income. Dropping out of school gives minority girls a higher status in the family because of the money they earn. Meanwhile, even if children are too young to work outside, they can do housework in order to reduce the burden in the family. Thus, for family-related factors, poverty is a main reason for dropping out.

Third, the culture of the Hui minority is one important internal factor for the dropouts. There are many factors related to culture—such as traditional customs, language, and religion (Teng, 2009)—that influence school dropouts. Culture originated in ancient times, but some traditional cultures still exist in the modern society. Incidentally, some traditional customs promote dropping out of school among Hui girls. For example, a Hui minority girl aged over 9 years old is regarded as a grown-up. Accordingly, they should wait for marriage at home and avoid going outside their household premises. According to the Law on Compulsory Education in China, children are obliged to go to school beginning at the age of 7 years (NPC, 2006). Many Hui minority girls give up schooling when they are over 9 years old. Tradition is therefore one key reason resulting in dropout. Hui minority girls over 9 years old are told to minimize their contact with strangers, especially boys. In the study, girls and boys were not separated in local schools. Thus, it forms a huge barrier for Hui minority girls in school. In the interviews, such a case was mentioned many times. Five or six years ago, one Hui minority girl left school with her classmate, a Han boy. They left school to work in an urban area. Parents and grandparents hope to avoid this kind of case from happening again; therefore, they prevent Hui girls from going to school. However, this is an uncommon phenomenon in this village. Due to cultural factors, separate schools for girls and boys have been implemented in some minority areas of China (*"Education,"* 2009) with the hope of reducing the chances of this kind of case happening again. In addition, language is an important factor in the dropout. No example was gathered in this study, but the barrier of language does exist in many minorities. In a minority nation, people have different languages. There are 55 minority groups and 129 languages in China (Sun, Hu, &

Huang, 2008). People have difficulty communicating with each other. As an example, there are three branches of Yao in the Guangxi Autonomous Region Lingyun County. Students in school could not communicate smoothly. If teachers do not learn the language of minorities, there will be a greater barrier for students. However, this did not happen in the place where the research was conducted. Nearly all students and teachers spoke Arabic, making it relatively easy to communicate. Finally, the Hui minority conforms to Islam as dictated by their history. Thus, parents want their children to go to mosques rather than to schools, an apparent influence of religion. Parents' thoughts and actions are affected by religion as well, and they normally decide not to send their children to school. In fact, culture is a broad concept as it includes many aspects. Hence, there are many reasons influencing the dropouts from a cultural perspective.

Finally, the curriculum is not attractive to the minority students. The curriculum is unified in local areas, and there is little diversity in the curriculum. In minority residential areas, the curriculum should have local characteristics. The local curriculum should not only promote knowledge of the history and culture in local minorities, but should also dissuade students from job hunting in local areas (Xu, 2002).

Diversity is an effective way to promote the development of minorities through diverse curriculums. At present, the curriculum is not flexible. Limited information exists on local history and culture in the curriculum. However, the current curriculum cannot provide ample knowledge for daily subsistence after graduation. As a result, students lose their interest in the curriculum and drop out of school.

IMPLICATIONS OF THE STUDY

Of the 55 minority groups in China, the Hui minority is a major branch (Y. Ma, 1984). The Hui minority is powerful because of religious influences. Many factors affect the dropout rates of minority girls. Hui minority girls are vulnerable. They should obtain equal education, the same as other students. The present study focuses on the dropping out of Hui minority girls, but there are many similar groups facing the same situation worldwide. As researchers in education, we have no ability to change the economic or political situation, but providing recommendations on the curriculum is one aspect for change. Relevant theory and practice should be utilized in minority education in order to avoid the dropping out of students.

Our study on dropping out of school in minority students shows the reasons why the government cannot accomplish the goals of compulsory education. Poverty, cultural differences, and the social environment are all important factors related to the dropout among minority girls. Dropping out of school is one phenomenon among minority students. This study takes the dropping out of Hui minority girls as an example. The study will make the global community aware of the situation of the minority girls in China. The theory of multicultural education originated in the United States. At present, that theory is being utilized to implement educational services in China, especially for minority groups. Multicultural education is based on equal rights and opportunities. It promotes a style of teaching and studying that takes into consideration cultural differences (Bennett, 1999). In a multicultural social background, it may be useful to develop respect and understanding of different cultures through educational reform in order for minority students to enjoy equality and justice in education (Xie, 1995). With the development of a multicultural world, multicultural education has also grown gradually. Multicultural education remains a sensitive global issue. It affects all countries and citizens, and involves all aspects of the educational system. Multicultural education reflects a certain view of the value of education, taking into consideration diverse beliefs and promoting international understanding and education for all. It aims to eliminate discrimination and bias through improvements in the educational system. All citizens, no matter their minority, ethnic, or national origins, should be able to develop their talents equally and amply (Chen, 2005). As Banks and Banks (1993) say, multicultural education is a thought, a philosophical view, a value tendency, a creative action in education, and a curriculum aimed at changing the current structure of education. For the issues on the dropout among Hui minority girls, this study serves as a reference for other minorities, whether they are located in China or in other countries.

REFERENCES

Banks, J. A., & Banks, C. A. M. (1993). *Multicultural education issues and perspectives*. Boston: Allyn & Bacon.

Bennett, C. I. (1999). *Comprehensive Multicultural Education: Theory and Practice*. Boston: Allyn and Bacon.

Chang, B. & Li, L. (2007). On problems and countermeasures of the curriculum guidance in elementary and middle schools. *Journal on the Development of Education, 7:* 20–21.

Chen, S. (2005). The historic mission of multicultural education under the view of globalization. *Journal of Research on Comparative Education, 12,* 37–42.

Cheng, L. (2006, June 29). Three features and six highlights in the revised version on law of compulsory education [Editorial]. *Xinhua Net.* Retrieved from http://news.xinhuanet.com/edu/2006–06/30/content_4769537.htm, 03/12/2009.

China Yearbook Editorial Department. (2006). *The People's Republic of China yearbook 2006*. Beijing: China Yearbook Press.

Dai, Q., & Dong, Y. (1996). History of bilingual education in Chinese minority. *Journal of Research on Education for Ethnic Minority, 4.* Retrieved from http://www.edu.cn/20011205/3012866.shtml. 02-09-2011.

Education. (2009, July 22). Education on Keerkezi minority. *China Minority Net.* Retrieved from http://mz.china.com.cn/?action-viewnews-itemid-2538

Jin, D., Zeng, P., Shan, Z., & Fu, A. (2007). Research on dropping out for middle school students in rural area. *Journal of Theory and Practice on Education, 15,* 46–49.

Lei, R. (2008). The exhibition and display of history and culture of the Hui: A research on making use of cultural relics of Chinese Hui people. *Journal of Hui Muslim Minority Study*, 3, 11–18.

Liu, Y. (2008, August 2). It is equal to reduce the fees on compulsory education in city. [Editorial]. *Xinhua News*. Retrieved from http://www.gov.cn/jrzg/2008-08/02/content_1062676.htm

Long, Q. (2008). The existing problems and its countermeasures of minorities' cultural curriculum resource exploitation. *Journal of Chongqing Three Gorges University*, 24.

Ma, F. (1997). *The current situation and development of the Hui minority in Shaanxi Province*. Beijing: Work Communication.

Ma, J. (2000). An analysis of the regional features of the distribution of the Hui nationalities' population compared with that of several other nationalities. *Journal of Hui Muslim Minority Study*, 4, 7–12.

Ma, T. (2008). Problems and countermeasures for Hui students in rural area of Yili. *Journal of Yili Prefecture Communist Party Institute*, 1, 88–91.

Ma, Y. (1984). *Common sense of minority in China*. Beijing: China Youth Press.

Ma, Y. (2000). Feature and approach of Hui minority education in Qinghai. *Journal of Research on Minority in Qinghai*, 3, 21.

Ministry of Education of the People's Republic of China. *Brief review of great events on education in 50 years (1980–1989)*. Retrieved from http://www.moe.edu.cn/edoas/website18/87/info4987.htm. The published date is 02–04–2002.

National People's Congress (NPC) Standing Committee (China). (1986). *The Law of Compulsory Education in People's Republic of China*. Beijing: Author.

NPC Standing Committee (China). (2006). *The Law of Compulsory Education in People's Republic of China* (New version). Beijing: Author.

Patton, M. (2002). *Qualitative Research and Evaluation Methods*. Thousand Oaks, CA: Sage.

Su, X. (2008, September 18). The brief introduction of Hui minority. [Editorial]. *China Net*. Retrieved from http://www.china.com.cn/aboutchina/zhuanti/hzfq/content_16501504_3.htm

Sun, H., Hu, Z., & Huang, X. (2008). *Languages in China*. Beijing: Commercial Press.

Teng, X. (2009). *Girls' education in multicultural society*. Beijing: Minority Press.

Wang, J. (2008). A longitudinal study of the problem of school dropouts of adolescent girls in ethnic minority poverty-stricken areas. *Journal of Research on Education for Ethnic Minority*, 1, 116–121.

Xie, N. (1995). Multicultural education in global society. *Foreign Social Sciences*, 23.

Xu, Y. (2002). Analysis of relationship between school-based curriculum and national curriculum development. *Educational Science Research*, 5, 18–20.

Yang, W., & Liu, X. (2006, September 27). The culture of minority is disappearing. *Xinhua Net*. Retrieved from http://news.xinhuanet.com/newmedia/2006-09/27/content_5141872.htm. 2009–12–03.

Yao, H., & Ren, Z. (2008). *Annual report on economic development in western region of China*. Beijing: Social Sciences Academic Press.

Yu, Z., & Du, M. (2007). Social analysis on low enrollment rate and high dropping out rate of minority rural area in western area. *Journal of Kangding Nationality Teachers College*, 16, 57–60

Yuan, L., & Tian, H. (2003). On the fairness of education resource distribution through selecting school. *Journal of Educational Science of Hunan Normal University*, 5, 75–77.

Zhang, M. (2002). Analysis of relationship between school-based curriculum and national curriculum development. *Journal of Guizhou Education College, 6,* 12–13.

Zhu, X., & Wang, X. (2000). Investigation and analysis of the reasons of students discontinuing their studies or dropping out of school in minority areas in Zhejiang Province. *Journal of Zhejiang Normal University, 2,* 80–84.

4 Multiculturalism in China

Conflicting Discourses in Universities

Zhenzhou Zhao

INTRODUCTION

A couple of years ago, I studied an undergraduate program at a university in Beijing, People's Republic of China (PRC). One of my roommates belonged to a Chinese minority group, the Mongols. We lived in a standard Chinese university student room—a tiny and crowded living space for six. Like the rest of us, this Mongol student spoke Mandarin, went to the same classrooms, and ate in the same canteen.

However, at times, our cultural differences adversely affected life in our community. This student maintained a strong interest in a Mongolian language radio program that was broadcast late every evening, although she could barely speak her mother tongue. One day, she returned from a large Mongolian gathering, excited and pleased. However, we, as members of China's Han majority, could hardly share her feelings. Her facial expressions conveyed obvious disappointment.

Some of the most telling experiences involved the television. My Mongol roommate would get very excited while watching TV programs about her people. However, the rest of us preferred watching other programs, and this led to misunderstandings.

During my final year at the university, I started to consider the notion of multicultural education, an emerging Anglo-American concept. It happened after a professor returned from a visit at the University of Toronto, Canada. Her classes triggered my curiosity on how affirmative actions for minority groups in China, called "preferential policies" in official parlance, were related to what was then a fresh idea for me. I wondered: Would it be possible for socialist China to embrace multiculturalism?

While globalization is softening political borders between countries, cultural borders resulting from resurgent attitudes toward ethnicity and race are playing increasingly important roles in defining individual identity and separating one person from another (Smolicz, Hudson, & Secombe, 1998). This is becoming extraordinarily important for multiethnic countries, such as China. Based on a historical review, Dreyer (1999) described the Middle Kingdom (i.e., "China" in the Chinese language) as a country that has adopted a "monocultural paradigm." In the post-Mao era, the situation remains unchanged:

> To the post-Mao leadership, as to its predecessors, whether Marxist or Confucian, multiculturalism meant diversity, diversity implied division, and division meant weakness. Before it was challenged by the West, Confucianism could not tolerate multiculturalism, since it believed all other cultures to be vastly inferior. After being challenged by the West, Confucianism and Marxism rejected multiculturalism because plurality engendered disorder and weakness against enemies. (p. 596)

However, studies on ethnic minority education in China have demonstrated that cultural diversity, especially in religion and language, continues to exist and is even flourishing under the socialist regime in the past six decades (Postiglione, 1998, 2009). Interestingly, Chinese intellectuals keenly use the theoretical lens of multiculturalism to analyze the situation of ethnic minorities in China's educational system (Zhang, 2005).

In the wake of my university experience, I embarked on a journey to study the cultural recognition of ethnic minority groups in educational settings. In particular, I focused on higher educational institutions (HEIs) because, in the words of Torres (1998), they are "the center of the storm in terms of diversity and affirmative action" (p. 439). In 2004, I traveled across half of China and investigated ethnic relations in three different universities. This chapter presents the multicultural experiences of minority college students, compares state policies and institutional entrenchments in universities, and discusses China's version of multiculturalism.

RESEARCH CONTEXT

China's ethnic landscape map is based on a nationwide ethnic identification program that began in the early 1950s. Although more than 400 groups applied for registration as distinct nationalities (*minzu*, which has recently been translated to "ethnic groups"), the Chinese government has recognized only one majority (Han) and 55 minority groups based on presumed objective nationality criteria formulated by Joseph Stalin in 1913 (i.e., common territory, language, economy, and psychological make-up manifested in a common culture) (Bilik, Lee, Shi, & Phan, 2004). There is great diversity among minority groups, from the largest group (Zhuang) to the smallest (Lhopa). They account for over 100 million people, but they comprise less than 10% of the national population.

For decades, the government has been committed to absorbing minorities into the official educational system for the purpose of building a homogenized, socialist-orientated national educational system (Hansen, 1999). The most important incentive is preferential treatment, specifically for ethnic minority students. The measures include native language school-ing, university examinations in minority languages, preferential admissions to universities, and specially designated ethnic minority colleges, as well as a program that provides a remedial year of preparatory study for students with academic needs (this program includes courses to improve Chinese language abilities). Statistical evidence supports the government's view that ethnic education has considerably developed since the Chinese Communist Party (CCP) took power in 1949 (Figure 4.1). Positive statistics create the image that minority students enjoy privileges in terms of resource alloca-tions. However, they leave unanswered questions about whether and how state-sponsored HEIs build a multicultural environment for students from diverse backgrounds, and how they help these students overcome barriers after their enrolment.

The most prominent preferential treatment offered to ethnic minorities is relaxation in university admission standards "to an appropriate extent" (Sautman, 1999, p. 175). In different provinces, bonus points for admis-sion that are accorded to minorities vary according to territorial area, HEI, and year. It should be noted that each member of a minority group is eli-gible for admission, regardless of where he or she lives; hence, those who are living in communities with Han Chinese also benefit. However, this policy is increasingly undermined by the fact that Hans illegally change

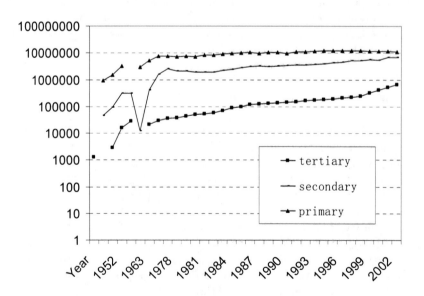

Figure 4.1   Number of ethnic students enrolled at different educational levels (1950–2003).
Source: China's Ethnic Statistics Yearbook *(Zhongguo minzu tongji nianjian)*, 2004 [Beijing: Ethnic Press *(Minzu chubanshe)*].

their registered ethnic status or registered residence to benefit from the preferential treatment, especially to access higher education. In 2009, the case of He Chuan-yang attracted widespread attention in the cyberspace and in print media. His father changed his ethnic status from Han to ethnic Tujia for him to obtain preferential treatment in the tertiary education entrance exams. This practice is very common. Despite the fact that He was one of the top scorers in Chongqing, his false identity caused his rejection by prestigious Chinese universities (Xiong, 2009). Some local scholars, such as Teng Xing at the Central University for Nationalities and Ma Rong at Peking University, have proposed that many factors should be considered when determining whether a student qualifies for preferential treatment. These factors may include regional disparities, local economic development, local culture, and social class. Scholars question whether preferences should be granted across the board. Indeed, this policy is increasingly becoming contentious. However, there are still no signs that it will be abolished because minorities are still quantitatively under-represented in China's HEIs, and lower requirement standards help improve their enrollment, regardless of whether or not students are authentic minority members.

Another manifestation of preferential treatment, as mentioned above, is the existence of more than 100 HEIs (among them, 13 are universities and the rest are colleges) created especially for ethnic minorities. These institutions offer minority students preferential admission and financial assistance in the form of subsidies. They also provide specialized courses and programs, such as ethnology, ethnic linguistics, ethnic history, and arts. These institutions have an essential mission: to cultivate minority talents to serve the state. In addition, their most prominent role is to train loyal cadres from minority groups to serve the state and to simultaneously encourage them to "love their own nationalities" (Mackerras, 1998, p. 284). However, some scholars, such as Teng Xing, argue that these institutions may work against their intended purpose; they may foster ethnic segregation and group consciousness. Overall, these educational institutions comprise a minor portion of the total number of China's HEIs; China has about 2,000 state-run and 1,000 private HEIs. More importantly, very few of these minority-geared institutions are well known or prestigious.

CONCEPTUAL FRAMEWORK

According to Allen's (2006) analysis on blacks, other people of color, women, and marginal groups, full and equal participation by members of disadvantaged groups in higher education is limited by "'racial macroaggressions' at the group, institutional, and structural levels"—and at the same time—by 'racial microaggressions' at the interpersonal, individual, and intra-psychic levels" (p. 224). To understand the campus climate and environment of minorities in universities, Allen (2006) proposed an external/internal framework that encompasses social and institutional forces. External forces refer to government programs and social policies, as well as sociohistorical movements. Internal forces include four dimensions in the institutional context that may influence educational programs and the racial climate of institutions, including

> a "historical legacy of inclusion/exclusion" for various race/ethnic groups; "structural diversity" in terms of numerical representations among different race/ethnic groups; a "psychological climate" of perceptions and attitudes between/among groups; and a "behavioral climate" characterized by intergroup relations on campus. (pp. 207–208)

In terms of external (social) forces in the Chinese context, minority members are granted preferential treatment by state policies. Huang and Nong (2003) argued that Chinese minority students enjoy equal rights in accessing higher education. In effect, the government highlights the meaningful admission of minority students to universities and turns them into models for their group members to emulate (Postiglione, 2000).

However, studies based on the experiences and perceptions of minority students often tell a different story (Clothey, 2005; Hansen, 1999; Zhao, 2010; Zhu, 2007). McCarthy (2000) asserted that the state does not commit itself to the promotion of minority cultures, although their religions, languages, and cultural practices are officially protected by the constitution. In the case of ethnic Tibetans, Zhu (2007) noted that the official state culture predominates the informal or manifest curricula in schools, and is transmitted to students for internalization through classroom teaching. This chapter uses "discourses" to explain such discrepancy. According to Fraser (1989), discourses are "patterns of interpretation" (p. 156), and meanings constitute social and institutional relationships. In other words, discourses are inherently related to politics because they empower some people on one side and subjugate others on another side by "highly controlling regimes of knowledge and disciplinary practices" (Hemmings, 2002, p. 293).

Discourse is not a simple linguistic concept; rather, it links language to practice, or what has been said and what has been done (Hall & Thomas, 1999). Furthermore, discourse involves socially constructed rules and regulations, which legitimize some statements and delegitimize others. For this reason, different discourses achieve different levels of status in institutions. Coates (1996) asserted that some forms of discourses become dominant in an institution because they appear to be "natural," thus "[making] invisible the fact they are just one among many different discourses" (p. 240). Furthermore, dominant discourses "tend to be reaffirmed through their institutionalization," and other discourses appear to be hidden or strange (Allan, 2003, p. 48). Consequently, people prefer to use what is dominant (Coates, 1996).

In another way, discourse functions to build social identities, consciously and unconsciously (Allan, 2003). As Pierre (2000) noted, "once a discourse becomes 'normal' and 'natural,' it is difficult to think and act outside it" (p. 485). However, resistance is possible against a discourse of domination, although such a discourse can control people's actions and even their bodies (Pierre, 2000). It should be noted that voice and discourse are not the same. The distinction between discourse and voice hinges on the fact that the former is institutional, interpersonal, and unauthored, whereas the latter is personalized for individuals or groups (Shohat & Stam, 1994).

This study reduces the four internal (institutional) dimensions to two discourses. The former two dimensions—historical legacy of the institution and structural diversity—are combined under institutional discourse. More specifically, this discourse refers to university policies and structures. Policy and structural discourses reflect authorities' concerns for political goals, that is, fostering ethnic unity, social stability, and national identity (Clothey, 2005). The latter two dimensions—psychological climate and behavioral climate—are jointly referred to as daily life discourse. This discourse may not be openly articulated in state policies, university documents, or campus media; it is taken for granted by all campus actors (i.e., administrative staff, teachers, and students). This chapter aims to examine institutional forces in universities, to answer research questions concerning university efforts to promote a multicultural learning environment, and to compare these efforts to the interpretation of minority students.

DATA COLLECTION

Fieldwork was conducted from July to December 2004 in three universities: Inner Mongolia Normal University (IMNU, *Neimenggu shifan daxue*), Beijing Normal University (BNU, *Beijing shifan daxue*), and South China University for Nationalities (SCUN, *Zhongnan minzu daxue*). They represent each of the three types of universities that minority students may access in contemporary China. According to Cheng (2006), there are three types of universities/colleges with respect to financing and management:

> those financed and managed by the national government through the Ministry of Education (these are meant to be flagship institutions of national priority); national institutions financed and managed by respective ministries; and provincial institutions financed and managed by provincial governments. (p. 99)

The three universities included in this study fit Cheng's typology. IMNU, which is under the authority of the autonomous regional government, is in Hohhot, the capital of Inner Mongolia Autonomous Region (IMAR). Its student population is mainly composed of Mongols and Hans, and it is the only university with both a Chinese language stream (students are called *Hansheng*) and a minority language (Mongolian) stream (students are called *Mengsheng*). BNU, a university run by the Ministry of Education, is a standard and predominately Han institution. It accommodates a very small number of students from diverse ethnic backgrounds. It is located in Beijing, a cosmopolitan city. SCUN, on the other hand, is mainly financed and managed by the Ethnic Affairs Bureau. It is a special university for training minority members in Hubei Province, although minority students only account for barely more than 50% of its population. The selection of the three universities is a strategy to maximize access to information (Stake, 1995).

Content analysis of selected relevant documents was carried out. University documents collected in this study included student handbooks, regulation documents, campus newspapers, student publications, and so on. All were issued by the universities to disseminate their ideologies; some were student requirements. These three universities displayed similarities in terms of administrative structures and student organizations. Interviews were conducted with administrative staff members who were in charge of student activities: members of the Communist Youth League Committee (CYLC, *Tuanwei*) at both university and department levels; staff at the Office of Student Affairs, canteen, and Psychological Consultation Center; teachers responsible for running campus media (e.g., campus radio stations and newspapers); and staff at the United Front Work Department (at BNU) and the Office of the Mongolian Language Teaching and Learning (*Mengyu jiaoyu yanjiu ke*) at IMNU. Academic staff members were interviewed, and classes were observed. In addition, interviews were conducted with student cadres who were in charge of student unions at both university and department levels; members of the Federation of Student Associations, Student Self-Administration Association, Art Troupe, and campus media (e.g., campus TV stations, campus newspapers, and radio stations); and regular students. In the interviews, a "client perspective" was adopted to empower students (Byrne, 2003). There were 122 interviewees (Table 4.1). Additionally, 15 Mongol students at a university for nationalities (including those in the pilot study and interviewed for fieldwork in Beijing), two well-known Mongol scholars, and two government officials were interviewed. The number of interviewees totaled 141.

FINDINGS

Data were sorted into two categories: institutional discourse, including the efforts of universities to help minority students cross cultural borders; and daily life discourse, including agent experiences and perceptions.

Institutional Discourse

In terms of university policies, the three universities are highly consistent, although IMNU and SCUN also highlight their ethnic characteristics. The policy discourse of a university is manifested in its policies and regulations,

Table 4.1 Number and Ethnic Identity of Interviewees

		Minorities	Han	Others	Total
IMNU	Academic and administrative staff	8	9	2 (unknown[a])	19
	Students	24	8		32
BNU	Academic and administrative staff		8	6 (1 foreigner, 5 unknown)	14
	Students	14	12		26
SCUN	Academic and administrative staff	1	5	4 (unknown)	10
	Students	14	7		21
Total		61	49	12	122

[a]*"Unknown" interviewees are high-ranking university administrators. It was quite difficult to conduct long interviews with them during the fieldwork, and there was not enough time to discuss their ethnicities.*

documents from university-sponsored campus media, student handbooks, and accounts from teachers and students. Three themes have emerged from the content analysis of documents from IMNU, BNU, and SCUN.

First, ethnic minorities are concerned about their customs and have positive views toward political involvement. For example, the third article in a section entitled University Students Behavior Criteria (*Gaodeng xuexiao xuesheng xingwei zhunze*) in the Handbook of Chinese University Students called for students to "respect different ethnic group customs and religious beliefs" (p. 26). This article is present in the student handbooks of all three universities. At IMNU, the *Chinese Communist Youth League Member's Civility Code (Tuanyuan wenming gongyue)*, contained in the CYLC Member Handbook, requires all members to "respect minority student languages, customs, and lifestyles" (p. 66). According to the SCUN Campus Order Regulations mentioned above, no one is permitted to bring non-Islamic food into SCUN's canteen, although non-Muslim students are not barred from eating at the canteen. Moreover, campus media describe the provision of aids to minority groups. For instance, the *BNU Express (Shida kuaixun)* reports that "ethnic Dongxiang teachers from Gansu Province were invited to visit the BNU Experimental Primary School and some days later, minority Dongxiang children came here again after they received financial donations from students at our school" (Issue No. 67, p. 5). Similarly, the *Student Home (Xuesheng zhijia)* (November 2003), a student publication, reports that students went to ethnic areas in Yunnan Province to improve local educational levels. These reports paint a picture, suggesting that "advanced Han as a whole helped the more backward minorities to develop" (Hansen, 1999, p. 261).

Second, ethnic minorities are economically backward, and they rely on external aids. Two articles in the Higher Educational Law of the People's Republic of China (passed on August 29, 1998, during the Ninth Session of the Standing Committee of the National People's Congress Fourth Conference) stipulate state aid for ethnic minorities:

Article 8: The state helps develop higher education and cultivate talent for ethnic minorities based on their characteristics and needs.
Article 9: Citizens have the right to obtain higher education. The state helps ethnic and poor students gain access to higher education.

Indeed, the IMAR government encourages Mongol students to choose their preferred ethnic study programs, although with some caveats. At BNU, ethnic minority students are eligible to receive more in monthly subsidies than Hans. SCUN implements regulations to help ethnic students after enrollment. Specifically, the university stipulates that undergraduates who major in ethnic studies are exempt from tuition, whereas students with other majors are charged from RMB 4,500 to 5,850 per year.

Third, all ethnic groups conform to the policy of ethnic unity as a component of Chinese nationality. The University Students Behavior Criteria (*Gaodeng xuexiao xuesheng xingwei zhunze*), which is detailed in the student handbooks of the three universities, requires that students "maintain ethnic group equality, unification, and cooperation in relations . . . and oppose any behavior that goes against national unity." More often than not, promoting unity among all groups involves three steps. First, emphasis is placed on ethnic unity as a university mission and as a criterion for student evaluations. For instance, while addressing the issue of how the youth love their country, the textbook *Cultivation of Ideological Morality* (*Sixiang daode xiuyang*) states that students should realize the importance of "unity among all ethnic groups and reunification of the motherland" (p. 8). Second, promoting unity involves promoting the Chinese nation (*Zhonghua minzu*); the promotion is found in speeches by leaders, regulations, and campus media. Examples include a call to "realize the Chinese nation's revival" in the *New Student Handbook* (pp. 6–7), "striving for the Chinese nation's development" in the *Undergraduate Curricula* (p. 7), and "fostering the Chinese nation's educational development" in the *Message of BNU's Alumni (Xiaoyou tongxun)* (p. 22) at BNU. These discursive practices contribute to an explicit goal: the "construction of a sense of unity with the Chinese nation" (Upton, 1999, p. 309). Finally, a lack of attention to minority culture helps promote unity. For example, there is no literature by minority authors or about minority groups in the Recommended Books for Developing University Students Cultural Cultivation (*Daxuesheng wenhua suzhi tuijian yuedu shumu*) listed in the *University Student Handbook in Inner Mongolia*.

Regarding the structural discourses of the three universities, IMNU and SCUN appear to represent more ethnic culture in the academia, curricula, campus media, and student organizations. A comparison of administrative discourses across the three universities is found in Table 4.2. As a university located in the ethnic areas, IMNU has a Department of Mongolian Language and Literature, bilingual classes in some departments, many courses pertaining to Mongolian culture and language, a Mongolian museum, Mongolian-language programs in the campus media, and two student associations especially for *Mengsheng*. SCUN has a Faculty of Ethnic Studies and Sociology, some courses on ethnicity, the Ethnological Museum, some programs focusing on minority culture in the campus media, and the Ethnic Studies Group (*Minzu yanjiuhui*, a student association). Yet, no minority language courses or programs are offered by the university. Each of the three universities has a canteen for Muslims. During interviews with administrative staff and Han students, it was found that the canteen is often referred to as a sign of official respect for minority groups. However, ethnic cultures are thinly represented in other service departments or in campus architectural styles. Compared with IMNU and SCUN, ethnicity does not play a crucial role in BNU's academic and administrative structure. There is an Office of Ethnic Affairs in the United Front Work Department, and there are several courses and occasional programs—offered by the campus media—which are relevant to ethnicity. Furthermore, there are very few ethnic activities at BNU and SCUN. Ethnic songs and dances during parties provide the main methods of minority cultural representation. In reality, this also happens at IMNU.

Table 4.2 Comparison of Structural Discourses across Three Universities

	IMNU	BNU	SCUN
Undergraduate majors relevant to ethnicity	19 of 42 majors	N/A	one preparatory class and one of 41 majors
Medium of instruction	Mongolian and Chinese	Chinese	Chinese
Languages in the campus media	Mongolian, Chinese, and English	Chinese and English	Chinese and English
Canteens	one Muslim canteen	one Muslim canteen	one Muslim canteen
Museums	Mongolian Museum	N/A	Ethnological Museum
Student organizations and associations	two Mongolian associations	N/A	Ethnic Studies Group

Daily Life Discourse

Daily life discourse can shed light on the true attitudes that universities hold toward minority students. Three themes have emerged from interviews with teachers and students (including Han members and minorities) in the three universities.

First, minorities are thought of as being favored (*chixiang'er*) or cared about (*shoudao zhaogu*). In these three universities, teachers and Han students use rather similar words to describe minorities in the campus, such as favored or cared about. This perception is not only grounded on the fact that minority students enjoy lower entrance requirements, but also on the way they are treated after enrollment. At IMNU and BNU, minority students are eligible to receive higher monthly subsidies than their Han peers. Students at SCUN report that they do not enjoy this kind of subsidy.

At BNU, Han students confirm that they care about minorities' ethnic lifestyles (*minzu xiguan*), especially the lifestyle of Muslims. Out of respect for the social customs of their Uyghur or Hui classmates, Han students never take pork inside dorm rooms, and they choose a Muslim canteen for any class gathering attended by Muslim minority students. At SCUN, Han students report that Tibetan and other minority peers apply to be covered by relaxed requirements to pass regular courses, such as Mao Zedong Thought (*Maozedong sixiang gailun*), on account of language deficiencies and low academic foundations (Dec. 2, 2004). Generally, the university approves such requests.

Second, ethnicity is downplayed and devalued. At IMNU, despite the fact that the Hans think that Mongol students are favored, data suggest some negative images about *Mengsheng*. It is important to note that negative *Mengsheng* images are not held by all teachers and students, or they may have held negative images in the past, but such were later rectified by close contacts with *Mengsheng*. Nevertheless, there is a widely held perception that *Mengsheng* are exposed to many negative images—and they admit this themselves. Male *Mengsheng* are generally stereotyped as "students who do not study hard," "lazy," "drink alcohol," "troublemakers," "do not follow rules," "skip classes," and "inactive and lacking in self-discipline." Females are seen as "introverts." A student cadre at the Federation of Student Associations claims that *Mengsheng* spend much of their time drinking, and they seldom participate in student associations (Sept. 5, 2004). Although associations actively try to attract them, *Mengsheng* seem to be indifferent toward these social functions. Han students report that *Mengsheng* often drink heavily outside the campus, and they fight with the Hans upon their return.

Interviews with BNU and SCUN teachers, administrative staff, and student cadres suggest that ethnicity is downplayed in terms of their work agendas. For example, regulations of the Federation of Student Associations at

BNU allow minority students to establish their own associations, although in reality, the university neither embraces nor prohibits this practice. Authorities often think of student gatherings as threats to state security, especially the gatherings of Tibetans and Uyghurs. According to a teacher working at the BNU president's office, the best way to show respect for minority culture is to allow the performance of ethnic songs and dances during parties. On the one hand, entertainment does not affect state security. On the other hand, minorities in these parties can express themselves through their distinctive cultural practices.

Although SCUN is a university for all nationalities, an administrative staff at the university's Communist Youth League—one in charge of all student unions and associations—claims that the university respects minority groups and has built a Muslim canteen, but ethnic issues are not highlighted. Any encouragement of ethnic identities by minority students inside the campus must be modest (Nov. 23, 2004). Accordingly, 46 ethnic groups are represented in the university, and highlighting ethnicity, in effect, does not contribute to the goal of ethnic integration. According to this teacher, the SCUN campus climate is similar to that of standard universities in China, although some measures are taken to promote ethnic activities. Interviews with administrative staff at BNU and SCUN—those in charge of in-campus student activities—show that both universities do not support the activities of any specific ethnic group, but only promote activities designed for all groups (Nov. 12 and 23, 2004). Accordingly, the latter course tends to create an image of ethnic unity. Indeed, national integration has been the ultimate goal of Chinese educational policies for minority groups, and the state is against anything that can lead to ethnic splittism (Postiglione, 1992a, 1992b). Despite the fact that the universities hold annual celebrations for Tibetan and Muslim festivals, ethnicity plays only a minor role in the daily lives of students, and other minority groups receive very little attention.

A theme relevant to the downplaying of ethnicity is the devaluation of minority groups. To some degree, Han students welcome minority students—simply to satisfy their curiosity about different cultures. After some time, however, minority members understand that the Hans are not really concerned, nor do they have a desire to learn more. Their interest is based only on curiosity. Furthermore, the Hans do not truly respect minority cultures; they view minority cultures as backward.

Moreover, minority students feel inferior. A Manchu student says that many students from Inner Mongolia feel hesitant about telling others where they come from because IMAR is seen as a backward ethnic area (Nov. 4, 2004). Exposed to negative stereotypes inside the campus, minority students have "lower academic achievements," they are considered "wild," and they are seen as "troublemakers." The admissions staff at BNU claims that the enrollment of minority students is due to government policy—because these students are not as qualified as their Han counterparts. A teacher in the Department of English claims that Mongol students are wild: "Those Mongols have a feature . . . forming cliques. Mongols are very wild, and a kind of people who often fight. Therefore, we cannot keep them together because fights easily occur" (Oct. 11, 2004).

A Han student describes students from Xinjiang as "different from [them], wild, and fierce looking" and as "troublemakers." The student has witnessed several campus instances that support his views (Oct. 24, 2004).

Third, daily discourse manifests invisible separateness. There is a type of division in the three universities. At IMNU, where the student body consists primarily of Mongols and Hans, Han teachers and students perceive that *Mengsheng* and *Hansheng* do not interact much in daily life. In fact, the concepts of *Mongol students* and *Mengsheng* make a difference at IMNU. *Mengsheng*, referring to students instructed in the Mongolian language, are mainly Mongol students. *Mengsheng* comprise about one-third of all enrolled undergraduates, and Mongol students account for 43.73% of the total undergraduate population.

In a study on the interaction between Mongol and Han students at a university, Li and Yang (2004), two postgraduates at IMNU, found that *Mengsheng* tend to interact with their own group members and exclude other students. This study found that *Mengsheng* and *Hansheng* students are differentiated at IMNU, although this differentiation is sometimes hidden. Despite common perceptions among agents, the universities still seem far from realizing their important goal of promoting intercultural communication between the two groups and creating a multicultural school climate.

At BNU and SCUN, only physically salient groups tend to be recognized as authentic minority members. Fresh students might introduce themselves according to their ethnic identities during the first class meetings. However, many interviewees report that they do not know the ethnic identities of their classmates or organizational colleagues. This is primarily because most minority students do not differ from the rest. Nearly all participants report that only students from Xinjiang (Uyghur, Kazak, etc.) and Tibet (Tibetans) can easily be recognized as minorities because of their salient features and physical appearances. Occasionally, they meet authentic minority members (*zhen shaoshuminzu*) other than Uyghurs and Tibetans, such as Miaos and Koreans. Moreover, Han participants claim that their Muslim Hui classmates also eat pork.

Students from Xinjiang and Tibet form cliques and observe their own cultural practices; this makes their presence so salient. For example, a Han student reports that one night, a large number of Xinjiang students prayed and sang together inside the campus after one member's father passed away (Oct. 21, 2004). Interestingly, when minorities are mentioned during the fieldwork, some participants immediately begin to talk about Uyghurs and Tibetans.

DISCUSSION AND CONCLUSION

The daily life discourse of enrolled minority students conflicts with the institutional discourse of universities in China. However, the former echoes some components of the latter (e.g., respect for minorities). This study attempts to explain the discrepancy with reference to multiculturalism in the Chinese context.

Since it was initially proposed in Canada in the 1970s, the idea of promoting multiculturalism has been applauded around the world. Meanwhile, it has taken different shapes (Joppke, 2004). Part of this concept is mirrored in the notion of "a united multiethnic state," which is promoted by China's Constitution, and a "pluralistic unitary structure" (*duoyuan yiti geju*) described by Fei Xiaotong (1992), a prominent anthropologist. The findings suggest that cultural diversity exists in China's higher educational system, but such diversity is manipulated and distorted. The Communist Party has used the state apparatus to declare itself "the guardian and developer of minority cultures" (Dreyer, 1999, p. 591). Yet, a top-down approach institutionalizes how ethnic minority cultures are represented. The classification of ethnic groups in China is largely based on Stalin's "four commons." In China, together with sex, date of birth, and place of birth, a person's ethnic identity is marked on his or her identification card for life. Ethnic identities are then manipulated by the state as a mechanism to manage and control the people.

China practices "state multiculturalism." It is established under the auspices of the state, and it does not represent a diversity of ethnic cultures on democratic grounds. State multiculturalism arbitrarily and forcibly shapes "imagined" ethnic boundaries, which are meanwhile subject to stereotypical representations through discursive and social practices. This is inseparable from the promotion of the state, although often in a hidden way. "Imagined" and fixed ethnic boundaries create borders that separate the majority from the minority and that affect the integration of minority students into the mainstream community (Anderson, 1991).

In China, ethnic culture is always viewed as inferior or backward; it is not something to be valued. In ancient times, people of ethnic groups were often considered barbarians (Dreyer, 1999; Jenner, 2001). Harrell (1996) used the idea of a "civilizing project" to describe the hegemony of the superior center (the Han) and the inferior periphery (minority groups). Consequently, minorities are subject to "internal orientalism" (Schein, 2000, p. 123), or they are taken as "inner colonial others" (Gladney, 2004, p. 367).

Since its founding in 1949, socialist China has not been blind to ethnic differences. Rather, out of concern for national unification, the nation's leaders have been allergic to the notion of group boundaries. Under the leadership of Mao, China made efforts to create a single, new Chinese Communist culture (Dreyer, 1999). In the post-Mao era, the state aspires to build an overarching and homogeneous identity in the name of the Chinese nation (*Zhonghua minzu*). Overall, minority groups are constructed as subjects to respect, to aid financially, and to preserve as part of the history of modern China. The value of ethnic culture, however, is not recognized in the discourse of authorities.

For the sake of equality, ethnic minorities are sought and actively recruited for admission to China's universities. However, universities often fail to foster student understanding and appreciation of one another's cultural differences in collegiate environments (Postiglione, 2004). Ethnic minority identities dissolve after students arrive on campuses, or they are only occasionally represented for designated purposes. A prominent example is the use of entertainment shows during campus parties. This is commonly used as a political propaganda technique to promote nationalism and state-building in universities. Furthermore, a problem arises when, as Gladney (2004) has pointed out, songs and dances are emphasized as the only valuable features of an ethnic minority culture; minority cultures are feminized or disempowered.

State multiculturalism does not truly recognize minorities. Therefore, not surprisingly, personal advancement is increasingly becoming a primary concern for minority college students. This mirrors the findings of other studies, such as Upton's (1999) study on a Tibetan region in Qinghai Province. Despite widespread bilingualism, "local linguistic and cultural traditions seem to be losing some of their power and relevance in the face of encroaching Chinese and global cultural forces" (Upton, 1999, p. 312).

Altogether, the culture of ethnic minorities is not given true respect and value within the ideology of state multiculturalism, although universities, to some extent, pay attention to cultural conservation and respect for minorities through policies and structures. Chinese authorities are fully aware of the fact that HEIs play a role in the reproduction of essential value orientations (Postiglione, 1992a). However, they should also come to realize the importance of (a) fostering an atmosphere that is conducive to the cultural survival of ethnic groups in schools, (b) bridging the gap between minority families and society, and (c) enhancing reciprocal understanding in cross-cultural interactions.

REFERENCES

Allan, E. J. (2003). Constructing women's status: Policy discourses of university women's commission reports. *Harvard Educational Review*, 73(1), 44–72.

Allen, W. R. (2006). Sticks, stones, and broken bones: Rhetoric and reality in the University of Michigan Affirmative Action cases. In W. R. Allen, M. Bonous-Hammarth, & R. Teranishi (Eds.), *Higher education in a global society: Achieving diversity, equity, and excellence* (pp. 203–226). Amsterdam: Elsevier.

Anderson, B. (1991). *Imagined communities: Reflections on the origin and spread of nationalism* (Rev. ed.). London: Verso.

Bilik, N., Lee, Y. T., Shi, K., & Phan, H. H. (2004). The ethnic and cultural process of *zhongguo* (China) as a central kingdom. In Y. T. Lee et al. (Eds.), *The psychology of ethnic and cultural conflict* (pp. 193–216). Westport, CT: Praeger.

Byrne, B. (2003). Reciting the self: Narrative representations of the self in qualitative interviews. *Feminist Theory, 4*(1), 29–49.

Cheng, K. M. (2006). Diversity in education: The Chinese version. In W. R. Allen, M. Bonous-Hammarth, & R. Teranishi (Eds.), *Higher education in a global society: Achieving diversity, equity, and excellence* (pp. 91–106). Amsterdam: Elsevier.

Clothey, R. (2005). China's policies for minority nationalities in higher education: Negotiating national values and ethnic identities. *Comparative Education Review, 49*(3), 389–409.

Coates, J. (1996). *Women talk: Conversation between women friends.* Oxford, UK: Blackwell.

Dreyer, J. T. (1999). China, the monocultural paradigm. *Orbis, 43*(4), 581–597.

Fei, X. T. (1992). Ethnic identification in China. In L. Poston Jr. & D. Yaukey (Eds.), *The population of modern China* (pp. 601–614). New York: Plenum Press.

Fraser, N. (1989). *Unruly practices: Power, discourse, and gender in contemporary social theory.* Minneapolis: University of Minnesota Press.

Gladney, D. C. (2004). *Dislocating China: Reflections on Muslims, minorities and other subaltern subjects.* London: Hurst.

Hall, D., & Thomas, H. (1999). Higher education reform in a transitional economy: A case study from the school of economic studies in Mongolia. *Higher Education, 38*(4), 441–460.

Hansen, M. H. (1999). Teaching backwardness or equality: Chinese state education among the Tai in Sipsong Panna. In G. A. Postiglione (Ed.), *China's national minority education: Culture, schooling and development* (pp. 243–280). New York: Falmer Press.

Harrell, S. (1996). *Cultural encounters on China's ethnic frontiers.* Hong Kong: Hong Kong University Press.

Hemmings, A. (2002). Youth culture of hostility: Discourses of money, respect, and difference. *Qualitative Studies in Education, 15*(3), 291–307.

Huang, M. G., & Nong, C. G. (2003). Lun minzu daxuesheng jiaoyu pingdeng quan de juti biaoxian [On equal rights of schooling for college students from minority nationalities]. *Guangxi youjiang minzu shizhuang xuebao* [Journal of Youjiang Teachers College for Nationalities Guangxi], *16*(1), 93–95.

Jenner, W. J. F. (2001). Race and history in China. *New Left Review, 11*, 55–77.

Joppke, C. (2004). The retreat of multiculturalism in the liberal state: Theory and policy. *British Journal of Sociology, 55*(2), 237–257.

Li, W., & Yang, X. F. (2004). Mengguzu daxuesheng xinli jiangkang de yingxiang yinsu ji jiaoyu duice [Factors of Mongol university students' psychological health and its implication for education]. In *Haixia liang'an jiaoyu lilun yu shijian yantaohui* [The collection of the Mainland and Taiwan Educational Theory and Practice Seminar], held at IMNU, Inner Mongolia (pp. 426–428).

Mackerras, C. (1998). The minorities: Achievements and problems in the economy, national integration and foreign relations. In J. Y. S. Cheng (Ed.), *China review 1998* (pp. 281–311). Hong Kong: Chinese University Press.

McCarthy, S. (2000). Ethno-religious mobilization and citizenship discourse in the People's Republic of China. *Asian Ethnicity, 1*(2), 107–116.

Pierre, E. A. S. (2000). Poststructural feminism in education: An overview. *Qualitative Studies in Education, 13*(5), 477–515.

Postiglione, G. A. (1992a). China's national minorities and educational change. *Journal of Contemporary Asia, 22*(1), 20–44.

Postiglione, G. A. (1992b). The implications of modernization for the education of China's national minorities. In R. Hayhoe (Ed.), *Education and modernization* (pp. 307–336). Oxford, UK: Pergamon Press.

Postiglione, G. A. (1998). *State schooling and ethnicity in China: The rise or demise of multiculturalism?* Paper presented at the 14th World Congress of Sociology, Montreal, Quebec, Canada, July 26–August 1, 1998.

Postiglione, G. A. (2000). National minority regions: Studying school discontinuation. In J. Liu, H. A. Ross, & D. P. Kelly (Eds.), *The ethnographic eye: Interpretive studies of education in China* (pp. 51–72). New York: Falmer Press.

Postiglione, G. A. (2004, December 4). Why are there no Tibetans in our universities? Hong Kong needs them for cultural diversity as much as they need a world-class education. *South China Morning Post*, p. E5.

Postiglione, G. A. (2009). The education of ethnic minority groups in China. In J. A. Banks (Ed.), *The Routledge international companion to multicultural education* (pp. 501–511). New York: Routledge.

Sautman, B. (1999). Expanding access to higher education for China's national minorities: Policies of preferential admissions. In G. A. Postiglione (Ed.), *China's national minority education: Culture, schooling, and development* (pp. 173–210). New York: Falmer Press.

Schein, L. (2000). *Minority rules: The Miao and the feminine in China's cultural politics*. Durham, NC: Duke University Press.

Shohat, E., & Stam, R. (1994). *Unthinking Eurocentrism: Multiculturalism and the media*. London: Routledge.

Smolicz, J. J., Hudson, D. M., & Secombe, M. J. (1998). Border crossing in "multicultural Australia": A study of cultural valence. *Journal of Multilingual and Multicultural Development, 19*(4), 318–336.

Stake, R. E. (1995). *The art of case study research*. Thousand Oaks, CA: Sage.

Torres, C. A. (1998). Democracy, education, and multiculturalism: Dilemmas of citizenship in a global world. *Comparative Education Review, 42*(4), 421–447.

Upton, J. L. (1999). Development of modern Tibetan language education in the PRC. In G. A. Postiglione (Ed.), *China's national minority education: Culture, schooling, and development* (pp. 281–340). New York: Falmer Press.

Xiong, B. Q. (2009, July 8). The incident of He Chuanyang and reforms of higher education admissions. *Dongfang zaobao* [Dongfang Morning].

Zhang, Y. K. (2005). Duoyuan wenhua jiaoyu shiye xia de shaoshu minzu gongmin jiaoyu [Citizenship education for ethnic minorities from a perspective of multiculturalism]. *Guangxi minzu yanjiu* [Guangxi Ethnic Studies], *79*(1), 21–26.

Zhao, Z. Z. (2010). *China's Mongols at university: Contesting cultural recognition*. Lanham, MD: Lexington Books.

Zhu, Z. Y. (2007). *State schooling and ethnic identity: Neidi Tibet schools in China*. Lanham, MD: Lexington Books.

Zhongguo minzu tongji nianjian [China's Ethnic Statistics Yearbook]. (2004). Beijing: Minzu chubanshe [Ethnic Press].

5 School Life and Ethnic Identity
A Case of Tibetan Student Narrative

Zhiyong Zhu

INTRODUCTION

I conducted a study on value orientations in the Chinese language textbooks for secondary school students from 1950s to 1990s in China. I wanted to examine the dynamic transmission of value orientations presented in Chinese language textbooks, classroom interactions, and on campus between students and teachers. I focused on Tibetan Neidi[1] classes (schools). Finally, I selected CZ Tibetan Secondary School as my research case school. However, when I entered the research context and observed preparatory grade Chinese language lessons, I found that Chinese teachers mostly focused on the analysis of words, sentences, and paragraph structure of the text. The value orientations presented in the texts of the Chinese language curriculum were not given much importance or extensively discussed between students and teachers. Two Chinese teachers told me it was because Tibetan students were still incapable of understanding and speaking the Chinese language well and that the teachers could not explore much more than the central thought (*zhongxin sixiang*) in the text stories. When I interviewed the students from different grades, most of them told me that there was a lack of Tibetan stories in Chinese textbooks. This observation made me rethink my research focus.

When communicating with students in the classroom and on campus, I sensed that most Tibetan students were often inclined to make comparisons between Neidi regions and Tibet. For example, when talking about the local community environment, they responded, "In your Neidi cities, pollution is very serious. In Tibet, water in the ditch can be drunk." In mentioning bugs on the ground, they complained about some Han Chinese teachers who trod on cockroaches in the classroom in front of the students. They explained that Tibetans do not take any animal's life, including insects. Such talk helped me understand more about Tibetans and Tibetan culture, the ethnic boundary between Tibetans and Han Chinese people, and what makes Tibetan students different. My interaction with them also helped refine my research questions on the relationship between school life and ethnic identity.

In 1984, the Central Committee of the Chinese Communist Party (CCCCP) issued the document "Directive on Establishing Tibet Classes and Schools in Neidi for Cultivating Talents" (*Guanyu zai neidi chuangban xizang xuexiao he juban xizangban peiyang rencai de zhishi*). In September 1985, under the examination and supervision of the National Education Department, the State Council Economic Work Consulting Team for Tibet, and the Education Commission of the Tibet Autonomous Region, junior classes and junior schools for Tibetan students were established in 16 cities or provinces across the nation. In the same year, the first 1,300 Tibetan five-year primary graduate students were selected and sent to these schools for further study. Students in this program temporarily migrate from Tibet to other Chinese cities (Iredale et al., 2001; Wang & Zhou, 2003), living in those cities for at least four years for junior secondary school education, and, at most, 11 years including secondary school education and higher education. They cannot visit their parents within the first four years of junior secondary school education. However, they are required to go back to Tibet to attend the General Examination (*tong kao*) together with other students from local schools in Tibet for the entry to senior secondary school education. They have to compete with local students in Tibet for the fixed quota of receiving senior secondary school education in Tibet and in other areas of Neidi in China. Generally, most of them have an edge in the examination over local students in Tibet. This preferential policy for Tibetan students in Tibet has been in place for over 20 years now. I conducted the project about Neidi Tibetan secondary school and examined the relationship between state schooling and ethnic identity from 1999 to 2003. This chapter reflects one part of the project and focuses on school life and ethnic identity through a case of a Tibetan student narrative (Zhu, 2007).

SCHOOL EDUCATION AND TIBETAN IDENTITY

Tibetans have been the custodians of Buddhism for more than a thousand years, and this religion has been the mainstay of Tibetan culture (Danzu, 1993). As Mackerras (1995) remarked, "To be a Tibetan has always been nearly synonymous with belief in Tibetan Buddhism, with Tibetans feeling very little difference between pride in being Tibetan and in believing in their own particular form of Buddhism" (p. 208). Buddhist teachings impart to Tibetans a love of nature, a belief in harmony between man and nature, homogeneity, kindness, tolerance, inner peace and hope, and, especially, the theory that all things are relative (Coleman, 1994; Danzu, 1993; Dreyfus, 1995; Korom, 1997; Wang, 1998).

Additionally, as the "land of snows," the living environment of the "rooftop of the world" has contributed to Tibetan culture, helping the Tibetans form the value orientations of admiring nature, whiteness, and purity. There are five traditions in Tibetan culture (Bon, Nyingma, Kagyu,

Sakyu, and Gelug), but they share the same goal, namely, to develop an enlightened insight into the nature of mind and phenomena, based on the compassionate motivation to benefit all beings (Coleman, 1994). Characterized by religion, Tibetan culture exercises an impact on the development of Tibetan education, especially state schooling (Geng & Wang, 1989; Mackerras, 1995).

Baden Nima (2000), a Tibetan scholar, analyzed the core of the Tibetan cultural spirit, which emphasizes *qiu shan* (seeking kindness) and *jianren buba* (being persistent and indomitable). However, he demonstrated that the *qiu zhen* (seeking knowledge) consciousness was not greatly valued in Tibetan culture. Thus, he maintained that Tibetan culture needs transformation, to follow in the steps of Chinese modernization and to absorb fine products of other cultures.

As a representative of Tibetan intellectuals, Baden Nima was also involved in cultural critique. He noted that Tibetan culture is not uniform and unchanging. On this basic point, he claimed that the content of Tibetan culture should penetrate all school curricula, and that the integration of Tibetan and Chinese culture should be transmitted through the curricula as well. Such educational content would enable students to construct Tibetan identity within the context of the Chinese nation. This claim is in line with that of Postiglione (1999) that what is taught and presented in school plays a role in the construction of students' ethnic identity.

Upton (1996) portrayed and discussed the dynamic nature of the ethnic identity of Tibetan intellectuals (mainly Tibetan educators, businessmen, and officials) through observation and interviews in the grasslands of a Tibetan community. She argued that Tibetan intellectuals act as defenders and preservers of the traditional culture represented by nomadic life (returning to grasslands and cultural roots), facilitators of the modernization of Tibetan culture, and promoters and reinforcers of a unified Tibetan identity, as approved by the central government through a standardized Tibetan language curriculum.

Upton (1999) discussed the historical development and cultural significance of modern school-based Tibetan language education in Songpan County of the Aba Prefecture in Sichuan Province. In this region, bilingualism is already widespread. However, she found that local linguistic and cultural traditions seemed to be losing some of their power and relevance in the face of encroaching Chinese and global cultural forces. Regarding school textbooks, she observed, "Contrary to the rhetoric that often surfaces in Western and Tibetan-exile reports about the Tibetan language curriculum in the PRC, the textbooks do contain a fair amount of material drawn from Tibetan sources and relevant to Tibetan cultural life in the broad sense" (p. 307). Nevertheless, she claimed that "the view of Tibetan history which is presented in the formal curriculum under the current political and cultural regime is far removed from the 'real history', which so many Tibetans at home and abroad currently crave" (p. 307). She recognized that the lessons play an important role in constructing a sense of unity with the Chinese nation among young Tibetans. In this sense, bilingual education emphasizes "integration" education but neglects "pluralistic cultures" education to a great extent. She contended that the design of curriculum content would threaten the power and relevance of Tibetan language education and cultural traditions, and the negotiation of students' ethnic identity.

To promote the cultural quality of ethnic minority students and their role in local economic development, the Chinese state has practiced a variety of preferential educational policies in ethnic minority areas (Sautman, 1998). The Tibetan students on whom this chapter focuses are temporary migrants to other parts of China for the state preferential educational policy for the Tibetan Autonomous Region.

RESEARCH METHOD

I did the fieldwork in CZ Tibetan Secondary School[2] from 2001 to 2002. In the study, I collected Tibetan students' diaries as narrative materials to look into how Tibetan students perceive other Tibetans, Tibetan classmates, Han Chinese teachers, students, themselves, and others. I also looked into how they respond to matters occurring in Tibet and Neidi regions, others' perceptions, and actions inside and outside of the school.

The idea of collecting these data came from a talk with a teacher in the school office in the officially approved fieldwork site. In a discussion about the students' lives with a head teacher of Chinese, he mentioned the students' diaries. He confirmed that it was valuable to know about the students' past and current life since they had come to the Neidi school. Before I interviewed the students, the teacher said he could recommend some students with whom I could talk about the diaries. In the same way, the other two teachers of Chinese also recommended students' diaries. Altogether they recommended 10 students, of which four were from Grade 3, four from Grade 2, and two from Grade 1. The criteria that the teachers used to recommend the students are as follows:

- Good at Chinese writing and expression
- Honest and courageous enough to express real experiences and feelings
- Influential among their peers in study, class work, etc.
- Thoughtful and insightful

I talked to the vice principal in charge of the school's academic program. Upon understanding the purpose of my research, he gave me permission to collect the students' diaries for research data. With the approval of the vice principal, I negotiated with the three Chinese language teachers again. These three teachers had been informed by the vice principal of my request.

The related students also expressed their agreement to the teachers. The three teachers of Chinese helped me obtain the students' diaries and suggested I ask each student for their earlier diaries as well as the current ones. After I received the current diaries of 10 students, I asked for their previous diaries. Due to the replacement of diary notebooks, some students presented me with only a small part of their diaries (fewer than 15 entries) in the new notebooks. Some students could not provide earlier diaries, which they had written since they came to the Neidi because, as the students explained, some diaries were lost while changing dormitories or classrooms, and some were thrown away with other used-up exercise books. Finally, five students' diaries were collected, the basic information of which is shown in Table 5.1. These five students wrote much more in their diaries (including the past diaries they presented to me) than the other five. They also expressed themselves more clearly than their counterparts in the same grade.

No student wrote every day, but all of them wrote at least one entry a week. They wrote more during particular periods, such as summer and winter vacation, but less in other periods, such as the mid-term examination and semester final exam review periods. The shorter pieces in the diaries were less than 100 Chinese characters in length, such as Dazhen's diary entry No. 2, and Tudan's diary entries No. 1 and No. 2. However, the longer entries contained more than 500 characters, such as Bianzong's diary entry No. 81 and Cilun's diary entry No. 36. Most diaries gave the date, week, and weather conditions, but some lacked this information. The students gave titles to some diary entries. Examples included "Friendship" (Dazhen, No. 92), "My Innermost Thoughts" (Dazhen, No. 116), "Sons and Daughters of Mountains in Tibet" (Cilun, No. 6), "On Fraud in Exams" (Cilun, No. 11), "Strong Impression on Military Training" (Dazhen, No. 18), "We Are Growing Up, Tibet Is Changing, and New Students Are the

Table 5.1 Basic Information about the Collection and Selection of the Five Students' Diaries

Student	Gender	Time of Registration at the School	Period of Diary	Collected Entries of Diary	Selected Entries of Diary
Dazhen	Female	Sept. 1998	Oct. 1998– Dec. 2001	173	41
Cilun	Male	Sept. 1998	Mar. 2000– July 2001	78	28
Bianzong	Female	Sept. 1999	May 2000– Dec. 2001	228	55
Tudan	Male	Sept. 1999	Sept. 1999– Dec. 2001	225	49
Yuzhen	Female	Sept. 2000	Sept. 2000– July 2001	90	30

Representatives" (Bianzong, No. 175), "Making Dumplings" (Yuzhen, No. 46), "The Future Dream" (Yuzhen, No. 89), and so on.

From the literature review on narrative analysis, it seems there is no single analytical framework that is functional for all narrative research. It depends on each research topic and the narrative materials. To some extent, a narrative analysis framework is rather loosely formulated, almost intuitively, using terms defined by the researcher (Manning & Cullum-Swan, 1994; Riessman, 1993). With reference to Maxwell (1996) and Lieblich, Tuval-Mashiach, and Zilber (1998), a model was developed for the classification of approaches to reading, analyzing, and interpreting life stories and other narrative materials, which contains two main independent dimensions: (a) holistic versus categorical approaches, and (b) content versus form. In the first dimension, the categorical approach can be adopted to focus on a problem or a phenomenon shared by a group of people, whereas the holistic approach is appropriate to explore the person or a group as a whole. In the second dimension, some researchers concentrate on explicit W-questions of the content of a narrative, such as what, why, who, where, and so on. On the other end of the second dimension, the researchers pay more attention to the structure of the plot, its relation to the time axis, its complexity and coherence, the feelings evoked by the story, the style of the narrative, and so forth.

Hence, a categorical approach is employed to analyze diaries on the basis of the content of each diary entry. To be able to dissect and rearrange the diary data into categories, coding is necessary. There are two frequently used coding methods: inductive (or emerging) and a priori codes. Inductive codes are defined as codes that are generated by the researcher directly from the data. A priori codes, on the other hand, are developed before or at the beginning of the research study (Johnson & Christensen, 2000). The preliminary research questions and related literature can often be used to provide guidelines for the coding (Marshall & Rossman, 1999). In this research, a priori codes were first used to generate general categories of students' schooling life experiences. Under these general categories, inductive codes were used to produce sub-categories. According to Cornell and Hartmann (1998), the asserted part of ethnic identity means who or what a person claims to be in interaction with others in various contexts. That is to say, their own assertion can be embodied by the perceptions of other people (including members of their own ethnic group and other ethnic groups) through interaction. Simultaneously, inductive codes were also employed. Other researchers and I read all of the collected diaries. The five students wrote down events that happened in the Neidi and in their past life in Tibet. According to the two coding methods, general categories of students' assertions about themselves in the diaries included the following:

- Viewpoints about Tibetan people and matters
- Viewpoints about classmates

- Viewpoints about Han Chinese people and Neidi development
- Self-introspection

The category of viewpoints about people and matters of Tibet mainly refers to the recollection of Tibetan people, matters before the students came to the Neidi, comments on present Tibetan people, and matters the students currently face. Viewpoints about classmates signify comments on current classmates in CZ Tibetan Secondary School. Viewpoints about Han Chinese people and Neidi development include opinions about Han Chinese teachers, students, and others, as well as Neidi development. Self-introspection primarily focuses on reflections on study goals, life values, personal characteristics and ideals, Tibetan language study, and other matters.

Based on the preceding general categories, I made the selection of diaries for the analysis of school life and ethnic identity construction from the collected diary entries in the fifth column as shown in Table 5.1. First, I asked three other researchers, whose research interests were not concerned with the ethnic identity of minority groups, to read through all of the collected diaries. Each diary entry was assigned a number in order (all of the diary entries were photocopied from the original ones). In the second reading, three scholars recorded numbers of the diary entries in accordance with the previously mentioned criteria on an additional card. They discussed contradictory entries together and reached a consensus for the next selection. Finally, the selection of diaries was made in the follow-up readings. The information from the selected diaries of each student is listed in the sixth column in Table 5.1.

Afterward, I carefully read every selected diary entry of each category to record notes on useful passages on note cards. While doing this, I tried to identify meaningful segments of diary entries and summarized the main topic using a phrase or a single sentence in the margin of the note cards to signify the segments. All relevant topics in diary entries were put into sub-categories. The whole structure of students' perceptions on themselves, Tibetans, Han Chinese people, Tibet, and the Neidi was then established. The relationships among categories and sub-categories also became clear. This chapter will demonstrate the relationship between school life and ethnic identity from the perspective of Yuzhen. The other students' experiences may be found in my book (Zhu, 2007).

DATA ANALYSIS

General Representation: Interviews and Essay Writing

After collecting the students' diaries, I interviewed each student in turn. After the interviews, the students were asked to write an open-ended essay in terms of the interview and their life experience.

Yuzhen was born in 1988 and a student of Grade 1. She was from the village of Muzu Gongga Prefecture of Lhasa District. Her parents were peasants but her father also drove a private minibus for business travel transportation. She had a younger sister. Yuzhen was the youngest student in the class, but her spoken Chinese was fluent. She was considered by the Chinese teacher as "the best student in writing Chinese compositions overflowing with emotion." Several of her classmates commented that she was "one of the influential students in the class." She was a member of the class students committee. Thus, she not only coordinated the teachers' management of the class and worked toward harmony in the relationship between themselves and other students, but also paid special attention to her own conduct. In this sense, owing to her personality, academic performance, management capacity, and so on, she became a public figure in her class.

In my interview with her, she mentioned the idea of "atheism," which her primary school advocated. However, she still believed in Buddhism.

Yuzhen: Yeah, I do believe in Buddhism. My parents both believe in it and they always go to temples to worship Buddha.
Researcher: Do you participate in some religious activities?
Yuzhen: Yes. For example, burning joss sticks to worship Buddha. My parents do it too. But our primary school advocated that we should not believe in religion. The school asked us to be atheists, but we still worship Buddha.

Yuzhen's father could speak Chinese fluently as a result of his business with a private travel agency. Before entering primary school, her father taught her Chinese language, math, and Tibetan language. Thus, she could speak a little Chinese before she went to school. According to educational regulations, she should have studied in the local primary school; however, her father wanted her to receive a better education in better conditions and a better environment. Thus, her father sought help (*zao guanxi*) to transfer her to No. 3 Primary School in Lhasa, where she joined the Chinese Language Class (*Han wen ban*). She started to learn Chinese from Grade 1. After five years of study, she had to go back to a local primary school in her hometown for the graduation exam and the entrance exam to the inland Tibet school.[3] She was the second student in that village admitted by an inland Tibet school.

Yuzhen had no experience of communicating with Han Chinese people while she was in the countryside. After she went to study in Lhasa, she got to know and communicated with some Han Chinese people, especially with his father's Han Chinese friends and a Han Chinese neighbor who treated her kindly. When she entered CZ Tibet Middle School, her father's Han Chinese friends in inland cities even came to see her. She claimed that she could identify Han Chinese people from their appearance and spoken Chinese.

Researcher: How did you know your neighbor in Lhasa was a Han Chinese?

Yuzhen: I just knew. Well, I could tell from appearance. Their appearance was not the same as Tibetans'. They were fairer and they speak Chinese.

Yuzhen was asked to write an open-ended essay in terms of her personal life experience in Tibet and the mainland after the interviews. She described Tibet as a "holy and beautiful" place. It has "immense Namu Lake, surging Yalu Tsangpo River, majestical Potala, mysterious Dhazhao Temple, vast prairies, clear streams, blue sky, and colorful wildflowers." Tibetans were regarded as an ethnicity, which featured "enthusiasm, naturalness and generosity (*dafang*), being good at singing and dancing, benevolence, honesty and unsophisticatedness (*chun pu*), unrestrained (*sa tuo*), boldness and unconstrainedness (*hao fang*)." Tibetans have their own "particular circle dance, opera, and beautiful songs." Tibetan people are "very hospitable to everyone, no matter whether they are Tibetans, Han people, neighbors, or from far away." Tibetan people did not "step on the insects on the ground because the insects had life, too." Such a self-image, mainly focusing on Tibetans' characteristics, indicated the way Tibetan students saw themselves and, even more importantly, the way they wanted to be seen by others.

Ethnic identity is produced and reproduced in the course of social interaction in different contexts (Cornell & Hartmann, 1998; Jenkins, 1994; Nagel, 1994). Besides the direct description of self-image of Tibetan ethnicity, Yuzhen illustrated her experiences of interacting with Changzhou City's local people in her essay writing as follows:

Some businessmen said, "The peasants here become rich if they have two cattle." I responded to them that, "The poorest families have at least two or three yaks in Tibet. Some families have more than one hundred yaks." They were very surprised. They still asked, "Are there any mosquitoes in Tibet?" "Of course not!" They looked at me jealously and said, "How comfortable you are!" Some people went so far as to ask, "Why do you come to study in the inland? Don't you have schools in Tibet?" I said, "If there are no schools in Tibet, how come I can write Chinese characters and understand Chinese?"

The student's experiences in interacting with Han Chinese people in the local community demonstrate different perspectives possessed by local Han Chinese people. Ethnic boundary exists between Tibetan and Han Chinese people, including skin color, geographical and economic conditions of their place of origin, and so on. The student's responses crystallized the role of ethnic identity in the interaction. That is to say, the local community context contributes to reproducing Tibetan students' ethnic identity construction. Generally speaking, Yuzhen seemed to take a milder look at Tibet and Tibetan people.

Yuzhen's Narrative in the Diary

Most diary entries are separate stories. Some stories describe and discuss a phenomenon or an event happening in the school or outside the school; some stories narrate and comment on an activity; and some present thoughts and reflections after watching TV news or a movie, reading an article, or learning a text. Basically, each story is made up of context and interaction between actors. Based on the discussion in the previous section, the construction of ethnic identity in the diary can be explored and revealed from the following categories:

- Viewpoints about people and matters of Tibet
- Viewpoints about classmates
- Viewpoints about Han Chinese people and inland development
- Self-introspection

One diary entry may include all or several of the categories mentioned in the preceding list. Yet, only the main topic of the diary is considered when it is classified into different categories. Sub-items are made up the same way. After reading Yuzhen's diaries, I find the category of viewpoints about people and matters of Tibet covers the viewpoints of people and matters in the family, primary school, and Tibetan social contexts. Viewpoints about classmates can be categorized into comments on unhealthy (*buliang xing-wei*), unacceptable, and positive behavior, and significance of thought and moral education. Viewpoints about Han Chinese people and inland development mainly focus on Han Chinese teachers, Han Chinese students, other Han Chinese people, and inland development. Self-introspection primarily includes sub-items of study goals and life values, and personal character and ideals.

Viewpoints about People and Matters of Tibet

The Family Context

Yuzhen presented the wishes for her by her parents and relatives when she left for the inland school—to study for herself and for the Tibetan people.

> On that day, many relatives and kind people presented me with the long, white *hada*. I felt upset as well as proud because I would leave them for a place far away from Tibet . . . I just took a pot of barley wine and walked around the house to raise a toast to them . . . At the airport, my parents, relatives, and friends exhorted me to study

hard for myself and for the Tibetan people . . . Good-bye, my beloved people! I will come back to Tibet with excellent results . . . After four years, I will repay my parents and the Tibetan people with an excellent performance. (Diary, No. 14)

Additionally, the thoughts of family members on the state government policy on Tibet were narrated in the diary.

> At the age of nine, I visited my grandpa. I found that great changes had taken place in his home. The house was larger and newer than before. He had a colored TV and some other electrical home appliances. I inquired about the reason . . . Grandpa explained, "The communist party is our benefactor and savior. The communist party emancipated us and we are free . . ." As a nine-year-old child, I didn't understand the meaning of benefactor, savior, emancipation, etc. Now I can understand them . . . The policy of the Party has warmed every Tibetan person. The spring wind of the Party has spread to the entire plateau of Tibet. The Party sends us a happy life. Tibet is prosperous and flourishing. I love my beautiful and mysterious Tibet. (Diary, No. 90)

The Primary School Context

Yuzhen described her feeling about attending the national flag flying ritual in primary school in Tibet.

> In No. 3 Primary School in Lhasa, we held the ritual of national flag flying every Monday morning. We were required to wear school uniform and bright red scarf. When I saluted the bright red flag, I felt an upsurge of love for the State. The flag was the symbol of our Chinese nation. Many martyrs have devoted their lives to the State. I was moved to tears when I thought of this . . . If every student can understand it and study hard, our state will become more and more beautiful. I love our national flag. The only thing that I need do now is study hard. We should be well-educated, self-disciplined people with high ideals and moral integrity so that we can develop our State and Tibet. (Diary, No. 12)

Yuzhen wrote an entry about a Han Chinese teacher in primary school and expressed her opinion of that teacher.

> Ms. Guo was the teacher who introduced me to studying. She was a kind Han who taught Chinese language. Like our family, she cared for us, loved us, and led us, innocent children, to the fount of knowledge . . . There was a time in class when I was not concentrating on the lesson. Her sudden question and my inability to answer it made me very embarrassed in front of my classmates. At that time, I hated her.

Afterwards, she advised me very patiently. As time went on, I came to know that she did it for my benefit . . . Furthermore, I understand her advice that "we can make mistakes but we cannot miss an opportunity." It will influence my study and life. (Diary, No. 88)

Moreover, Yuzhen thought it was worth learning from her close friend:

In primary school, my close friend was Jiayong Qucuo, a Tibetan girl . . . After six years, I had found that she was conscientious in her work and treated others very honestly. Sometimes she has an eccentric character. . . . She does not pocket money that she picks up . . . I should learn from her and look on her as my close friend forever. It was regretful that she did not pass the entrance exam to inland Tibet school. I felt sad about it. (Diary, No. 21)

Yuzhen wanted to be a teacher when she moved back to the primary school in the rural area after having studied for five years in the primary school in Lhasa.

During the school year in Gagang Primary School after I transferred from No. 3 Primary School in Lhasa, I knew many children from mountains. On Sundays, we went to herd sheep, swim, and pick flowers. Gradually, I found that those children were very rustic. They did not know about the city. They had a narrow outlook. I felt I was very rustic, too. I did not know how to farm and herd sheep. At that moment, I had an ideal to be a teacher in the village . . . Go to the countryside and impart science and culture. Let them receive a better education . . . If I were a teacher, I would teach them to be thrifty, unite with students as a family, and not to discriminate against any student who failed in academic performance. (Diary, No. 87)

The Tibetan Social Context

To Yuzhen, Tibet presented different kinds of scenes in different seasons. Tibet was full of mystery.

Tibet is a fertile place. I live in the boundless grassland. As the sun reveals its smiling face, the herders drive flocks of sheep and goats to the hillside. The children take their horses to the green meadow. Immediately, the quiet village comes alive. In spring, the grass starts to grow. The river water is melting . . . In winter, the village is covered with a large white cotton quilt . . . The thick and white snow seemingly makes a fairyland for the people. Tibet presents quite different scenes in the four seasons. I love Tibet. (Diary, No. 27)
    Tibet has beautiful scenes—the flowing and limpid streams, bunches of fresh flowers, grains, and wild fruits. The horses gallop on the

plateau. I secretly made a decision to study hard to build my lovely homeland, Tibet. (Diary, No. 20)

Tibet is a mysterious and ancient place. There is one prosperous city, Lhasa. It is well known that Tibetan people firmly believe in Buddhism. Therefore, you can see resplendent and magnificent monasteries everywhere. Dazhao Monastery is one of them. (Diary, No. 64)

Viewpoints about Classmates

Unhealthy Behavior

Yuzhen believed and advocated that discipline played a great role in ensuring students' successful study in school.

> As the Chinese teacher came into the classroom, someone made a strange noise. That student must have a poor sense of discipline and supercilious. The teacher got angry and inquired about who had done it, but no one responded . . . The teacher had to ask us to write a statement to adhere to school rules after the class bell rang. The class was finished this way. Classmates! We should abide by the rules, which are the only reliable guarantees for success in our studies. (Diary, No. 40)

Yuzhen pointed out the wasteful behavior of her classmates and criticized such an attitude.

> Today, a cooked egg was found in the dustbin in the classroom. An egg is very nutritious. Why was the egg put there? Is the school rich enough? Why not save it for others? Perhaps some people are eager for it . . . Many questions come to my mind. In short, it is wrong to waste. Perhaps the person who threw the egg away thought that an egg was insignificant, for our state has a vast territory and abundant resources. I think this attitude is completely wrong. Though our state has a vast territory, the resources are limited. (Diary, No. 67)

Positive Behavior

Yuzhen reminded classmates about cherishing good opportunities to study at an inland school.

> Today was National Day. The school held the "Fourteen-Year-Old Youth Ritual" . . . Flying the national flag evoked my love for our state. All students wore bright-colored Tibetan robes . . . In the afternoon, we saw the film "Beautiful Mother," which tells how a single mother supported her disabled son so he could go to school . . . Today our Tibetan students come to study in the inland in bright and spacious

classrooms. It is a good opportunity to realize our ideals. We should work hard and repay our parents' and the Tibetan people's kindness. (Diary, No. 9)

Yuzhen also hoped her classmates could repay the state and Tibet with talents and skills in the new century.

Today was the last day of the year 2000 . . . We greet the new 21st century . . . The new century will have high requirements on the successors of the State and Tibet . . . The State spends a large amount of money cultivating us. Classmates! When you waste your rice, do you think of how hardworking the peasants are? When you leave tap water running and walk away, do you think of the reduction of the water resources of our state . . . ? Only if you are mindful and contribute your love, will the world become a nicer place . . . The 21st century is the time for science to develop. If we have no talents and skills, we cannot repay the State and Tibet. (Diary, No. 44)

Yuzhen dreamed of her homeland Tibet at night, but her classmate's words reminded her of the significance of studying in the inland.

In the morning, Suoqu asked me what was wrong. I told her that I had dreamt of my homeland. She said, "Do not be sad. In four years' time, we can go back. Here, the school also cares for descendants of ethnic minorities . . . Currently, the first task for us is to study hard, unite with classmates, master skills, and improve abilities so as to build Tibet." (Diary, No. 63)

Yuzhen felt very excited about the ideals of her classmates in the speech class to be some kind of scientist in the future.

In speech class, the teacher asked us to make a speech. The topic was "My Ideals" . . . The ideal of No. 18 student was to be an inventor; Number 19's[4] was to be a mathematician . . . Hearing their speeches made me reflect. Science in our state is under-developed. If such talents as inventors, mathematicians, etc. could be found in great numbers among us, how wonderful it would be! China would flourish, and our Tibet would be more prosperous. (Diary, No. 65)

Yuzhen felt happy to be able to get together with older sisters for the celebration of Tibetan New Year.

Tibetan New Year is the most traditional festival for Tibetans. To celebrate it, we students prepared many kinds of food including Tibetan food and decorated the dorm with pictures and colorful ribbons. It was full of festival atmosphere. On New Year's Day, our older sisters invited us to visit their dorm. It was a good time to get together with them. We not only enjoyed all kinds of food but also performed singing, sketches, dancing, and games . . . Sporadic laughter rose in the dorm at times. (Diary, No. 56)

Significance of Thought and Moral Education

Yuzhen summarized the factors related to adolescents' crimes. She wrote that Tibetan students should love the state and the people.

> This afternoon, we went to the Accountancy School near our school to visit the "Exhibition on Preventing Adolescents from Committing Crimes" . . . The reasons why adolescents commit crimes include social, school, family, and personal factors . . . I hope all of our Tibetan students can study hard. Do not waste time and this opportunity. Love the state and the people. However, how can we love the State? I think, for us, studying hard is the real proof of loving the State. (Diary, No. 34)

Yuzhen also gave prominence to quality and morals in social competition while discussing the award for the civilized class.

> The flag for the title of civilized class has been taken from us . . . We are members of the class collectively. Whether we can win the title back depends on our efforts. We must do well not only in hygiene but also in study. Classmates! The society of the future is characterized by science, technology, and information. We will be eliminated from the contest without some degree of culture and knowledge. Without quality and morals, we will still be eliminated. For the future of our class, of the state, and of Tibet, let us work hard today. (Diary, No. 35)

Yuzhen advocated that all students learn morals from Lei Feng:

> This month is a "civilization and courtesy month" (*wenming limao yue*). On March 5, 1963, Chairman Mao delivered the call to "learn from comrade Lei Feng" . . . Lei Feng did countless good deeds in his life . . . He served the people and studied hard . . . He lived a very simple life. From him, we can see many virtues in the Chinese nation. Let us learn these virtues: diligence in studies, being thrifty and hardworking, and arduously struggling . . . Let us maintain these virtues in our behavior. (Diary, No. 60)

Viewpoints about Han Chinese and Inland Development

Han Chinese Teachers

Yuzhen made the following comments on a life guidance teacher.

> From Tibet to the inland, I have met many teachers . . . However, one teacher impressed me very much . . . She was our life guidance teacher, Mrs. Han, who was strict with us and very conscientious in her job. She examined each dorm very carefully . . . She patiently taught us to fold quilts. In our spare time, we always talked to her about our Tibet. Sometimes she acted as our doctor and our mother . . . I do not know if she retired or was dismissed. On the day she left, we felt very sad. Afterwards, she came to see us, and we were very excited to talk with her like mother and daughter. (Diary, No. 71)

Han Chinese Students

Yuzhen experienced Tibetan–Han friendship through a formal activity.

> This morning we took the bus to No. 15 Middle School for a "Tibetan-Han hand-in-hand activity . . ." When we got off the bus, Han Chinese students welcomed us with enthusiastic applause. First, we tried to make contact. I got a Han Chinese friend and we played together . . . In the afternoon, we played games. Time flew quickly. We had to go back to school. When we got on the bus, I said goodbye to my friend. I was almost crying. She seemed to ask me to write to her. It was enough to express our Tibetan-Han friendship. (Diary, No. 45)

In the inter-school activity, her new Han Chinese friend introduced her to the Han Chinese custom of wrapping dumplings.

> I was really happy on the day of "Tibetan-Han hand-in-hand activity." Wrapping dumplings is a Han Chinese custom. It was the first time I had wrapped dumplings. Our Tibetan people have no such custom. My Han Chinese friend took me to wash my hands first. We were allocated to the sixth table. The table was covered with a plastic paper. She said, "You wait here and I'll fetch the stuffing." I understood "stuffing" as "string" [The Chinese pronunciation of "stuffing" (*xian*) is the same as "string" (*xian*)]. I was extremely puzzled. Did we need "string" to wrap dumplings? While I was thinking about this, she came back with the "stuffing." I suddenly saw the light . . . I imitated her and she taught me how to do it. Using this method, I made the first dumpling. Gradually, I wrapped the dumplings better and better . . . The dumpling tasted delicious. This was the first time I had wrapped dumplings with Han Chinese friends. (Diary, No. 46)

Yuzhen thought she, as a Tibetan, should practice writing Chinese characters well.

> This morning the teacher took us to visit the art museum. The paintings by children from the kindergarten are really wonderful, but I cannot draw anything. I feel ashamed. There are many books in the museum. The handwriting in the books looks beautiful. Now I am learning Chinese. As a Tibetan, I must practice my Chinese handwriting well and master these skills. (Diary, No. 2)

Inland Development

Yuzhen set up her lofty aspirations and high ideals to help develop Tibet after visiting the city of Shanghai.

> Our three-day visit to Shanghai has finished . . . Looking at the magnificent buildings, wide roads, the beautiful environment, and Jing Mao Tower, my thoughts are far away . . . When I stepped into this strange and prosperous city, I felt very fresh and happy. It also invoked me to think of the holy and fertile land—Tibet. Tibet has its boundless land, blue sky, and flowing and limpid streams. Though Shanghai is not as holy as Tibet, it has high buildings, crisscrossed roads, cheerful people, and cars . . . Suddenly it seemed that I saw smiling faces with the enthusiasm of Tibetan people. They show hope on their wrinkled faces. They wished we would not be "people with very limited outlooks" any more. They wished we would walk out of the remote mountains . . . Instantly, I felt I had a grave responsibility resting on my shoulders. Since the opening and reform of the State, great changes have taken place in Tibet. However, compared with the inland, Tibet is still backward. To cultivate more talents for Tibet, the State invests a lot of money in running inland Tibet schools/classes so that our Tibetan children receive better education . . . We carry the hopes not only of Tibetan people but also of the State, because Tibet's tomorrow is in our hands. We are the tomorrow of Tibet and the State . . . Classmates! Exert yourselves in the struggle for the future of Tibet! (Diary, No. 89)

Self-Introspection

Study Goal and Life Value

Yuzhen always reflects on behavior. When she saw her classmates studying seriously, she thought about what she herself has done in school.

> After morning exercise, I saw Tudeng Yangjie reciting texts on the playground. She studied hard and seriously. This made me think to myself

... Now I am a middle school student. I am growing up. It is unnecessary for others to persuade or force me to study ... If my parents know that I spent a lot of time playing, they would feel disappointed. How hard my parents have brought me up! If I cannot enter high school after four years, how can I face my parents, classmates, and my Tibetan people? How can I go back to build Tibet? Thus, I have to seriously study so I can help develop Tibet in the future. (Diary, No. 23)

An ideology and politics lesson led Yuzhen to review her life values in the current school.

We did not have the Ideological and Politics lesson in the classroom today. The teacher brought us to the canteen. He asked us to look at the large-scale painting on the wall and said a few words about it. I thought that it was only a figure painting at the time. Some students talked about it. "It is an old Tibetan man working hard in Tibet." "Every single grain is the result of toil" ... After listening to the explanation, I felt ashamed. I thought of my father. He exerted painstaking efforts for me. We have no reason not to study hard here. Our fathers' generation produced every single grain of rice with their sweat and toil. Han Chinese brothers and sisters in the canteen get up early every morning to prepare breakfast for us. They have done it for fifteen years! Fifteen years! This lesson greatly inspired me. (Diary, No. 30)

She came to understand her study goal after reading the story of "The Little Match Girl."

I like the story of "The Little Match Girl" ... Thinking about myself, I feel ashamed. Compared with the little girl, I am not worried about meals and clothes. It seems like I live in heaven. It is unreasonable for me not to study hard. What a big difference between the little girl and me in two different societies! We grow up in the care of the Party ... Thinking about such a poor girl, I feel ashamed. I should work hard and master skills so as to help build the state and my beautiful Tibet. (Diary, No. 68)

The development of Changzhou City provoked Yuzhen's strong identity of ethnicity and helped enhance her study goal.

Fang and I went to the supermarket downtown. The supermarket is very large. There are all kinds of merchandise. We bought some things and left. I looked around and found many high buildings along the street. These buildings made me think of Lhasa. Seeing such a large supermarket makes me want to build one in Lhasa. When I grow up, I will establish a large supermarket in Lhasa and develop Lhasa to be like Changzhou. I think this is what I will do. This day will come. Let me grasp this chance of studying in the inland and work hard for our folks in Tibet. Let us make Tibet as beautiful as inland cities. As long as we show our love, the future of Tibet should be splendid. The only way that I can show love is to study diligently. We will go back to Tibet in the future. For the future of Tibet, we should not forget our study goal in the inland. (Diary, No. 26)

Personal Character and Ideal

After studying a text about happiness, Yuzhen recalled past happiness she had experienced at different stages and then had a better comprehension of the meaning of happiness.

> After learning "What is Happiness," I can really understand the implications of happiness . . . At a very young age, I thought happiness meant having a family with better conditions . . . When my neighbor was enrolled in an inland Tibet school, I thought that was happiness if I could be a student of an inland Tibet school. After learning this text, I understand that if you do voluntary service and good deeds for others, you will feel happy. Now the service that I should do is just to study. We should do good things for our class and the school. In the future, we can do good things for Tibet and our state. (Diary, No. 25)

Yuzhen hoped to be a doctor in 20 years' time:

> In twenty years, I will be a doctor. In 2021, I will become the Dean of Lhasa People's Hospital. I will be very busy. I will do several operations on patients every day. One day I will feel tired after three operations and want to take a rest. Suddenly, the phone will ring again. "Hello, Doctor Yuzhen? We have an emergency. We need to operate. Please come to the hospital!" A new Tibetan baby is born! He and his mother are saved! The whole family will show me their gratitude, too . . . I would like to serve my Tibetan people. (Diary, No. 77)

Discussion: School Life and Ethnic Identity

Explicitly, according to what Yuzhen narrated in the diary, it can be concluded that she internalized the state ideologies intended by the school. She came to understand the relationship between the Chinese Communist Party's policy on Tibet and Tibet's development. She also experienced the advantages that the state preferential educational policy had brought her. She interpreted the aim of inland Tibet schools as developing talents for Tibet. Patriotic education drove her to realize that studying hard was the true way of loving the state. Thus, to build the state and Tibet has been the most important aspect of her study goals and life values. The beautiful scene and mysterious elements of Tibet encouraged her love of Tibet. However, the backward situation in Tibet and the gap between the development of the inland and Tibet that Yuzhen saw personally propelled her to form a kind of responsibility to develop Tibet. The formation of this kind of responsibility is part of the school's ideological education. The organization of a visit to Shanghai is an approach to practicing ideological education. She encountered Han–Tibetan friendship through interaction with Han Chinese students in a formal inter-school activity. The ethnic difference was certainly identified in the interaction, such as diet customs.

It is noteworthy that through the analysis of the dairies, the cultural characteristics of Tibetans can be sensed in different contexts, such as the *hada* and its implications, Tibetan clothes, Tibetan food (ghee tea, *zang ba*, and barley wine), Tibetan customs and etiquette (*guo lin ka, tang ka, san kou yi bei*), Tibetan festivals (*Wang guo* Festival, Tibetan New Year), Tibetan dances and songs, the natural beauty of Tibet, and the Tibetan language. The representation of these cultural symbols in practice informs others about "who and what" Tibetans are. Additionally, the students write about these cultural characteristics consciously or unconsciously in the diary, which demonstrates the construction of their ethnic identity in words. Because the students hand the diaries over to the teachers, the expression and explanation of Tibetan cultural characteristics also reveals that the students want to show Han Chinese teachers what or who "we" Tibetans are.

To sum up, the students not only construct their ethnic identity in different contexts, but also narrate their ethnic identity in words through their diaries to themselves and to the readers. However, due to individual life experience, the students constructed their ethnic identities differently, as perceived from the classification of ethnic identity construction by Cornell and Hartmann (1998), though in the same schooling context. Through the analysis of the diaries, ethnic identity—being "Tibetan"—organizes much of the students' thoughts and actions in Neidi school daily life. Yuzhen was very inclined to carry on the ethnic identity assigned by the school and the state.

NOTES

1. The area refers to inland and coastal regions of China, compared to frontier and boarder regions like Tibet. In this chapter, Neidi Tibet class/school indicates classes or schools built in inland and coastal regions for Tibetans from Tibet Autonomous Region.
2. The CZ Tibetan Secondary School is located in the southwest part of Wujin District in CZ City in Jiangsu Province in the eastern costal area of China, which is very close to Shanghai City.
3. In China, the law states that children should enter schools at the place where his or her registered permanent residence is located. Students can study at

a school on a temporary basis, but he or she must go back to the registered school for examinations to graduate and enter a high school.
4. As soon as Tibetan students enroll in CZ Tibet Middle School, they are given a student number. Because most Tibetan students' names include four Chinese characters and some names are identical, it is difficult to distinguish them in some contexts. Thus, sometimes, the students and the teachers call students' numbers instead of their names on campus and even in classes.

REFERENCES

Coleman, G. (1994). *A handbook of Tibetan culture: A guide to Tibetan centers and resources throughout the world*. Boston: Shambhala Press.

Cornell, S. E., & Hartmann, D. (1998). *Ethnicity and race: Making identities in a changing world*. Thousand Oaks, CA: Pine Forge Press.

Danzu, A. (1993). *Zangzu wenhua sanlun* [On Tibetan culture]. Beijing: Zhongguo youyi chuban gongsi.

Dreyfus, G. (1995). Law, state, and political ideology in Tibet. *Journal of the International Association of Buddhist Studies 18*(1), 117–138.

Geng, J., & Wang, X. (1989). *Xizang jiaoyu yanjiu* [Studies on Tibetan education]. Beijing: Zhongyang minzu xueyuan chubanshe.

Iredale, R., Bilik, N., & Su, W., Guo, F., & Hoy, C. (2001). *Contemporary minority migration, education and ethnicity in China*. Northampton, MA: Edward Elgar.

Jenkins, R. (1994). Rethinking ethnicity: Identity, categorization and power. *Ethnic and Racial Studies, 17*(2), 197–223.

Johnson, B., & Christensen, L. (2000). *Educational research: Quantitative and qualitative approaches*. Boston: Allyn & Bacon.

Korom, F. J. (1997). *Constructing Tibetan culture: Contemporary perspectives*. Quebec: World Heritage Press.

Lieblich, A., Tubal-Mashiach, R., & Zilber, T. (1998). *Narrative research: Reading, analysis, and interpretation*. Thousand Oaks, CA: Sage.

Mackerras, C. (1995). *China's minority cultures: Identities and integration since 1912*. New York: St. Martin's Press.

Manning, P. K., & Cullum-Swan, B. (1994). Narrative, content, and semiotic analysis. In N. K. Denzin & Y. S. Lincoln (Eds.), *Handbook of qualitative research* (pp. 463–477). Thousand Oaks, CA: Sage.

Marshall, C., & Rossman, G. B. (1999). *Designing qualitative research* (3rd ed.). Thousand Oaks, CA: Sage.

Maxwell, J. A. (1996). *Qualitative research design: An interactive approach*. Thousand Oaks, CA: Sage.

Nagel, J. (1994). Constructing ethnicity: Creating and recreating ethnic identity and culture. *Social Problems, 41*(1), 152–176.

Nima, B. (2000). *Wenming de kunhuo: Aangzu jiaoyu zhi lu* [Perplexity on civilization: Road to Tibetan education]. Chengdu: Sichuan Ethnic Press.

Postiglione, G. A. (1999). *China's national minority education: Culture, schooling and development*. New York: Falmer Press.

Riessman, C. K. (1993). *Narrative analysis*. Newbury Park, CA: Sage.

Sautman, B. (1998). Preferential policies for ethnic minorities in China: The case of Xiangjiang. In W. Safran (Ed.), *Nationalism and ethnoregional identities in China* (pp. 86–118). Portland, OR: Frank Cass.

Upton, J. L. (1996). Home on the grasslands? Tradition, modernity, and the negotiation of identity by Tibetan intellectuals in the PRC. In M. J. Brown (Ed.),

Negotiating ethnicities in China and Taiwan (pp. 98–124). Berkeley: University of California, Institute of East Asian Studies.

Upton, J. L. (1999). The development of modern school-based Tibetan language education in the PRC. In G. A. Postiglione (Ed.), *China's national minority education: Culture, schooling, and development* (pp. 281–339). New York: Falmer Press.

Wang, C., & Zhou, Q. (2003). Minority education in China: From state's preferential policies to dislocated Tibetan schools. *Educational Studies, 29*(1), 85–104.

Wang, L. (1998). Sky Burial: The Fate of Tibet (*Tianzang: Xizang de minyun*). Mississauga, Ont.: Mirror Books Ltd (Mingjing Chubanshe).

Zhu, Z. (2007). *State schooling and ethnic identity: The politics of a Neidi Tibetan secondary school*. Lanham, MD: Lexington Books.

6 Constructing Tibetan Students' National and Ethnic Identities in the Tibetan School Education

Zhiyan Teng

INTRODUCTION

I have been engaged in ethnic minority education research for several years and participated in a number of projects. During the past three years, I have participated in an important research project, the Relationship between Religious Belief and Modern School Education in the Northwest Ethnic Minority Areas, which was undertaken by the Research Center for the Educational Development of Minorities at the Northwest Normal University in China. The Tibetans are an ethnic minority who practice Tibetan Buddhism, which made me conduct an investigative research about the relationship between Tibetan Buddhism and the Tibetan modern school education. This investigative research work made me understand the Tibetans and the Tibetan students, and I gradually became interested in them. Of course, the research, to a certain extent, also relates to the problem of the Tibetan students' identity.

In addition, following the events of March 14, 2008, in China and of some Tibetan separatists' constantly conducting separatist activities, many teacher and professional organizations have raised questions about how Tibetan school education forms Tibetan students' identity. An important topic of discussion includes how the Tibetan school education influences the Tibetan students' views on ideas, such as conflict and peace, and the relationship between ethnic minority and national identities. As a Chinese minority education researcher, I feel this is a challenging research problem and is worthy of study; therefore, I began to think deeply and research the relationship between Tibetan school education and the Tibetan students' identity construction based on previous studies. It has far-reaching significance for the Chinese nation's stability, national unity, and prosperity.

School education is the main means of adolescent socialization. It further consolidates and expands adolescents' self-awareness and collective consciousness, which have been formed in the family by teaching adolescents knowledge, skills, and values systematically, and it establishes the adolescents' national common culture and political value system recognition and identity through more regular and rigorous educational training.

The Tibetan people established schools and had a modern school education system after the People's Republic of China was founded in 1949. The Tibetan modern school education system has developed rapidly since the introduction of China's economic reforms. As a result of the joint efforts of the Chinese government officials and Tibetan schools, the latter established a universal nine-year compulsory education, which has improved greatly the level of scientific and cultural knowledge of Tibetan students. These efforts greatly contributed to Tibetan social and economic development, and played an active and constructive role in the formation of the Tibetan students' ethnic and national identities. How does the Tibetan school education influence the identity construction of Tibetan students? In the context of school education, what is taught and shown will play an important role in the students' identity formation.

First, I begin with an overview of various discussions on school education and identity construction and explain why there is a need to study the school education and the identity construction of Tibetan students. Second, I describe the Tibetan minority population. Third, I explore China's minority policy context and the Tibetan school educational practice context. Fourth, I examine the situation of Tibetan students' ethnic identity and national identity construction. I conclude this chapter by making recommendations on how to achieve long-term impact, as well as on how to implement steadily the objectives of harmonizing the ethnic and national identities.

LITERATURE REVIEW ON SCHOOLING AND IDENTITY OF TIBETAN STUDENTS

Every country in the world faces problems related to ethnic identity and national identity; this is most true in multiethnic countries like China. In the context of a state-sponsored school education system, how minority students construct an ethnic identity and a national identity has become a major issue in multiethnic countries. Discussions about school education and identity construction of Tibetan students have particular implications for the field of education in China because they help us further understand how schooling influences the identity construction of Tibetan students.

Chinese Minority School Education and Ethnic Identity

China is a multiethnic country consisting of 56 ethnic groups. Since the 1950s, the Chinese government has attached great importance to the education of ethnic minorities and has established modern schools in 55 ethnic communities. Many domestic researchers have focused on bilingual education and educational achievements in the school education of minorities, but only few researchers have paid attention to how the content and form of minority school education affect the ethnic groups' thoughts about their own status in the whole nation and expression of their own ethnic identity and culture in the whole country. Since the 1990s, some Chinese scholars (cf. Liu, 1997; Teng & Zhang, 1997) and Western scholars (cf. Hansen, 1999; Trueba & Zou, 1994) began to take an interest in ethnic minority education and ethnic identity.

Since the 1990s, Chinese scholars have researched and discussed the relationship between the Chinese nation and ethnic minorities and the role of minority school education in state integration. They have explained the possibilities and basic conditions of ethnic assimilation and ethnic amalgamation within the Chinese nation (Aqitu, 1994). Some scholars also have discussed the consistency problem between the ethnic identity and national identity (Li, 1999). Most studies have focused on the discussion about what the ethnic identities of ethnic minorities should be and how the minority school education should integrate ethnic minorities into the nation.

Western scholars think that the rising voice of ethnic identity, from the local perspective, is not in favor of the integration of the China state (Shih, 2000). Mackerras (1995) claimed that the unified national curriculum for the implementation of China's minority education policy does not mean that minority cultures and languages were suppressed. However, he pointed out that religion played a certain role in raising ethnic identity; therefore, the educational institution in ethnic minority areas as a whole plays a role by resisting clear ethnic identity feelings (Mackerras, 1995). Postiglione thinks that the influence of the school education on ethnic identity depends on what schools teach, how they teach, and how they assess. Therefore, he suggested that ethnic minority schools should properly highlight cultural diversity in order to be able to raise the understanding of different ethnic groups and to strengthen ethnic identity within the Chinese nation structure (Postiglione, 1999).

Education and Tibetan Identity

In the 1990s, quantitative studies on Tibetan students' identity gradually increased. At present, research by Chinese scholars about the identities of the Tibetan people focus on three aspects: (1) the acculturation and ethnic identity of Tibetan students in mainland Tibetan schools or classes (Yan & Song, 2006; Zhu, 2007); (2) the status of cultural identity among Tibetan undergraduates; and (3) the relationship among ethnic identity, cultural adaptation, and mental alienation among Tibetan undergraduates. Researchers think that the Tibetan students' ethnic cultural identity is not weakened even when they learn about the Chinese language and Chinese culture (Wan, 2006; Yong & Wan, 2003). They think that the number of Han Chinese friends, periods of learning Chinese, and the parents' ethnic identity have an impact on the Tibetan undergraduates' ethnic identity and cultural adaptation (Wan & Wang, 2004; Wan, Wang, & Li, 2002).

However, these quantitative studies do not fully reflect the process of how Tibetan students adapt to school education and cannot help us understand how Tibetan students and their families construct the meaning and the way of school education in their community life. Only by ethnographic methods can researchers understand the reality of school education in Tibetan areas, identify the characteristics of school education, clarify measured data, effectively use these quantitative data, and explain the problems existing in the Tibetan school education and related identity problems.

Upton (1996) discussed the dynamic nature of the Tibetan intellectuals' (mainly Tibetan educators, businessmen, and officials) ethnic identity. In her view, Tibetan intellectuals are not only traditional nomadic culture advocates and holders but also promoters of modern Tibetan culture and facilitators who develop and strengthen a unified Tibetan identity that is transmitted through the standard Tibetan language courses approved by the central government. In addition, Upton (1999) thinks that the contents of textbooks in schools play a very important role in young Tibetans' formation of an ethnic identity that unites it with the Chinese nation. She claims that the design of course content will be a threat to the strength and significance of Tibetan education and cultural traditions, and it also affects the ethnic identity of students.

Since its "Reform and Opening," China has entered a more intense period of social change due to the strong impetus of modernization and globalization. With the development of Tibet's economy and tourism, the modernization process has brought various shocks and changes in the relatively more traditional Tibetan areas. On the one hand, it greatly increased the awareness of seeking development and progress to change Tibet's backwardness. On the other hand, the Tibetan people's awareness of cultural autonomy gradually increased, and traditional culture was increasingly taken into account. In this context, how do the Tibetan ethnic identity and national identity come into conflict and arrive at integration? How does Tibetan school education affect the formation of identity in Tibetan students? What is the status of Tibetan students' identity? Can a win–win situation be created wherein a gain in ethnic identity would strengthen and not weaken the national identity? Studies on these issues have important theoretical and practical significance for the in-depth understanding of the relationship between Tibetan culture and mainstream culture and between the Tibetan development and national unity, good psychological adjustment of cultural crossroads, and maintaining the stability of a multiethnic country, such as China.

DESCRIPTION OF THE TIBETAN MINORITY POPULATION

The population of Tibetans in China is 5,416,021. The Tibetan people in China live mainly in the Tibet Autonomous Region, Yushu, Hainan,

Huangnan, Haibei, Guoluo and Haixi Tibetan Autonomous Prefecture in Qinghai Province, Gannan Tibetan Autonomous Prefecture and Tianzhu Tibetan Autonomous County in Gansu Province, Ganzi Tibetan Autonomous Prefecture and Aba Tibetan and Qiang Autonomous Prefecture and Benli Tibetan Autonomous County in Sichuan Province, and in Diqing Tibetan Autonomous Prefecture in Yunnan Province. The Tibetan minority population living in the Tibet Autonomous Region is 2,427,168; the Tibetan minority population settled in Sichuan, Qinghai, Gansu, and Yunnan provinces is 2,927,372; the Tibetan minority population scattered in other regions is around 62,000 (Census Office of the State Council, 2000).

The Tibetan language belongs to the branch of the Tibet-Burmese language group of the Sino-Tibet language family. It has three dialects: Weizang, Hekang, and Anduo. Their written language was created around 7 AD and has three types of scripts. In their long history, the Tibetan people have created numerous historical and literary records, which are the largest collection of all the minority groups of China.

A rich and colorful culture is also a long-standing tradition of the Tibetans. The unique-styled Budala gong, built in 7 AD, is a representation of Tibetan palatial architecture. Many beautiful Tibetan handicraft articles can be traced back 500 to 600 years. The remarkable ones are "Kadian" (a kind of carpet) and "Bangdian" (a kind of apron), which are woven from wool and threaded by a special process.

Tibetans have many traditional and religious festivals every year. "Luosa," the Tibetan New Year's Day, is the most important one. Exchanging "Hada" is a very popular etiquette in Tibet. The main food of Tibetans is "Zanba," whereas the buttered tea and the highland barley liquor are their favorite drinks.

Most Tibetans practice Tibetan Buddhism. Tibetan Buddhism has penetrated into all areas of Tibetan culture and life. Sincerely believing in the "samara" of life, firmly believing in retribution of sins and the pursuit of virtues and benignity are the core values of the Tibetan people.

LEGAL AND POLICY CONTEXTS OF THE TIBETAN STUDENTS' IDENTITY CONSTRUCTION

As the fundamental law of the country, the 1982 Constitution of China establishes a number of basic systems to protect the ethnic identity and promote national identity in ethnic education. This is the prerequisite and fundamental basis of the overall national education policy in the country. Under the Constitution, promoting the common prosperity of all ethnic groups is the fundamental objective of China's national development; all ethnic minority groups have the freedom to use and develop their own languages; maintaining the equality of all ethnic minority groups and helping ethnic minority areas to accelerate economic and cultural development are the country's basic tasks. The Constitution establishes the ethnic regional autonomy system. The self-government institutions of the national autonomous areas have the power of autonomy in administering local education. The PRC Regional Autonomy Law for Minority Nationalities (1984) further provides the right of autonomy for the education in ethnic autonomous areas and protects ethnic minority educational legislation. In accordance with the educational principles and laws of the state, the self-government institutions in ethnic autonomous areas work out their local educational programs, including the establishment of schools, school systems, school forms, teaching content, teaching language, and enrollment procedures of schools at all levels. The practice of regional autonomy not only ensures the rights of the ethnic minorities to exercise autonomy as masters of their homelands but also adheres to the principles that accelerate ethnic equality, ethnic unity, and co-prosperity of each nationality.

The ethnic regional autonomy system affects the identity of ethnic minorities in two ways. First, through the implementation of ethnic regional autonomy and the establishment of autonomous institutions, local traditional social organizations and management systems have gradually been replaced by autonomous systems. The local administration system is established in accordance with the provisions of the decree of the unified central government system to achieve reunification of the country. At the same time, ethnic minorities can exercise their autonomy rights by participating in national political and economic activities. In this process, the identities that are traditionally based on geographical and blood ties begin to change. The national identity of ethnic minorities is established and strengthened gradually. As a higher level of identity, the national identity surpasses the "tribal" or "village" identity of minorities. Second, by setting up autonomous regions, autonomous prefectures and autonomous counties and townships, blood ties and geopolitical identity (traditionally limited to the family or the village) gradually extend to the identity of county, prefectures, and even the autonomous regions. With the national institutional arrangements, the traditional closed single-family or village identity is gradually broken and forms the ethnic identity and the national identity linked to the national system in a greater range.

Language is the carrier and an important base of culture; it is also identified as an important symbol in recognizing of groups of people. The PRC Constitution 1982 and the National Common Language Law state that all ethnic groups have the right to use and develop their own spoken and written languages; the state popularizes the nation's commonly spoken Chinese (Article 19 of the Constitution); and the state popularizes the commonly spoken Chinese and standard Chinese characters (Article 3 of the Law of National Common Language). These provisions organically combine the diversity and uniformity of the language; they not only respect the right of ethnic minorities to learn, use, and develop their own spoken and written languages but also protect the rights of various ethnic groups to learn languages from each other, especially to learn and use the commonly spoken Chinese and standard Chinese characters. This not only reflects the relations, including ethnic equality, ethnic unity, and co-prosperity of each nationality but also shows that China is a unified multifamily of nations. Document No. 14 (2002), issued by the State Council, aims to vigorously promote the minority primary and secondary schools' bilingual education, correctly handle the relationship of using minority language and Chinese language teaching, and deploy the minority primary and secondary schools' bilingual teaching. Minority primary and secondary schools gradually form a curriculum that teaches the minority language and the Chinese language, and the areas where conditions permit should offer a foreign language course. We should place bilingual teaching materials in the local education development plans and compile Chinese teaching materials of minority students in accordance with the new full-time Chinese national primary and secondary school syllabus. We should actively create conditions for the primary schools and secondary schools using minority language in order to offer Chinese language courses gradually from the first grade. The state should pay attention to bilingual teaching, research, development, and publication of educational materials. All the governments of the Tibetan autonomous areas have also laid down the specifications giving consideration to both Tibetan and Chinese language courses. For example, the Provisions of Tibet Autonomous Region Study, Use, and Development of Tibetan Language (2002) declare that in compulsory education period the schools should use the Tibetan language and the national common language as spoken and written teaching languages, offer the Tibetan language and the national common language courses, and provide foreign language courses.

EXPERIENCING THE TIBETAN SCHOOLING PRACTICE CONTEXT

How do Tibetan schools carry out and implement the National Policy? In order to gain insight into how Tibetan schools actually work, I visited two schools in the Gannan Tibetan Autonomous Prefecture and two mainland Tibetan classes in Gansu Province.

The Practice of Ideological Education in Tibetan Schools

The Tibetan schools fully implement the Chinese government's guiding principles for education and minority policies, apart from promoting overall student development in moral character, intelligence, physical training, and aesthetic education. These approaches contribute to strengthening the backbone of the Chinese nation. In particular, they not only contribute to socialist construction in Tibetan areas, but they also support the leadership of the Communist Party of China. Consequently, these safeguard the unification of the country, as they adhere to the unity of nationalities.

An education official, in his speech at a Tibetan middle school ceremony, clearly showed what identity the Tibetan students should have. Here are some excerpts:

> The Tibetans are an industrious and intelligent national, and the people have a fine tradition of patriotism. To every student, you are an aspiring young people with love of motherland and knowledge. You are not only the builders of the future of Tibetans, but also a glorious herald of friendship between the Chinese and Tibetans. We hope you will carry forward the fine traditions of the Tibetan people, and with the Han people live in harmony, loving each other dearly, to make a contribution to enhance the friendship between the Han and Tibetan nationalities. We hope that the fine atmosphere of study comes to stay among students, and all of you will study and learn hard in order to lay a solid foundation for the construction of your homeland. Besides, everyone has to be ideal. Morality, culture, and discipline transforms. (Field notes, Mr. He, 2007)

To some extent, the love of country and Tibet and Sino-Tibetan friendship ideology were put forward in the first place when the education official posed the question "who are you." His definitions about students' identity were in accordance with national policy, and his speech was also encouraging students to construct their ethnic identity in the real context of the school. He also emphasized that the purpose of the students' learning is to build the Tibetan area, hoping students can construct an ethnic identity, and he persuaded them to devote themselves to the future development of the Tibetan region. Certainly, this kind of ethnic identity cannot politically threaten the propagation of national ideology but should follow the pattern of pluralism and integration within the unity theme of the Chinese nation. The teacher's idea highlights also the specification of ethnic identity.

> China is a united multiethnic country. The Tibetan people, as a member of the family of the Chinese nation, have created and promoted their brilliant, distinctive culture during intercommunion with other ethnic groups in a long history. Until now, the Tibetan culture is a bright pearl of the Chinese nation and the world's cultural treasure. As a master of the new era, the Tibetan people inherit, develop, and share the Tibetan traditional culture together, creating modern civilization life and cultural undertakings to make the Tibetan culture rise to unprecedented prosperity and development. With China's reform and opening and in the modernization drive, especially with the further development of the implementation of the Western development strategy, the Tibetan people are modernizing with a brand-new attitude toward the world, and the Tibetan culture will also make a newly great progress. (Interview, Mr. Wu, 2007)

This discourse stressed the relationship between the Tibetans and Chinese nation, and between Tibetan culture and other ethnic minority cultures composing the Chinese national culture; it also praised the Tibetan people's creativity and the development of Tibetan culture, which emphasized the ethnic minorities' harmony and national unity as well. Thus, this assigned identity adopted "the pattern of pluralism and integration within the unity of the Chinese nation (Fei, 1989, p.1)." Furthermore, these words are also often spoken in teachers' history and geography classes in Tibetan schools; what follows is an example.

> Tibetans made an important contribution to the forming of a national unified country, which is one of the most important nations with a long history and excellent traditional culture. After a long history of formation and development, Tibetan language, literature, art, music, dance, painting, drama, architecture, sculpture, history, medicine and astronomy have not only been endowed with rich cultural tradition of content, but their own unique style and form fully embody the Tibetan people's wisdom and creativity, and also add luster to the Chinese national historical and cultural treasures. (Field notes, Mr. Gongbao, 2007)

Thus, from the preceding words, the education in Tibetan schools shows that they not only attach importance to the dominant position of national identity to enable Tibetan students to internalize concepts, such as "Chinese nation," "national unity," and "Sino-Tibetan friendship," but they also show respect for the Tibetan culture and history. These enable Tibetan students to form the concept of "serving the hometown" and "building a hometown." Tibetan school administrators and teachers are devoted to ideological education, including teaching on the concepts of "I am Chinese," "patriotism and national unity," and "unity of nationalities and Sino-Tibetan solidarity" in order to help students form both a Tibetan ethnic identity and a national identity.

The Practice of Bilingual Education in Tibetan Schools

Language is the vehicle and the basis of culture; it is also a symbol of ethnic identity. The core issue concerning Chinese minority education is that of language. At present, Tibetan schools are implementing bilingual education; this includes the native language of Tibetans (Tibetan) and the common language in China (Chinese).

Presently, in the Gannan Tibetan Autonomous Prefecture, bilingual education can be divided into two models. (1) In the Tibetan-oriented model, each course is taught generally in Tibetan, whereas Chinese is designed as a common subject. This kind of teaching model is mainly carried out in schools (including external teaching sites) of agricultural and pastoral regions under the administrative level of county, the county-based primary schools and high schools, and some of the junior high schools in cities. In this way, before the year 2001, there were no Chinese classes designed for primary students until they reach a higher grade (generally until Primary 3). However, after 2001, Chinese has been offered to the students of Primary 1 in the schools in towns, whereas other subjects are taught in Tibetan. In the agricultural and pastoral regions, schools can teach Chinese to the students of Primary 1 according to their teaching conditions—teaching hours being six to eight classes per week—whereas other subjects are taught in Tibetan. (2) Teaching is done mainly in Chinese, whereas Tibetan, which is offered as an independent subject, is used as a complementary language. This model is adopted in the junior high schools in cities and most of the schools in counties. (Interview, Mr. He, 2008)

Due to the differences of the two models, the language environments are also varied in different schools, which leads to a large gap in language acquisition between those students. In the case of Tibetan-oriented model, the teaching language being Tibetan and the textbooks written in Tibetan, the students can do better in Tibetan in comprehensive skills, and the ethnic identity is well formed among these students. In the Chinese-oriented model, both the teaching language and the textbooks being Chinese, students are better equipped in the Chinese language, which facilitates the construction of national identity.

The Practice of Non-formal Curriculum in Tibetan Schools

In addition to the formal curriculum, Tibetan schools also make use of varied non-formal curriculum to strengthen the students' national identity and ethnic identity. Generally speaking, the non-formal curriculum refers to those that have not been included in the school's training, curriculum guidelines, and teaching materials, whereas the students have to acquire social information, meanings, beliefs, values, and manners. The non-formal curriculum has varied contents and forms, including rituals, slogans, and activities. Non-formal curriculum that contains national consciousness may cultivate students' national identity, whereas that which reflects ethnic culture may facilitate the manifestation of ethnic differences in schools and thus promote the ethnic identity.

Rituals can pass on social rules and values and make participants reflect on their own status in the social system. They are also capable of promoting identity construction; they can embody and transfer certain customs, regulations, beliefs, or a worldview. Furthermore, school-opening and flag-raising ceremonies in Tibetan schools each week have the function to transmit national consciousness and to promote national identity. (Field notes, 2009)

In Tibetan schools, propaganda galleries and school newspapers often manifest the typical Tibetan culture characteristics, such as the hada, yaks, a Buddha drawn by students, experiences of Tibetan life, stories of Tibetan childhood, descriptions of Tibetan customs and rituals, and performance of Tibetan songs and dances. Schools not only acquiesce but support the expressions and presentations of the meaning of these activities. Meanwhile, they create different situations, especially in extra-school activities, to encourage individuals or groups to represent their personalities. In the meantime, the students themselves are creating opportunities and situations to express and represent their ethnic sentiments. Those representations are not only the transition of national consciousness but also the practice of ethnic identity among the Tibetan students. (Field notes, 2009)

To sum up, Tibetan schools in China have carried out the basic principle that both national identity and ethnic identity should be considered altogether; they have cultivated cross-cultural adaptive abilities in Tibetan students. In terms of basic knowledge, skills, and attitudes, the students are persuaded not only to accept the common culture in order to construct their national identity, but also to sustain their own ethnic culture in order to construct their ethnic identities so that the two can coexist harmoniously.

DOUBLE IDENTITY CONSTRUCTION AMONG TIBETAN STUDENTS

In order to gain insight about the status of the Tibetan students' identity construction, I interviewed some Tibetan students in the Tibetan middle schools in Gannan Tibetan Autonomous Prefecture and the mainland Tibetan classes in Gansu Province.

Cognition of Diversity in Unity

Tibetan school education, on the one hand, actively guides students to recognize their own cultural backgrounds, understand their own cultural origin and change, and inherit and develop their own ethnic minority culture. On the other hand, it also requires students to learn the common culture and guides students to understand, respect, and develop other cultures; this achieves good results. This can be seen from a Tibetan middle school student's statement.

> We live in a diverse society; our country is a multiethnic multicultural meeting country, all of which confirms a picture of modern China. As a student, there are too many things to learn, but I think we should learn the Chinese language well because it is very useful. Of course, we also have to learn the Tibetan language because this is our own traditional culture. Furthermore, the Tibetan traditional culture is very famous in the world; many countries, including the United States, Japan, and other countries study the Tibetan traditional culture. As a Tibetan, we have a responsibility to carry forward the Tibetan traditional culture.

The Tibetan culture is an important component of the Chinese traditional culture, and we need to continue to learn it.

Tibetan students have a clearer understanding of their own ethnic minority culture and of the Chinese national common culture that pass through the learning in primary and secondary schools. They have learned to recognize the richness and pluralism of culture and have respected the existence of values and space of all kinds of cultures. (Interview, Cireng, 2009)

The Feeling of Diversity in Unity

In the Tibetan students' conversation and their diary accounts, they repeatedly claim, "I am a Tibetan, and I'm proud of being a Tibetan." (Interviews, Nima and Danzheng, 2009)

They have such an understanding of Tibet: Tibet is sacred, beautiful, lovely, rich, and full of mystery and treasure. The Tibetan people are warm, hospitable, and with a generous nature, honest, non-artificial, and good at singing and dancing. The Tibetan people believe in Buddhism and they benevolently love others, serve others, and are dedicated to others. The Tibetan people have very good thinking skills and have a generous moral character, pure heart, and a strong sense of shame.

Thus, we can say that Tibetan students, emotionally, first of all keep in mind that they are Tibetans and are full of feelings of national pride and cohesion.

When I talked with Tibetan students about their attitudes on associating with other ethnic groups, especially with the members of the Han, most of them replied that there is generally no difference because we are all Chinese. (Interviews, Zhaxi, Zhaozheng and Danzeng, 2009) For example, a Tibetan student described the following thoughts in his diary: "Around us, it seemed that there is a big warm hand supporting us and helping us. They are not our family, but better than family. They work hard for us day and night, shade sunshine in summer, keep warm, and resist against wind and snow in winter." (Diary, Kazhuo, 2009)

The implementation of the ideological education in Tibetan school education has made students understand the thread of the "Diversity in Unity of the Chinese Nation." Students emotionally have known that they are "a factor" for "diversity" and a part of the unity. Thus, they have accepted their own ethnic culture and have respect for other cultures as well. They also have come to know that all ethnic groups are equal brothers and make an indelible contribution to the Chinese nation's rejuvenation and development. They have conscientiously formed an integrated whole identity in the pluralistic context. Therefore, the construction of an ethnic identity is consistent with the pattern of diversity in unity of the Chinese nation in the school education context.

Therefore, the Tibetan students have formed a good sense of belonging, responsibility, and pride in their own ethnic culture and national co-culture. They demonstrate not only a positive ethnic identity but also a positive sense of national identity. In their own words to express this: "I am a Tibetan," "We are all Chinese."

CONCLUSION

Most countries in the world are multiethnic and how to coordinate the relationship between ethnic identity and national identity is a common issue. Multiethnic countries have to face the challenge of the imbalance between ethnic identity and national identity because of the inherent differences in the object and source that can be recognized. Moreover, economical and cultural factors also lead to inconsistencies between them. Many scholars hold that conflicts exist among ethnic, national, and cross-border identities, and they even point out that ethnic and supra-national identities can be considered as a denial to national identity (Gorenburg, 2000). Huntington (2004) strongly supports such a view in his work "Who Are We? The Challenges to America's National Identity," in which he puts forward that sub-national and cross-border identities proved to be the deconstruction to the national identity of the United States and are major factors threatening the safety of America.

Therefore, many people think that harmonizing the tensions and conflicts between ethnic identity and national identity is impossible and that inevitably they are in the opposition to each other. Based on this point of view, some people hold that national assimilation is available, whereas others think that people should build pure ethnic identities according to the results of national self-determination (Cui, 1999).

However, national assimilation and national self-determination have been determined to go against the social reality and have a bad influence on the unity and stability of a country. No doubt, authorities in countries hope that their national populace not only submit to their own national culture but also accept mainstream culture; that is, the minority in one country should combine ethnic identity with national identity, which has become a major issue for many multiethnic countries. If we want to realize this objective, we have to solve the following two problems: it is necessary, first, to balance the pace of development between the national economy and regional economy and, second, to educate people to respect the cultures of different minorities.

The realization of ethnic identity mainly depends on national socialization and education guidance, whereas education guidance is the most effective way to improve the realization of national identity. Thus, educators have the responsibility to cultivate the national populace with good physical and mental qualities. The most important thing is to educate them to develop the consciousness of an ethnic identity and a national identity. Apart from this, we should not ignore the choice of suitable knowledge, culture, and correct values used in a specific schooling context, which are closely related to the harmonious combination between national identity and ethnic identity.

China has 55 minority groups, and our government insists that minorities should acknowledge not only their own nation but the whole country as well. As mentioned earlier, our government and schools have the responsibility to accelerate the harmonious combination between ethnic identity and national identity. On the one hand, every educator should encourage students to study hard in order to become an educated society member; on the other hand, for Tibetan students, we need to educate them to return to their homeland willingly and make contributions toward the unity and development of our country. In the schooling context, although the students probably build an ethnic identity and a national identity of different types and in different degrees, they internalize ethnic and national ideologies at the same time, which proves that the schools not only provide the stimulus for the delivery of national ideology but rebuild the construction of students' ethnic identity.

REFERENCES

Aqitu, Q. (1994). The national assimilation media and the principle of confirmation. *Journal of Inner Mongolia University (Humanities and Social Sciences)*, 26(4), 93–100.

Census Office of the State Council.(2003). *Tabulation of 2000 Population Census of China(Volume 1)*, Beijing: China Statistic Press, 18–46.

Cui, Z.(1999). National Self-determination Rights, Human Rights and Sovereignty, *Reading*, 245(8), 25–29.

Fei, X. (1989). *The Pattern of Pluralism and Integration within the Unity of the Chinese Nation*. Beijing: Minzu College of China. p1.

Gorenburg, D. (2000). "Not with One Voice: An Explanation of Intragroup Variation in Nationalist Sentiment", *World Politics*, 53(1), 116.

Hansen, M. H. (1999). *Lessons in being Chinese: Minority education and ethnic identity in southwest China*. Seattle: University of Washington Press.

Huntington, S. P. (2005). *Who are we? The challenges to America's national identity*. Beijing: Xinhua Publishing House.

Li, Y. (1999). Ethnic identity and national identity: Identity of ethnic and national consciousness in the Chinese society. *Journal of Chongqing Normal University (Edition of Social Sciences)*, 20(2), 3–12.

Liu, X. (1997). A marginal return: The problematic in Zhang Chengzhi's reinvention of ethnic identity. *Journal of Contemporary China*, 6(16), 567–581.

Mackerras, C. (1995). *China's minority cultures: Identities and integration since 1912*. New York: St. Martin's Press.

Postiglione, G. A. (1999) *China's national minority education: Culture, schooling and development*. New York: Falmer.

The PRC Regional Autonomy Law for Minority Nationalities (1984). Retrieved February 28, 2001, from http://www.people.com.cn/item/flfgk/rdlf/1984/111202198401.html

The Provisions of Tibet Autonomous Region Study, Use, and Development of Tibetan language (2002), from http://www.chinatibetnews.com/kejiao/2002-08/16/content_2883.htm

Shih, C. Y. (2000). Book review: Lessons in being: Chinese-minority education and ethnic identity in southwest China/China's national minority education: Culture, schooling and development. *Journal of Asian Studies, 59*(2), 406–408.

Teng, X., & Zhang, J. (1997). The national identity and the ethnic identity of the minority school. *Journal of South-Central University for Nationalities (Humanities and Social Sciences), 88*(4), 105–110.

Trueba, H. T., & Zou, Y. (1994). *Power in education: The case of Miao University students and its significance for American culture.* Washington, DC: Falmer Press.

Upton, J. L. (1996). Home on the grasslands? Tradition, modernity, and the negotiation of identity by Tibetan intellectuals in the PRC. In M. J. Brown (Ed.), *Negotiating ethnicities in China and Taiwan* (pp. 98–124). Berkeley: University of California, Institute of East Asian Studies.

Wan, M. (2006). *Multi-culture view: Research on values and nationality self-identity.* Beijing: Ethnic Publishing House.

Wan, M., & Wang, Y. (2004). Ethnic identity of Tibetan undergraduates. *Acta Psychologica Sinica, 36*(1), 83–88.

Wan, M., Wang, Y., & Li, J. (2002). A study of Tibetan undergraduates' national and cultural identity. *Journal of Northwest Normal University (Social Sciences), 39*(5), 14–18.

Yan, Q., & Song, S. (2006). Students' problems in cross-cultural study and countermeasures in the ethnic educational model of running schools in other place: Taking Tibetan classes and Xinjiang classes in the hinterland as examples. *Journal of Research on Education for Ethnic Minorities, 17*(2), 65–68.

Yong, L., & Wan, M. (2003). On the factors that influence the Han and Tibetan culture identity status of the Tibetan undergraduates. *Studies of Psychology and Behavior, 1*(3), 181–185.

Zhu, Z. (2007). The construction of ethnic identity in the context of state-prescribed school curriculum: A sociological analysis. *N.W. Ethno-National Studies, 54*(3), 44–55.

Part II

Minority Students in Hong Kong

7 Critical Perspective on New Arrival Children from Mainland China in Hong Kong
Government Policies, School Practices, and Teacher Responses

Stella Chong

INTRODUCTION

In 1995, returning from the US as a school psychologist, I became a teacher in Hong Kong. At that time, Hong Kong was still a British colony (the region was returned to the sovereignty of China in 1997). In-service student teachers who were mainly teaching remedial classes in mainstream schools constantly spoke of their apprehensions when teaching new arrival children (NAC) from mainland China. It was initially puzzling: aside from their places of origin, how different could these students be? Hongkongers and mainland Chinese have the same ancestors; historically, the ancestors of many Hongkongers were immigrants from China too! Class discussions drove me to conduct a literature search on NAC. However, surprisingly, a dearth of information was found. This led me to investigate; NAC later became the focus of my dissertation (Chong, 2004).

This chapter begins with a discussion on the historical emergence of NAC, as well as on NAC-related government policies and educational provisions. Subsequently, an overview of the latest literature on NAC is presented, the research study is introduced, and the research methodology is described. Findings with respect to school responses toward minority students are emphasized. Thereafter, factors within the educational system that may enhance or constrain prospects for the democratic schooling of NAC are examined from a critical perspective. Implications are drawn from the discussions.

HISTORICAL EMERGENCE OF NAC

Before World War II, people from mainland China freely traveled to Hong Kong. (The term "mainland" is adopted throughout this chapter to distinguish mainland China from Hong Kong, Macau, and Taiwan.) The influx of mainlanders to Hong Kong was most acute during four historical periods:

the civil war (1948–1949), the implementation of the "touch base policy" (a policy, which was adopted in 1974, allowing those who could evade capture to stay in Hong Kong; the policy was abolished in 1980), after the Cultural Revolution in 1978 (International Social Service, 1997), and finally after the reunification of Hong Kong and China in 1997. Mainlanders are not truly "new immigrants" because Hong Kong is part of China. Thus, the term "new arrivals" is used (Hong Kong Council of Social Service, 1982).

Since 1980, the settlement of mainlanders in Hong Kong has been tightly controlled. A strict quota system of 75 one-way permits a day was set; it was later raised to 105 in 1994. A year later, the number was increased to 150 (Asia Pacific Migration Research Network, 2009). Several new immigration policies (e.g., the Admission Scheme for Mainland Talents and Professionals in July 2003, the Capital Investment Entrant Scheme in October 2003, and the Quality Migrant Admission Scheme in June 2006) were further instituted to attract talents and capital into the city (Immigration Department, 2008). These policies aim to sustain the young population and to maintain economic vitality in Hong Kong. NAC in the fourth period are more economically affluent and skilled than those in first, second, and third periods.

Population of NAC from Mainland China in Hong Kong

Hong Kong is comprised of four main regions and 18 districts. According to the latest statistical figures from the Education Bureau (2009a, 2009b), 1,312 NAC are enrolled in Hong Kong schools (December 2008 to May 2009, with a monthly average of 218 students). The percentage of enrollment by region is as follows: New Territories East (37.8%), Kowloon region (31.9%), New Territories West (20.4%), and Hong Kong region (9.9%). Of the 18 districts, the 10 heaviest enrollments are found in Shatin (343), Tuen Mun (122), Kowloon City (118), Wong Tai Sin (118), North District (96), Yuen Long (60), Sai Kung (59), Tai Po (57), Kwun Tong (56), and Kwai Chung and Tsing Yi (54). These children are concentrated in less affluent areas, and the concentrations are heavier in areas that are closer to the mainland borders (58.2% in the New Territories East and West). Nevertheless, the number of NAC from the quota system has been decreasing since 2001 (Kwoh, 2006). Meanwhile, the number of children born to parents without identity cards has been increasing rapidly, from 620 in 2001 to 9,237 in 2005. In the first ten months of 2006, 12,398 nonresident children were born (Clem, 2006). The Education Bureau is becoming aware of the potential educational needs of these children whose parents are not permanent residents.

Government Policies and Educational Provisions

From kindergarten to Primary 1 and from Primary 6 to Form 1, there are two ways of admission: centralized allocation and self-allocation. To some extent, the self-allocation procedure allows parents to choose where to enroll their children, but final decisions rest upon school administrators (Education Commission, 2006). The centralized procedure purportedly aims to offer equal opportunities for all and to reduce the pressure, among children, to enter elite schools. Thus, it becomes the primary means of catering to the needs of disadvantaged children. However, this admission procedure is not devoid of problems.

In 1996, the government established the Central Placement Unit (CPU) to handle the school enrollment of NAC. The CPU sorts NAC according to their residential areas and assists them in finding schools. The CPU's role is virtually confined to providing a list of available schools in specific places and advising parents to apply for admission. There is, in reality, no legally binding admission policy stipulated by the Education Bureau.

There are four government-sponsored programs that aim to help NAC adjust to their new environments. First, the Induction Program is a 60-hour course for children aged 6 to 15 years. The course is designed to promote the personal development, social adaptation, and basic learning skills of NAC. Second, the English Extension Program is another 60-hour English remediation program for newcomers aged 9 to 15 years. Third, the School-Based Support Scheme is a block grant given to schools with NAC enrollees. The grant is used to provide remedial lessons, to purchase resource materials, and to organize extra-curricular activities, among others. Fourth, the full-time Initiation Program aims to provide a transitional adjustment period for newcomers in an alternative mode of schooling prior to their enrollment in mainstream schools. The program is currently operated in five schools, and it runs in a cycle of six months from September to March every year (Education Bureau, 2009a).

In Hong Kong, secondary schools are classified into Anglo-Chinese schools (60–90%) and Chinese schools (10–40%) (Morrison & Liu, 2000). English medium instruction (EMI) schools are generally perceived by the public to have higher status than Chinese medium instruction (CMI) schools. Most NAC, who have English language problems, are generally placed in CMI schools or lower band schools (Band 3 is the lowest in a three-tier quality structure). According to the Education Bureau, effective September 2010, there will no longer be a pure division of schools into CMI or EMI (Education Bureau, 2009b). This new policy intends to counteract the labeling of CMI schools and to address concerns over the transition of CMI students from junior to senior secondary and/or post-secondary levels where EMI teaching is widely utilized.

However, all students enrolled in mainstream schools who experience learning difficulties will be placed in one of the following programs: a resource class (a pullout program for remediation) or the Intensive Remedial Teaching Program (IRTP). Under the IRTP, students attend all their regular classes, but they are provided extra remediation before or after school. There is a higher proportion of NAC and students with special needs in these classes.

LITERATURE REVIEW

The Hong Kong Family Welfare Society has been serving new arrivals from the mainland since the 1940s (Tong, 2000). Nonetheless, there is scant information on NAC. Two of the earliest publications issued in the early 1980s, the *Report on Working Group on "New Arrivals"* (1982) and the *Report on the Social and Economic Adaptation of the Chinese New Arrivals in Hong Kong* (1985), were from the Hong Kong Council of Social Service. In the 1990s, some studies were conducted by voluntary or nongovernmental organizations, such as the Hong Kong Professional Teachers' Union (1994), the Boys and Girls Clubs Association (1996), the Hong Kong Federation of Youth Groups (1995), and the International Social Service Hong Kong Branch (1997). These studies mainly surveyed the educational conditions and adaptation mechanisms of new arrivals in Hong Kong. During the turn of the 21st century, there was a surge of new studies.

Rao and Yuen (2001) found that NAC encounter the following challenges: securing age-appropriate school placements; adjusting to the new school, education system, curricula, social environment, and changes in family ecologies; and facing prejudice, segregation, and marginalization. According to a study in 2004 by the Society for Community Organization, 91% of newcomers experience discrimination (Kwoh, 2006). In Ng's (2003) study, one mother said, "My children do not even like to be identified as new immigrants because the image of mainlanders has been so vilified in Hong Kong." Hue (2008) theorized that some new arrival students use the meritocratic approach to offset their sense of being discriminated and to make sense of their cross-cultural experiences.

Interestingly, in a sample of five upper-grade primary schools (local students = 264, NAC = 283), Cheung and Hui (2003) found that NAC have a significantly higher sense of school belongingness and a lower sense of rejection than local students. This result may not be surprising because NAC may feel less alienated and rejected when they compose the majority in schools. Accordingly, NAC may feel more bonded in schools than local students. In another study involving a primary school (N = 387), Chan and Chan (2004) ascertained that NAC do well in their academic work but less well in their family relationships and self-esteem than local students. In contrast, Tam and Lam (2005) found that migrant adolescents (N = 243) have higher self-esteem than local-born youth (N = 750); such differences are perhaps attributable to the educational levels and years of Hong Kong residence of their parents.

Young immigrants exhibit better levels of adjustment to challenges and better mental health than local-born youth. This phenomenon is caused by several factors, including contentment and gratitude, a strong family concept, "face" (i.e., defending honor for oneself and family), an urge for knowledge, a sense of crisis, faith in life, and acceptance of their marginal identities. According to Wong, Lam, Yan, and Hung (2004), a high level of social competence (e.g., self-control, empathy, assertiveness, and the ability to read social cues) is also crucial in mitigating acculturative stress, leading to better mental health. Wong (2008) further studied the effects of stressful life events and social support on the mental health of youth from the perspective of resilience. He maintained that apart from social competence, the ability to endure hardships and peer support seem to be the protective factors that remarkably affect the mental health of newly arrived youth.

Cheung and Leung (2009) conducted the most extensive research on secondary school students from the mainland (N = 1,243). They found that in the face of discrimination, early social integration into the host society and disconnection from their native homes are essential to successful acculturation. However, fluency in the host language, although it appears conducive to the success of acculturation, may not mitigate the adverse effects of discrimination because the Cantonese of new arrivals is nonetheless different from the Chinglish style (i.e., mixing of Chinese and English words in Hong Kong Cantonese) that local Hongkongers speak.

Conceptually, pre-1997 and post-1997 studies on newcomers have common themes that embody four key domains: cultural (e.g., cross-cultural identity), educational (e.g., school adjustment), social (e.g., discrimination), and psychological (e.g., mental health). The political domain is left largely unexplored. Most of the investigations were rather "tame"; little critical analysis was conducted beneath the surface of the problems. In contrast, since the 1970s, debates on immigrants in the West have centered on critical issues, such as the creation of minorities, the politics of education, equality, justice, and power relations (Cummins, 2000; Freire, 1970; Nieto & Bode, 2008; Sleeter & Grant, 2009; Taylor, 1992). Discourses on these issues are rarely examined in Hong Kong.

RESEARCH STUDY

This research identifies factors that may enhance or constrain the democratic schooling of newcomers. Democratic schools are those that listen to student voices; treat everyone as equals; promote fairness and human dignity; and eliminate social, gender, racial, and cultural divisions. NAC arrive in Hong Kong daily, and they are changing school enrollment patterns; hence, it is imperative to understand the effects and implications that migration brings.

METHODS

This research consists of multiple case studies in nine primary schools found in six of the eighteen school districts of Hong Kong. The percentages of NAC in the nine schools ranged from 4.4% to over 95%. Nine principals (mid 40s to late 50s in age) and ten teachers (late 20s to mid 50s) participated in this study. Of the 19 interviewees, 11 were males. The first interview was with a former student of the researcher, and the former student also invited their school principal to participate in the study. The rest of the interviewees were identified through the snowballing technique (successive references from interviewees). Data obtained from this sampling procedure were cross-validated with other data collected from various sources, such as conversations with principals, government policy documents, literature, media documentaries, and various databases. This triangulation procedure was a multimethod approach in comparing, combining, and contrasting different kinds of data to show their complementary patterns, as well as to cross-check their validity. Two sets of unstructured open-ended interview schedules were sent to the schools prior to the interviews. All interviews were taped and transcribed. Transcripts were sent to individual interviewees for feedback. Findings of the study were interpreted based on critical pedagogy.

RESEARCH QUESTIONS

This study investigates three major issues:

1. How do school administrators and teachers respond to students with culturally diverse backgrounds?
2. What factors within the school organization may enhance or constrain prospects for the democratic schooling of newcomers?
3. What policy and teacher education implications can be drawn from the study?

RESEARCH FINDINGS

The following section provides an overview of the responses of school administrators and teachers toward NAC.

Responses of School Administrators

In admitting newcomers, five of the nine schools are guided by the principle of "teaching without categorizing" (有教無類), a philosophy attributed to Confucius. This philosophy implies that students—whether they are rich or poor, good or bad, smart or not—should not be labeled but taught according to their abilities. Other schools emphasize values, such as caring, faithfulness, honesty, diligence, and persistence, which fundamentally characterize the general Asian culture. Findings suggest that school philosophies contradict with the personal philosophies of administrators. Many fall short of actualizing their official school guiding philosophies. For example, two principals openly admit that they will bar

NAC from their schools if their academic performance or behaviors are detrimental to the school. Another states that he will not admit those who are deaf, blind, and physically handicapped, including nearby transfer-ins with records of behavioral, emotional, or academic problems. Some principals admit NAC provided that these students are willing to be demoted to lower grades. The following excerpts from two principals tell the story:

Principal 1: I am most afraid that they will take drugs. Although we don't have too many of these cases yet, we have encountered them. So if I had realized their problem in the very beginning, I wouldn't have accepted them because I couldn't allow them to pollute our students' minds.

Principal 2: There is no unconditional admission for NAC. With compulsory education, it seems that we are offering some free gifts, we, therefore, have to be more selective about whom to give to . . . We cannot admit them all. We have to pick and choose. Otherwise, it is not fair to other parents . . . We have to be fair to other local children, too. There are children who had tried four to five times to pass the exam but failed.

Recent conversations with several principals prove this reality. For example, one secondary school principal claims that NAC may not pass their entrance exams:

Yes, they have to sit for an exam . . . many cannot pass the entrance exam . . . that is why they change school, of course there are some problems, perhaps because of academic problems, so they may not pass our entrance exam. (Personal communication, June 10, 2009)

One primary school principal does not fully welcome NAC, stressing that cultural differences may pose academic problems:

Basically, I don't welcome them very much, because the culture differences between the two lands are great . . . a lot of values we uphold, newcomers don't . . . their social values, whether to abide to rules or not . . . are very different, therefore, they are hard to teach, very hard to teach. I won't intentionally accept them . . . Fortunately, our school is good enough, we don't have to worry to accept them; we can sing a higher note. (Personal communication, July 6, 2009)

The belief structures of these principals are based on two assumptions. First, education is for privileged normal children, not for those who are marginalized, such as children who are unable or unwilling to learn, or children who have physical or emotional deficiencies. Second, conformity to institutional rules and norms is a prerequisite to schooling. These two underlying assumptions are deeply embedded in the Hong Kong school system.

Responses of Teachers

Data reveal the resourcefulness of teachers in managing various demands posed by the daily influx of NAC. This resourcefulness is conceptualized under a five-tier coping mechanism.

Reliance on Self and Personal Practical Knowledge

Teachers always try to build on their past experiences; they commit themselves to tackling problems as they arise. One teacher with minimal prior knowledge or training in teaching NAC tries to impress his students with his "outside-the-textbook" knowledge to keep their attention in class:

> You need to find out how you can reach the unmotivated so that they would . . . pay some attention in class. If I have spoken ten sentences, they listen to three, there is still learning. So what strategy should I use? . . . you have to think of something they don't know in China, talk a little to arouse their interest, then go back to the book, then they may get three out of ten of what you taught.

Other teachers tend to exercise their professional judgment or personal practical knowledge in dealing with newcomers. The most common strategies that teachers use include watering down the curriculum, teaching kindergarten-level English, providing easier work, giving extra supplementary work, providing remedial classes, and using a different or more lenient grading system. However, there are teachers who believe that treating children equally is treating them fairly; otherwise, schools are either unfair or are practicing discrimination:

> During examination, we [teachers] treat them just the same because we don't want to label them. How would we know whether they have improved or not if we don't use the same measurement to measure [their achievements]? If we use a shorter ruler to measure them, they thought they have made progress, but in fact, they haven't. We encourage them to catch up. We don't want to shorten the distance for them to race. If they have to reach 100 meters, we don't want them just to reach 50, for they will never reach the destination. So we have to have a standard measurement.

Some teachers do not appear to understand that it is unjust to assess all students using a formal standardized measurement; a standard measurement penalizes the underprivileged and favors the most privileged (Bourdieu,

1976). In responding to the challenges posed by NAC, few teachers dare to venture beyond school boundaries; most teachers simply stick with their common sense logic and regulations. This submission to unity and to the dominant culture is unfortunately rooted in Hong Kong's academic tradition, and teachers submit reflexively.

Reliance on Colleagues

Teachers report that exchanging ideas and experiences, sharing information with one another, and group problem solving among caring staff help relieve them from shouldering the burdens alone.

Reliance on Parents

Teachers recognize that without parental cooperation, their actions will simply be partially successful. Some teachers conduct home visits; others think that it is more important to make parents feel at home when they come to school. Some think that enlisting parents as volunteers will improve teacher–parent communication and enhance the academic performance of students.

Reliance on Pupils

The majority of teachers find that providing more opportunities for children to help one another not only alleviates their teaching burdens but also benefits children themselves (e.g., it improves their self-confidence). Furthermore, some teachers realize that by acting as both teacher and friend (or as confidants), they are building good rapport with NAC, thus improving cooperation and learning.

Reliance on Professionals

When the immediate resources of teachers are exhausted, they turn to professionals, such as social workers, for help. They may also attend special seminars organized by established community organizations, such as the police force in the areas of smoking and drugs, where professional advice and support can be sought.

Indigenous Features that Enhance or Constrain the Democratic Schooling of NAC

Data triangulated from various sources were critically reviewed from five perspectives (i.e., political, cultural, economic, educational, and social) to ascertain factors that may enhance or constrain the democratic schooling of NAC.

Political

Several government policies appear to be conducive to democratic schooling. First, the integration policy in 1999 emphasizes the fundamental right to regular education of children with diverse needs (Education Department, 2000). Second, in 2000, the Hong Kong government recognized the establishment of a tradition-rich and culturally diverse educational system as one of the aims of the Education Reform. Third, the School-Based Management Scheme in 2005 allows schools to adopt their own systems of governance based on participatory decision-making, transparency, and public accountability (Education & Manpower Bureau, 2006). Fourth, the extension of the 9-year free educational system to 12 years started in SY 2008–2009. The extension aims to address the diverse needs of students, to reduce the pressure created by public examinations, and to make learning more rewarding (Education Commission, 2006). All of these policies are laudable because they result in a virtual paradigm shift from a historically autocratic to a more democratic rule, and from exclusive to inclusive education, which runs along the line of democratic schooling for all students.

However, there are major loopholes in government policies that run against democratic schooling. For example, the constitution does not sufficiently protect the basic rights of students from underprivileged groups. The present study found that many NAC are barred from good school bands. By not stipulating a compulsory admission policy when school space is available, the government seems to be legitimizing the continuity of a status quo that works for the benefit of the dominant culture. Consequently, newcomers from distinct cultural backgrounds are greatly disadvantaged. Furthermore, by pushing aided schools to switch to the Direct Subsidy Scheme (DSS) in the name of providing more choices and quality schooling (at a time when the academic standards of graduates are decreasing), the government is protecting the elite culture. The push for the adoption of DSS appears to be pressuring prestigious schools toward privatization and, simultaneously, toward segregation, separating the bright from the dull, and the privileged from the underprivileged. This scheme, in the name of offering a diversified educational system, obscures the implicit agenda of the dominant class, that is, to maintain the status quo. The scheme separates the haves from the have-nots, and the elites from the marginalized, thereby jeopardizing democratic schooling.

Cultural

Culturally, some recognizable features in schools, such as the ideology of "teaching without categorizing" (有教無類), enhance democratic schooling. Fundamentally, Confucius believed that through education, each person can "become human" (成人), that is, having good morality and "becoming talented" (成材). "Becoming talented" means achieving one's potential.

Unfortunately, as proven in this study, such good philosophies have not been actualized in most schools. The current education that over-values elitism and that is built on rigorous examinations has failed to observe the Confucian objectives of becoming human and becoming talented. Professor Lee, a Nobel prize chemist, succinctly criticized this elite-oriented examination system as "using intelligence to harm morality" (以智害德), "using intelligence to harm the body" (以智害體), and "using test questions to harm intelligence" (以題害智) (Lee, 1999).

According to Freire (1972), the society is creating an educational system to submerge "marginals" into "cultures of silence." This "culture of silence" is further reflected in data from the majority of schools that emphasize the acculturation of ethnic minority students. Schools want to rapidly "Hongkongize" NAC and other ethnic minorities by expecting them to adopt the local language and to model local behavioral patterns. Perhaps, the emphasis on collectivism and respect for authority in the Asian culture may partly explain why self-denial is seen as unproblematic, and why many newcomers are willing to relinquish their identities at the request of authorities, believing that they may have better futures if they do so.

Schools must appreciate cultural diversity and aim to promote cultural acceptance by celebrating cultural pluralism and by acknowledging that the loss of indigenous identity is detrimental to healthy personal development. In addition, the loss of students' indigenous identity defeats the aims of the Education Reform: to strive toward a culturally diverse and tradition-rich educational system.

Economic

All new educational policies intend to achieve some planned changes. However, the supply of education in meeting different demands is often limited by available resources. Mismatch often wastes many resources and generates problems related to equity and equal opportunities in education. For example, in considering the waste of resources as a result of low birth rates, about 60 schools were closed in recent years (Kwoh, 2006); others were forced to merge. In this study, one of the village schools was closed, and it merged with another school. On the one hand, the merging of the village school with the urban school may have the advantage of eliminating the segregation of newcomers, and saving maintenance costs and other physical and human resources. However, on the other hand, the merger may greatly disadvantage newcomers. For instance, forced closure ignores participatory decision-making, as well as the right of parents and children to choose their future schools. Often, newcomers are assigned to the lowest band schools where vacancies are available, and this sometimes results in the need to travel long distances.

As mentioned earlier, with DSS funding for elitist education, which is backed by dominant middle-class parents and business sectors, many underprivileged students are denied their rights to the best possible education because they cannot bear the costs. They may be exposed to qualitatively different types of educational knowledge, such as a "practical" curriculum that prepares them to become marginally employed workers, instead of a sophisticated curriculum that can lead them to legal, medical, or managerial fields. There is the danger of turning many lower band schools into ghettos for the poor, slow, dull, or unmotivated. Such an elitist view of education may contribute to the reproduction of unequal class structures and the promotion of social inequalities, thereby jeopardizing democratic schooling.

Educational

Data from the present study fully illustrate how individual schools deny the admission of NAC. In the name of upholding standards and fairness, schools apply formal criteria and equal treatment to all. This serves to perpetuate the cultural privileges of the most privileged. Many NAC, who start school on a different footing because of their diverse backgrounds, are greatly disadvantaged when a difference-blind principle is applied to them. By enforcing universal standards, children are put in an unequal position, which constitutes social injustice, inequality, and oppression, all contrary to the principles of democratic schooling.

Cummins (2000) postulated that the most important factor in school failure among ethnic monitory children comes from unequal power relations and its role in cultural subordination. In this study, power relations are clearly revealed. Schools have the power to accept or reject, to demote or promote, and to recognize or not recognize newcomers through coercive power relations. Similarly, minority parents are likely to feel disempowered before school authorities. Many do not know their rights and entitlements. Even if they do, they may still feel powerless because they may be constrained by the overriding Asian value of respect for authority, coupled with the fact that the fate of their children is in the hands of authorities. Although dialectic relations among children may not be as explicitly imbued with power relations as the relations between minority groups and those in authority are, teachers may inadvertently help to reinforce such differential power relations between Hongkongers and ethnic minorities. For example, young Hongkongers whose linguistic and cultural capital are deemed superior may be asked to peer-tutor newcomers; while young Hongkongers are "superiorized" in the process, newcomers are "inferiorized."

Social

Socially, when it comes to NAC, the majority of schools commit either one or more of the three types of ethnic stereotyping: institutional, cultural or ideological, and individual stereotyping. For example, stereotyping occurs when schools directly or indirectly deprive NAC of their rights to, or opportunities for, appropriate education or entitlements (institutional stereotyping); when NAC are portrayed negatively by school authorities and various media (cultural or ideological stereotyping); and when a principal or teacher excludes or attempts to inferiorize NAC through blatant acts (individual stereotyping). Of the three, institutional stereotyping appears to have the most life-limiting effects because it oppresses minority groups, and it helps perpetuate differential power relations between groups (Essed, 1990).

Taylor (1992) contends that a person or group can suffer greatly if their identity is mistakenly recognized or unrecognized, and if society mirrors back to them a despicable picture of themselves. This can imprison the person in a false, distorted, and reduced mode of being. This seems applicable to NAC because they are socially labeled as "mainland boys" or "mainland girls"—derogatory terms that connote stupidity and unfashionableness—when they demonstrate conspicuous behaviors. Such blatant or subtle ethnic stereotyping makes their daily lives difficult. As members of the stereotyped social group, they are systematically reduced, molded, and immobilized. Although some schools note that there are NAC who manage to succeed in the end, Taylor warned that if we look too closely at individual success cases, we will miss the macroscopic situation of the oppressed social group. Some individuals may benefit; however, the overall structural inequality, which oppresses those who are marginalized, remains intact. Without doubt, this inequality is detrimental to democratic schooling.

IMPLICATIONS OF THE STUDY

Although this research study focuses mainly on the impact of NAC on the educational system, the study's policy implications may be generalized to other ethnic minority groups.

Government Level

Policy for Democratic Schooling

Primarily, as recommended by the United Nations Committee on the Rights of the Child, the government should establish a children's commission or an independent body to monitor children's rights (Connolly, 2006). The government should ensure that the basic human rights of children, such as equal access to education, equal opportunities to pass through the system, equality in educational quality, and equal access to life chances, are protected (Farrell, 1999). This implies that a policy of nondiscrimination and equal opportunity must be prominently instilled in school policies. Such policy must have a clear, legally binding requirement of more open admission to protect children's right to education and to safeguard the human dignity of parents when knocking on school doors. Without legal enforcement, as illustrated in this study, different schools may interpret the policy according to their own perceptions. Hence, an indigenous and minority-specific concept of educational equality must be formulated to serve as basis for the development of a policy that ensures *vertical equity*, that is, the "unequal treatment of unequals" (Darnell, 1983, p. 306). Only through democratic schooling, where equality and nondiscriminatory practices are upheld, will children from diverse backgrounds be given a fair chance of survival or perhaps upward social mobility to free themselves from marginalization.

Policy for Multicultural and Multilingual Education

As a result of globalization, cultural and language pluralism will inevitably become a future phenomenon in most industrialized societies. Evidently, multiculturalism enriches rather than impoverishes society. To be a proactive government with foresight rather than a reactive government that "ad hocs" issues as they arise, the government should ensure that multicultural education becomes part of its educational plans. Multiculturalism can neither remain invisible nor stay in the peripheries of mainstream education. Along this line, the government needs to endorse multi-language policies that affirm the identity of different racial minorities. Language is part of one's identity (Banks, 2001); hence, only through a healthy sense of cultural identity can a person have the strong desire to function effectively in two cultures. The government should therefore aim at expanding its biliterate and trilingual policies to multi-literate and multilingual policies. Such a forward-thinking plan is likely to motivate students to learn whatever foreign languages they desire rather than being forced to learn just one (i.e., English). Children will be more motivated to learn languages when they see its relevance. Simply pushing children to learn one foreign language without assuring that they see its significance or value means a waste of time, energy, and resources; it further creates a sense of failure among them. Only by opening more doors to learning different languages and embracing diversity will the government truly achieve the goal of an educational system that understands and appreciates the values, symbols, and traditions of several cultures. Only then can the educational system function at a competent, meaningful, and global level.

School Level

Flexible Grade Level System

Data reflect that the school system is inflexible in handling students with a wide spectrum of abilities, especially newcomers who have different languages. They are often demoted simply because they lack knowledge in one subject area (i.e., English). Unless schools are ready to accommodate individual differences by adopting a more flexible grading system and by recognizing that diversity is a valuable resource to be extended and preserved, the personal development and self-actualization of children will be retarded. Two areas need cautious attention. First, flexibility should not be misinterpreted or translated into streaming children to differential ability groups and thereby reinforcing social inequality. Second, the age factor should be taken into consideration when arranging the grade and curriculum, so that age-appropriateness is observed and meaningful learning is realized.

Flexible Curricular and Assessment Approaches

The current curriculum and the assessment system in most schools appear too rigid. In this study, it is clear that stakeholders place great emphasis on children's academic learning. They tend to use a deficit paradigm in assessing the achievement of students, which may trigger a self-fulfilling prophecy of failure. Literature has shown that the way educators perceive students significantly influences the quality of education that students receive, which in turn may determine the success or failure of students in schools (Towndrow, Koh, & Tan, 2008). Thus, the view of diversity as a problem needs to be re-framed (Nieto, 2002). Teachers need to differentiate the curriculum from the way students are assessed. To enhance equality and quality of education, teachers must expand their scope by looking holistically at the potentials and talents of children, and by employing different approaches to accommodate their learning differences. If full inclusion is truly one of the goals of Hong Kong education, teachers must go beyond their traditional teaching approaches to benefit all children, not just the few elites.

Parental Involvement

To foster institutional or policy changes, parents need to be part of the steering force. Unfortunately, the school culture of Hong Kong tends to discourage the active participation of parents in their children's education. Likewise, parents, especially those belonging to minority groups, also tend to become "invisible parents" because of the perceived hostile or unwelcoming school environment, or because of other, personal reasons (Liu, 2009). If the best interests of children are truly on their agenda, schools need to regard parents as close partners from the start and be sensitive to their situational dilemmas.

Furthermore, with respect to the growing number of non–Hong Kong resident parents giving birth in Hong Kong, the government should consider taking a proactive role in collaborating with hospital authorities to survey parents while they are still in Hong Kong and to determine if these prospective NAC will attend Hong Kong schools. The government can then effectively design educational opportunities for potential newcomers.

Implications for Future Teacher Developments

This study demonstrates that schools are undergoing rapid changes because of the continuous inflow of newcomers and because many educators are unprepared to teach them. The unpreparedness of teachers appears directly related to current teacher education programs. To date, Hong Kong has paid little attention to multicultural education. None of the eight universities in Hong Kong has an explicit module on multicultural education. Removing multicultural education from the curriculum of Hong Kong's higher educational institutions would be a grave mistake.

In the 21st century, teacher education programs must emphasize the unique visionary challenge of producing culturally proficient teachers and educational leaders to live out the dream of a truly democratic society (i.e., a society that commits itself to social justice, liberty, civic equality, and fraternity), and to ensure ethical integrity in a society of people who are not afraid to condemn exclusion, manipulation, and misery. The new generation needs the kind of education that enhances and expands every human being's ability to understand and transform the world, and that makes use of approaches that transcend national, class, and ethnic boundaries—so that all may exercise their basic human right to develop their cultures and live fuller and more humane lives (Freire, 2005).

REFERENCES IN ENGLISH

Arnove, R.F. & C. A.Torres, (Eds.). *Comparative education: The dialectic of the global and the local.* Lanham, Md.: Rowman & Littlefield.

Asia Pacific Migration Research Network. (2009). *Migration issues in the Asia Pacific.* Retrieved December 15, 2009, from http://www.unesco.org/most/apmrnwp7.htm

Banks, J. (2001). *Cultural diversity and education: Foundations, curriculum, and teaching.* Boston: Allyn & Bacon.

Bourdieu, P. (1976). The school as a conservative force: Scholastic and cultural inequalities. In R. Dale, G. Esland, & M. MacDonald (Eds.), *Schooling and capitalism—A sociological reader* (pp. 110–117). London: Open University Press.

Chan, Y. M., & Chan, C. M. (2004). Self-esteem: A comparison between Hong Kong children and newly arrived Chinese children. *Research in Education, 72,* 18–31.

Cheung, C., & Leung, K. (2009). Resources mitigating the impediment of discrimination to the acculturation success of students migrated to Hong Kong. *International Journal of Intercultural Relations, 33*(5), 372–382.

Cheung, H. Y., & Hui, S. K. F. (2003). Mainland immigrant and Hong Kong local students' psychological sense of school membership. *Asia Pacific Education Review, 4*(1), 67–74.

Chong, S. (2004). *A critical perspective of culturally diverse children in the changing school population in Hong Kong.* Unpublished doctoral thesis. University of Toronto, Canada.

Clem, W. (2006, December 9). Mainland mums a teaching challenge. *South China Morning Post,* p. EDU3.

Connolly, N. (2006, February 11). Legislators press for anti-bias law to protect mainland migrants. *South China Morning Post*, p. EDT3.

Cummins, J. (2000). *Language, power and pedagogy: Bilingual children in the cross-fire*. Clevedon, UK: Multilingual Matters.

Darnell, F. (1983). Indigenous cultural minorities—Concepts pertaining to their education. In Center for Education Research and Innovation and OECD (Eds.), *The education of minority groups: An enquiry into problems and practices of fifteen countries* (pp. 293–315). Aldershot, UK: Gower.

Education and Manpower Bureau. (2006). *School-based management document*. Hong Kong: Author.

Education Bureau. (2009a). *A chart of special arrangement in support of NAS children* (in Chinese). Retrieved from http://www.edb.gov.hk/index. aspx?nodeid=635&langno=2

Education Bureau. (2009b). *Fine-tuning the medium of instruction for secondary schools*. Retrieved from http://www.legco.gov.hk/yr08–09/english/panels/ed/ papers/ed0529-edbecp4802n-e.pdf

Education Bureau. (2009c). *A Chart of special arrangement in support of NAS children*. Retrieved December 15, 2009, from http://www.edb.gov.hk/index. aspx?nodeID=635&langno=1

Education Bureau. (2009d). *Fine-tuning the medium of instruction for secondary schools*. Retrieved December 15, 2009, from http://www.legco.gov.hk/yr08-09/ english/panels/ed/papers/ed0529-edbecp4802n-e.pdf

Education Commission. (2006). *Progress report on the education reform (4)*. Hong Kong: Government Printing.

Education Department. (2000). *Toward integration* [CD-ROM]. Hong Kong: Education Department.

Essed, P. (1990). *Everyday racism: Reports from women of two cultures*. Alameda, CA: Hunter House.

Farrell, J. (1999). Changing conceptions of equality of education: Forty years of comparative evidence. In J. Farrell, *Comparative and cross-cultural perspectives*, course materials, volume 2 (pp. 1–46). Toronto, Ontario: University of Toronto.

Freire, P. (1970). *Pedagogy of the oppressed*. New York: Seabury Press.

Freire, P. (1972). *Cultural action for freedom*. Harmondsworth, UK: Penguin Books.

Freire, P. (2005). *Education for critical consciousness*. London: Continuum.

Hue, M. T. (2008). Cross-cultural experiences of immigrant students from mainland China in Hong Kong secondary schools. *Ethnography and Education, 3*(3), 229–242.

Immigration Department. (2008). *Hong Kong: The facts*. Hong Kong: Information Services Department, Immigration Department.

International Social Service. (1997). *A study on the Chinese new immigrants in Hong Kong*. Hong Kong: Author.

Kwoh, L. (2006, January 23). Mainland children happy to stay home. *The Standard*, pp. A10–A11.

Liu, E. W. (2009, May 15). More work needed to reach out to "invisible parents" who feel excluded from schools. *South China Morning Post*, p. EDU11.

Morrison, K., & Liu, I. (2000). Ideology, linguistic capital and the medium of instruction in Hong Kong. *Journal of Multilingual & Multicultural Development, 21*(6), 471–486.

Ng, D. (2003, June 21). Mainland prejudice "should be illegal." *The Standard*, p. B03.

Nieto, S. (2002). *Language, culture, and teaching. Critical perspectives for a new century*. Mahwah, NJ: Erlbaum.

Nieto, S., & Bode, P. (2008). *Affirming diversity: The sociopolitical context of multicultural education*. Boston: Pearson/Allyn & Bacon.

Rao, N., & Yuen, M. (2001). Accommodations for assimilation: Supporting newly arrived children from the Chinese mainland to Hong Kong. *Childhood Education*, 77(5), 313–318.

Sleeter, C. E., & Grant, C. A. (2009). Making choices for multicultural education: Five approaches to race, class, and gender. Hoboken, NJ: John Wiley & Sons.

Tam, V. C. W., & Lam, R. S. Y. (2005). Stress and coping among migrant and local-born adolescents in Hong Kong. *Youth & Society, 36*(3), 312–332.

Taylor, C. (1992). *Multiculturalism and "The Politics of Recognition."* Princeton, NJ: Princeton University Press.

Towndrow, P. A., Koh, C., & Tan, H. S. (2008). *Motivation and practice for the classroom*. Rotterdam, Netherlands: Sense Publishers.

Wong, D. F. K. (2008). Differential impacts of stressful life events and social support on the mental health of mainland Chinese immigrant and local youth in Hong Kong: A resilience perspective. *British Journal of Social Work, 38*(2), 236–252.

Wong, D. F. K., Lam, D., Yan, P., & Hung, M. (2004). The impacts of acculturative stress and social competence on the mental health of mainland Chinese immigrant youth in Hong Kong. *British Journal of Social Work, 34*, 1009–1024.

REFERENCES IN CHINESE

Boys & Girls Clubs Association. (1996). *A report of the adaptation of newly arrived school children from mainland China*. Hong Kong: Author.

Hong Kong Council of Social Service. (1982). *Report on working group on "new arrivals."* Hong Kong: Author.

Hong Kong Council of Social Service. (1985). *Report on the social and economic adaptation of the Chinese new arrivals in Hong Kong*. Hong Kong: Author.

Hong Kong Federation of Youth Groups. (1995). *A survey of the adaptation of newly arrived youth from mainland China*. Hong Kong: Author.

Hong Kong Professional Teachers' Union. (1994). *A survey of the educational condition of the newly arrived secondary students from mainland China*. Hong Kong: Author.

Lee, Y. Z. (1999). *Chinese culture and education* [Press release]. Retrieved from http://www.cuhk.edu.hk/ipro/990928c.htm

Tong, C. Y. (2000). *Stories of landing—True stories of new arrival families*. Hong Kong: Ming Cheung Publishing.

8 Culturally Relevant Counseling Practices for New Immigrant Students

Betty C. Eng

INTRODUCTION

Each culture has complex and unique counseling needs. Hence, scholars and practitioners acknowledge the need for culturally relevant counseling theories and practices. This chapter discusses the counseling needs of new immigrant students (NISs)—also called Chinese immigrant students, new arrival students, cross-border students, and international students—in Hong Kong. Unquestionably, NISs share much of the same cultural ancestry with their Chinese counterparts in Hong Kong; however, they also have distinct needs. From these needs, tensions and conflicts often arise, and issues of identity, culture, language, and sense of belongingness have become major counseling concerns.

This study explores multiple identities shaped by the "one country, two systems" relationship between Hong Kong and China, by the Confucian heritage culture, and by indigenous stories. The discussion, although localized in Hong Kong, has global implications for practitioners, educators, and policymakers. Through student narratives and other data sources, the counseling needs of NISs are examined for the construction of culturally appropriate and relevant counseling theories and practices.[1]

Roots of the Inquiry

It is from the author's personal immigration, assimilation, acculturation, and transformation experiences that this research is predominantly premised. I am a Chinese American who was born in China and raised in the US. As an immigrant, counseling practitioner, and educator, I identify and empathize with the personal and emotional needs of immigrant children raised in foreign countries and cultures. Confronted with new and sometimes alien and unwelcoming places, immigrant children from China require support and resources from their host communities.

To understand life is to understand experience (Dewey, 1938). Using the research approach developed by Clandinin and Connelly (2000), I earlier conducted a five-year research project that sought to understand the identity, culture, and sense of belongingness of NISs. To accomplish this project, I embarked on a journey from China to the US and to Hong Kong—a journey that spanned three family generations and that showed how experience has shaped my identity, culture, and sense of belongingness. Using my life history as the basis of the project, I found that the experience of immigration results in competing and contentious perceptions regarding traditional Chinese values and the values of the dominant society.

Seeking an understanding of identity, culture, and sense of belongingness, I went to Hong Kong where I became a counselor in an international and multinational school, a teacher-educator for over 10 years, and currently a teacher of counseling at a university. I found that Hong Kong Chinese students are also struggling with their own understanding of identity, culture, and sense of belongingness—similar to my own experience during the Asian American movement in the 1970s in the US. For over 150 years, until 1997, Hong Kong was under British control. The period of British colonization heightened and intensified questions of culture, identity, and sense of belongingness. The dilemma of Hong Kong students is expressed in the following questions: "Am I Hongkonger or Chinese?" "To whom is my allegiance and loyalty?" "Where do I belong?" and "Who is it that I wish to become?" These questions are complex, multifaceted, fluid, and forever changing.

Recovering and reclaiming life stories are acts of empowerment; in this sense, what is personal *becomes* political. The life stories gathered in this study reveal systematic political and social injustices that must be carefully considered in guidance and counseling. Hence, these acts of recovery and reclamation should guide culturally relevant counseling theories and practices for NISs.

This study, set in an elementary school, explores the academic, personal, and social needs of NISs. Counseling implications and the need for culturally relevant counseling theories and practices are discussed.

DESCRIPTION OF THE MINORITY POPULATION

Immigrants in the Midst of Internationalization

Hong Kong's diversity is caused by numerous influences that shape the culture and language of its residents. First, Hong Kong has a long history of colonization, which led to the amalgamation of Eastern and Western influences in the region. Second, Hong Kong hosts diverse sociopolitical ideologies. While there are residents who adhere to the communist ideology, there are also those who—influenced by over 150 years of British rule—espouse capitalist ideals. Third, Chinese traditions, which can be traced back to Confucianism and Taoism, interact in unique ways, promoting cultural diversity in Hong Kong.

Hong Kong is an international center, and it is composed of a society of immigrants. However, it is only in recent years that complex historical, social, and political issues have been addressed in terms of diversity and inclusiveness. This shift is attributable to the call for globalization, which compels people from around the world to recognize their connectedness. With growing democratization, issues of social justice and equity are now being addressed among cultural minorities, including new immigrants in Hong Kong.

New Immigrant Students

With Hong Kong's return to China in 1997, many Chinese immigrants have been legally allowed to enter Hong Kong (Wong, Yan, Lo, & Hung, 2003; Yuen, 2004). Approximately 41.2% of the legal daily quota of immigrants (150 immigrants) from China are children under the age of 14. Furthermore, 20% of the immigrants are adolescents or young adults, aged 15 to 34. Previous research by community organizations (e.g., Hong Kong Federation of Youth Groups, 1995; International Social Service–Hong Kong Branch, 1997) has highlighted obstacles and difficulties encountered by young immigrants. Among the sociocultural issues are academic stress, adjustment to language, schooling, cultural integration, acculturation, peer relationships, low self-image, and lack of family support.

NISs and Local Hong Kong Youth

In their comparative study of NISs and Hong Kong-born youth, Sun, Fung, and Kwong (2000) discovered that contrary to their expectations, immigrants have better mental health status than locals. Specifically, immigrants who have higher cross-cultural competence have better mental health outcomes (Anderson, 1994; Hannigan, 1990), proving that social competence is a significant predictor of emotional well-being. Elksnin and Elksnin (1995) defined social competence as a combination of social skills and adaptive behaviors that may include (1) the appropriate application of social skills, (2) the ability for self-regulation or monitoring, (3) the consideration of the cultural context within which social competence is defined, and (4) social qualities (e.g., self-esteem, self-reliance, and problem-solving skills). In addition, individuals who are socially competent are more likely to succeed in social interactions. According to Wong et al. (2003), NISs have better mental health than Hongkongese youth because they find the obstacles they encounter in Hong Kong more acceptable and tolerable compared with the severe hardships they experience in China. Compared with NISs, Hongkongese youth have relatively poorer mental health because they have better social and economic qualities of life, leading to higher life expectations and greater vulnerability to stress. Therefore, they need to be more competitive. It is also suggested that the lack of traditional values and identity among Hongkongese youth contribute to their inability to deal with stress.

Non-Chinese Speaking Students

Numerous ethnic minorities add to Hong Kong's diversity. In Hong Kong, 5.1% (343,950) of the total population belongs to ethnic minorities (Census and Statistics of Hong Kong, 2001). Ethnic minorities include Filipinos (41.4%), Indonesians (14.7%), mixed racial background such as Chinese Indian (5.7%), Britons (5.5%), Indians (5.4%), Thais (4.2%), Japanese (4.1%), Nepalese (3.7%), Pakistanis (3.2%), Americans/Canadians (2.7%), Australians/New Zealanders (32.0%), Koreans (1.5%), and others or not specified (5.9%). About 99% of these ethnic minorities are long-term residents; the rest are mobile residents.

School-age children from these ethnic minorities are characterized as non-Chinese speaking (NCS) students who present special challenges to the educational system of Hong Kong. Racial tensions and discrimination in education, employment, public service, and sociopolitical participation are issues raised by community organizations, such as Hong Kong Unison, a charitable nongovernmental organization.

The foregoing discussion provides a brief background of the communities that make Hong Kong culturally diverse. For Chinese immigrants from mainland China, there are yet other complex cultural issues, such as their employment in professional fields along with Hong Kong's long-term or permanent immigrants, which must be addressed. These issues do not only affect Hong Kong; they also affect all other regions where mainland Chinese immigrate.

EDUCATIONAL LANDSCAPE OF HONG KONG

Understanding Hong Kong's educational landscape, particularly its recent reforms on counseling, is helpful in understanding the needs of NISs. Traditionally, the primary purpose of education in Hong Kong has been the transmission of information. Driven by examinations at every stage of student matriculation, Hong Kong's traditional educational purpose has led to teaching by rote learning and to spoon-feeding. To reform the educational system, the government seeks to promote holistic student development through the whole-school approach (Hong Kong Education Commission, 2002):

> To meet the needs of society in the 21st Century, the Education Commission in 1998 embarked on a two-year comprehensive review of the overall education system in Hong Kong . . . Students are the focal point of the entire reform. By creating space for schools, teachers, and

students, the reform is implemented to enable every student to attain all-round development in the moral, intellectual, physical, social, and aesthetic domains according to his/her own attributes so that he/she will be capable of lifelong learning. It is also hoped that each student will develop the ability for critical and exploratory thinking; be innovative and adaptable to changes; be filled with self-confidence and a team spirit; be willing to put forward effort toward the prosperity, progress, freedom, and democracy of society; and contribute to the future well-being of the nation and the world at large. (p. 3)

This seemingly progressive shift in Hong Kong's educational policies provides timely opportunities for exploring personal narratives to gain new teaching and learning insights. Moreover, this progressive shift suggests new directions for guidance and counseling toward a holistic educational approach. Hong Kong's Curriculum Development Council (2001, 2002), a governmental body that guides and establishes educational curricular goals, promotes a "learning to learn" approach that engages learners in critical thinking and reflection. It has introduced a newly re-organized personal, social, and humanities educational curriculum that encourages self-directed inquiry. This reform promotes the intellectual, personal, and social development of students within an educational culture that supports lifelong learning. With this shift in curricular orientation that embraces holistic student development, it seems that guidance and counseling will play a much more critical and important role in schools than before (Eng, 2007). This applies not only to guidance and counseling teams in schools but also to classroom teachers, principals, and parents.

According to the Careers and Guidance Services Section of the former Education Department of Hong Kong, a whole-school approach to guidance was recommended by Hong Kong's Education Commission in 1990 "to create a positive environment in the schools in which students' problems are responded to in a positive and constructive manner" (p. 29). Schools that effectively practice the whole-school approach are characterized as having four key collaborating entities: teachers, students, management, and a developmental guidance program. According to the Hong Kong Education Commission (2002), with the implementation of the whole-school approach to guidance,

guidance has come to be considered as a way of fostering behavior and facilitating students in personal, social, and school adjustment (Hong Kong Education Commission, 1990). During the last ten years, guidance services have accordingly evolved from a remedial "casework" approach to a more preventive and developmental approach (Hui, in press). Hui and Lo's (1997) study has shown the feasibility of integrating developmental guidance programs into the whole-school curriculum. Guidance as a responsibility of all teachers is now affirmed, and a school's provision of guidance services is suggested as an indicator of quality education. (Hui, 1998, p. 436)

Although the reforms follow the whole-person and whole-school approaches, creating opportunities for personal and social development, difficulties still arise in the implementation of the reforms. Nevertheless, the groundwork for these recent educational changes has already been established.

NIS NARRATIVES

This study seeks to investigate the academic, personal, and social needs of NISs in Hong Kong, as well as the counseling implications of these needs. Through this investigation, the challenges encountered by NISs (i.e., those caused by teacher and societal perceptions of who they are) and the effects of these challenges on school interactions are explored.

Using the narrative inquiry approach of Clandinin and Connelly (2000), stories of experiences from students, mothers, and teachers were gathered through six months of intensive research in various Hong Kong elementary schools and community centers. The study explored the linguistic, cultural, and identity development of NISs and their families. For purposes of this study, NISs are students who were born in China and who immigrated to Hong Kong within the last four years.

Data were collected from semi-structured interviews and participant observations in one key elementary school, Sun Gai Primary School.[1] The school is found in a low-income area in Hong Kong. The participants included six teachers, six students, and five mothers. Additional data were collected from mothers in a Women's Resource Center and from focus group interviews with teachers and students in other schools. Classroom interactions and school activities (e.g., assemblies and recess, in- and out-of-school settings) were extensively observed, and "triads" (i.e., students, their parents, generally their mothers, and their teachers), the school principal, and the school counselor were interviewed. Following classroom observations, participation in classroom and school settings, and conversations with students, parents, teachers, and other school personnel, descriptive field notes and research journal entries were written. Government documents were analyzed for relevant demographic information and student program profiles. The journal entries, interview transcripts, field notes, and document analyses were computerized, and all data were filed in a computer system. Other sets of information were obtained through a review of documents from the Education Bureau (EDB), the government body responsible for educational planning, and from a small body of research focusing specifically on the school experiences of NISs.

The examination of issues related to NISs in Sun Gai Primary School is critical because most NISs are currently scattered throughout Hong

Kong, and many of them are in low-income areas, such as Sun Gai. This study focused on one student, Ah Fai, and his relationship with his teachers and family.

Stories of Experience: Ah Fai

"What are you writing in your notebook? May I see it?" Ah Fai, a Primary 3 student (equivalent in age and level of schooling to a third-grade student in the US) asks as we sit at the back of the classroom during our first day of observation. Ms. Lee, his English teacher, calls him to attention. At another point in the lesson, without raising his hand, Ah Fai exclaims in Cantonese, "I don't understand this sentence!" as he tries to comprehend English words in his workbook. He turns around and looks inquiringly toward us, the researchers, for help.

In an interview, Ah Fai speaks of his home in China and his experiences in Hong Kong since he, at the age of 6, arrived in 2002. Ah Fai was born in Shenzhen, a developed border city adjacent to Hong Kong, and he views himself as "half mainland Chinese and half Hongkonger." Ah Fai fluently speaks Hong Kong Cantonese, which he learned in Shenzhen. He also speaks Helao, his first language and his family's village dialect. In Lu Feng, his grandparents' home in China, he and his family speak Helao. He likes Lu Feng because it is spacious, and he can play with chickens, swim, fish in the river, and play games with his cousins and neighbors. The school in Lu Feng has a huge park with trees where children can play. On the other hand, Hong Kong is a small place, but accordingly, it has a Disneyland. Ah Fai has forged friendships in both places; his Hong Kong friends are primarily his classmates because his family does not have relatives in the region. In fact, many mainland students in the area do not have friends, and they are not allowed to leave their apartments because parents view the area as dangerous (the area is infested with gangs). In addition, some mainland students are bullied by their Hong Kong classmates.

Ah Fai speaks English poorly; he finds the language difficult. Consequently, English is his least favorite subject. Nevertheless, Ah Fai claims that he strives to improve his English by seeking help from his classmates and even from a classmate's older brother. He also returns to school to attend special tutorials in preparation for tests or examinations in English. The English language, a language NISs have not studied extensively in the mainland, poses an obstacle to their success in school because their levels of English proficiency determine the classes in which they are placed (NISs are often placed in grades with younger students).

Stories of Experience: Teachers

Teachers contribute to Ah Fai's academic development. Interestingly, teachers at Ah Fai's school cannot distinguish NISs from locals. One can say that NISs have so successfully assimilated into the Hong Kong system that they no longer require special attention. However, in the case of Ah Fai and his mother, there is a picture of current and largely unmet critical needs (i.e., academic performance, personal, and social needs). In addition, teachers have unfavorable opinions regarding NISs, and these opinions are often based on the English proficiency of these students, their perceived level of effort in learning the language, their parents' sources of income (often government assistance), and societal prejudice against them. A common story is the importance of English proficiency and how it defines the academic success, identity, and sense of belongingness of students. Unfortunately, teachers frequently focus on the limited (or the lack of) English language skills of NISs, and the level of English development is the most dominating and most frequently cited student characteristic by teachers. Although many NISs and their families have their respective regional Chinese dialects and not Cantonese (the language most Chinese in Hong Kong speak) as their first language, the Chinese language is rarely cited as a factor in the social and educational adjustments of NISs. Moreover, teachers continue to hold very negative perceptions and stereotypes about NISs and their families, although they tend to consider the needs of these students.

Ms. Lee, Ah Fai's homeroom and English teacher, indicates that, "newly arrived mainland students are rich." She provides examples of how they have good quality writing papers and expensive erasers, and she speaks about how they become lazy and how they exert no effort in looking for jobs because the public welfare system supports them. She further states that many mainland Chinese collect unemployment packages and that some mainland students do not work hard because in the future, they will become just like their predecessors. This seems to be a universal story. Although teachers and others say that "mainland students are the same to [them] as Hong Kong students," they are also quick to assert that "[mainland students] are welfare cheats and lazy!" The counselor in Ah Fai's school, for example, states that the students are the same; yet, when pressed, she speaks of poverty, hardship, arranged marriages, and parents' lack of education. The counselor believes that children will succeed if they are motivated, but she claims that most NISs these days are not that strong, and their parents do not care much about their education.

Stories of Experience: Parents and Family

The narrative of Ah Fai's mother further illuminates questions raised about Ah Fai. In contrast to Ah Fai's energy and boldness, his mother is reserved; she appears tense and wary. She speaks Cantonese with a heavy accent, and she appears self-conscious and ill at ease. She does not have friends or relatives in Hong Kong, and she spends most of her time at home, cooking and caring for her family. She does not know how to use the public transport system, and she does not go far from the neighborhood of the estate where the family lives.

Ah Fai's mother comes from the city of Lu Feng; she has lived in Hong Kong for just a year. She and her husband married in 1994, and she gave birth to Ah Fai in 1996. In 1997, a daughter was born in Shenzhen. Her husband is also from Lu Feng who, at 48, illegally entered Hong Kong; he has been living in Hong Kong for "many years" now. Her family was separated for about three to four years until immigration allowed her daughter to enter Hong Kong. Ah Fai followed, and finally, she arrived in 2004. During this period of separation, her husband shouldered the full responsibilities of parenthood. Such cross-border marriages or relationships are common, and the separation of family members is expected.

Ah Fai's father is now unemployed because of a back injury, and his mother does not work outside the home. Financially, they are hard-pressed. They manage by "buying and doing with less of everything." To curb expenses, they only buy inexpensive vegetables and fish for family meals. Rather than seeing a doctor, they purchase medicines from the local drug store.

Ah Fai's mother becomes most animated and expressive when asked about her children's studies. The English language is a focal point in defining the academic performance and achievement of her children:

> Their English is not good. My daughter is in Strengthening Remedial Class. Their English is bad. They need to rely on themselves. My daughter always gets no points from her dictation. My son's dictation is also bad. I usually ask him to write them several times before the dictation. I don't know how to teach them. But the principal and the teachers are good to us.

Ah Fai's mother admits that she does not know how to teach her children. As a parent who is trying to help her children succeed academically, she feels helpless, isolated, and displaced. Her experiences (i.e., coming to Hong Kong as a stranger, being separated from her friends and family in Lu Feng, and being reunited with her children and husband) seem to present competing identities and sense of belongingness. Whereas her son states that he is "half mainland Chinese and half Hongkonger," we wonder whether she can say the same thing as assuredly and as forcefully as Ah Fai does. Will she find her place in Hong Kong? Will she find support? What does the future hold for her and her family?

ANALYSIS AND FINDINGS: LEARNING FROM THE INQUIRY

Ah Fai's narrative reveals multiple identities shaped by language and culture. From our observations, we find him to be highly spirited, curious, and eager to learn. Will his positive outlook be nurtured and be supported by his teachers, school, and family? He aspires to become a policeman or a fireman—professions that require both rigorous physical and written examinations. Given the Hong Kong context and the current policies of the EDB, will his poor English language performance hinder his studies? Will his level of English proficiency affect his identity and sense of belongingness, and will it shape or even define his future? He likes both Lu Feng and Hong Kong. Is having a multiple identity (i.e., he is both mainland Chinese and Hongkonger; he speaks Heleo, Cantonese, and an improving level of English; and he can move back and forth from these languages and cultures) advantageous or detrimental? We realize the difficult obstacles that beset Ah Fai and wonder what will become of him in the future. We wonder if it will be by choice or by force that Ah Fai will become another "early school leaver" after completing his last opportunity—the final three years of compulsory education in junior secondary school at around age 14 or 15—to become a member of the workforce. Such questions emerge from Ah Fai's narrative, and they raise concerns for other students in Hong Kong.

Although NISs continue to immigrate to Hong Kong and experience difficulties in their adjustment, academic performance, and acceptance, their needs seem to have faded into a state of invisibility. As a social, political, and educational issue, the influx of NISs was at its height after Hong Kong was handed over to the sovereignty of China in 1997. At that time, politicians and educators were concerned of a possible "takeover" by Chinese from the mainland, although they were assured of a "one country, two systems" jurisdiction. With the influx of immigrants from mainland China, Hong Kong worried about the possible exhaustion of social services, employment opportunities, and educational resources. As these worries subsided, funds for the orientation and settlement of immigrants were redirected; Sun Gai Primary School, Ah Fai's school, was not spared. Furthermore, research interest in NISs waned as research funds were re-allocated for other issues. The examination of Ah Fai's experiences in Hong Kong, however, reveals complexities that must be addressed. Although this study focuses on one student—Ah Fai—the challenges this student encounters hold true for a large and increasing number of other NISs in Hong Kong schools.

The stories in this study illustrate some of the challenges that NISs and their parents encounter as they negotiate a sense of ethnic identity and belongingness in Hong Kong schools. In Hong Kong schools, NISs and their mothers experience academic, personal, and social difficulties. The school-based practices implemented to meet the needs of diverse students reveal that limited funds are being spent on NISs; special NIS programs have been discontinued, and in general, little accommodation is made for their special needs. These limited resources contribute to poor performance in school tests, to a sense of alienation for some students, and in extreme cases, to suicide. Although NISs share many cultural and ethnic commonalities with

Hongkongese students, they speak different languages, have different levels of English proficiency, and have had different school experiences. They struggle with English language acquisition, financial stability in the family, and acceptance by teachers. Although the school system no longer views NISs, such as Ah Fai, as a priority requiring special attention, the unique personal and social needs of NISs remain evident.

Given Hong Kong's history of colonization, teachers identify English language proficiency as the point of critical difference between Hongkongese students and NISs. It is less likely that NISs have achieved high levels of English proficiency in China, and this is identified by their teachers and recognized by their mothers as a significant disadvantage in their bid for academic success in Hong Kong schools. The inadequacy of financial resources to support academic tutoring assistance and the lack of linguistic skills to assist their children leave mothers feeling helpless, and at times, hopeless, in their attempts to support the academic success of their children.

Another striking realization in this study of immigration and settlement is the power of language and culture in shaping identities even in communities that are apparently very similar. As an ethnic Chinese, an immigrant mainland Chinese, who most likely speaks Cantonese in his or her home region, is expected to have much in common with a Cantonese-speaking Hongkongese. This expectation, along with the consequent expectation of easy adaptation by Chinese immigrants, has contributed to limited support for settlement programs and to a redirection of resources originally earmarked for supporting immigrants. Meanwhile, the experiences of Chinese immigrants reveal not only significant financial, social, and academic hardships, but also a general misunderstanding about their plight as they attempt to succeed in their schools and communities. These challenges capture the power of historical and political influences that not only shape school contexts but also affect the social expectations of teachers and community members in Hong Kong. Furthermore, these challenges reinforce the notion that the rejection of minority groups accounts for the academic success of Asian students. This realization also calls for schools and educational systems worldwide to assume responsibility for providing necessary academic and social adaptation support for all immigrant students, rather than to rely on presumed inherent differences among members of some racial or ethnic groups as an explanation for the superior academic performance of some students.

IMPLICATIONS: CULTURALLY RELEVANT COUNSELING THEORIES AND PRACTICES

According to Sue and Torino (2005), to make counseling meaningful and relevant, it is essential to use counseling modalities that genuinely reflect the realities of client's life experiences, identities, and cultural values:

Cultural competence is the ability to engage in actions or create conditions that maximize the optimal development of client and client systems. Multicultural counseling competence is defined as the counselor's acquisition of awareness, knowledge, and skills needed to function effectively in a pluralistic democratic society (ability to communicate, interact, negotiate, and intervene on behalf of clients from diverse backgrounds), and on an organizational or societal level, advocating effectively to develop new theories, practices, policies, and organizational structures that are more responsive to all groups. (p. 3)

To be a culturally competent counselor, one must first become *aware* of and be sensitive to his or her own beliefs, values, and biases regarding human behavior. Second, one must be *knowledgeable* of the background, experiences, values, and beliefs of culturally diverse groups. Third, one must be *skilled* in providing support by sending and receiving verbal and nonverbal responses accurately and appropriately, by carrying out culturally appropriate interventions, and by predicting the strengths and limitations of such interventions.

Contextualization for Hong Kong

In response to criticisms claiming that Hong Kong's educational system encourages spoon-feeding and breeds a recitation-based, memory-oriented, and examination-driven curriculum, recent educational reforms aim to promote a "learning to learn" approach at all educational levels; this suggests a movement toward the rise of a non-directive approach to guidance and counseling (Atkinson & Wampold, 1982). A non-directive approach places students at the center of guidance and counseling. In this approach, students define the issues, needs, and problems. Throughout the counseling process, they are viewed as active participants engaged in the resolution of issues, in the search for intervention measures, and in the application of strategies. In this way, the thoughts and feelings of students are respected and integrated into the counseling process, thereby empowering them. The approach requires a shift in the role of the counselor in the Asian context—the counselor becomes a facilitator and a guide, not the sole source of authority and wisdom.

According to Postiglione and Lee (1995), Hong Kong's post-colonization period and the region's movement toward a more democratic society suggest an increased interest in liberal ideas that embrace a non-directive approach to guidance and counseling. Among classroom teachers in Hong Kong, there is a growing interest in humanistic and holistic teaching philosophies that cater to the needs of students. Examples of these philosophies include the ideas of Rogers (1951), known as the father of counseling in the US, and the postmodern counseling approach (i.e., narrative therapy) developed by White and Epston (1990) and McLeod (1997). Roger's person-centered therapy is an evidence of the shift in thinking toward a non-directive approach where the person being served, not the counselor, is empowered by being allowed to define his or her counseling issues and by being given the authority to resolve his or her concerns. Narrative therapy facilitates and processes the authoring and reconstruction of life stories that clarify experiential realities or lived experiences.

However, as expected in any transition from one way of thinking to another, there are tensions, barriers, and conflicts as illustrated in this statement by an elementary school teacher who is pursuing a master's degree in counseling:

> As much as I yearn for and believe in a person-centered approach to counseling, I am disappointed and frustrated to find myself incapable of practicing it in my school. Because of this, I do not believe I can ever become a good counselor.

This teacher has been recently introduced to Rogerian theory, but she finds it impossible to practice Roger's concepts in her school. Her statement speaks of the difficulties she encounters in her school—difficulties that demand a highly directive approach where teachers are expected to dominate and control students. In a directive approach, the teacher is expected to be the primary source of authority, while students participate as passive learners. On a daily basis, the teacher is expected to punish or reward students with the designation of grades for assignments and examinations. For both learners and teachers, there is little time for meaningful reflection or personal and social development. As such, this teacher and future counselor tends to dominate the counseling process by giving answers and solutions—rather than by enabling students to explore and define issues and solutions. Moreover, this teacher was socialized to expect answers and solutions from people in authority. This experience was embedded in her way of thinking and in her professional practice. Thus, it is not surprising for this student of counseling to experience tensions in striving to be a person-centered or non-directive counselor in a highly hierarchical and directive Hong Kong context.

In the guidance and counseling of students with diverse needs, such as Ah Fai, one may be faced with dilemmas and tensions created by the shift from a directive to a non-directive approach to guidance and counseling. In such cases, this study's findings may prove significant. First, an awareness and acknowledgment of this struggle are needed. By getting in touch with these feelings, one creates a heightened sense of "wakefulness" toward how this tension might affect the counseling process. For established authorities, such as teachers, social workers, and counselors, the guidance and counseling of students, such as Ah Fai, may present more pressures to utilize a directive approach (i.e., to provide quick and easy answers and solutions). They are more likely to utilize a case approach that responds to the need for immediate solutions rather than a developmental approach that engages in an evolving journey of self-exploration, understanding, and personal development.

Selected Strategies for Counseling Students with Diverse Learning Needs

Eng (2007) developed strategies for counseling students with diverse needs. Adapting these strategies to the needs of students, the needs of the counseling process, and the specific cultural context should be considered.

Journal Writing

Journal writing is an effective way of expression that is conducive to counseling. For NISs who find writing an obstacle to expression, drawings, photos, music, and poetry are alternatives. This is particularly effective for students with language needs who, for fear of rejection on account of cultural differences, find it difficult to express themselves. For students who are conditioned to view writing as an academic subject, which is the case for many Chinese students in Hong Kong, the opportunity to write freely and frankly—without fear of punitive assessment—is a new experience. Assuring students that the activity is not graded and that writing errors are not penalized, and providing supportive counselor feedback are helpful. The writing of journals, as records of significant events and as chronicles of reflections on the meaning of experiences, must be encouraged. Journal entries may be kept confidential, or they may be shared during counseling sessions as determined by the student and the counseling process. Research on journal writing, involving Hong Kong university students, initially found that journal writing promotes a high degree of self-disclosure, revealing highly sensitive and complex issues, such as lack of self-confidence, lack of acceptance among peers, fear of failure, and antagonism toward immigrants from China. The "anonymity" of journal writing, compared with face-to-face encounters, provides a safer place for self-disclosure.

Language of Feelings and Self-Disclosure

Particularly in Chinese cultures, feelings are not commonly expressed or welcomed. Among Chinese students, self-discipline and a saving face attitude often inhibit the deep and full expression of emotions. Enabling students to express their feelings is often the first step in counseling. Emotionally expressive words may be helpful in encouraging further elaboration, which facilitates in-depth explorations. Among the Chinese, emotions are often expressed through metaphors or stories. "The negative results from the examination made me feel like I had been blown apart by a typhoon" is an example of how metaphors can provide colorful and powerful ways of exploring feelings. Role-playing and the use of dolls among younger students can also facilitate the exploration of feelings and the eventual development of a language of feelings.

Serial Testimony

This activity, which was originally developed for workshops to explore controversial topics (e.g., racism and sex discrimination), can be adapted for purposes of counseling. In this activity, students sit in a circle and describe an important or significant experience in their lives. Some may choose to share a happy event, and some may opt to share experiences on fear of failure, discrimination, and acts of violence. Each person is given 10 minutes to share the experience while others actively listen. No comments or judgments are given after the completion of each testimony, and the process continues until everyone has shared his or her story. After everyone has testified, responses are shared. For students with diverse needs, this activity can be a powerful experience because it provides them with the opportunity to share difficult or challenging experiences in a safe and protected environment that is free from judgment or blame.

Individual Counseling

Individual counseling sessions with students are helpful, particularly in establishing the reasons and purposes of counseling. Sensitivity and caution are needed to prevent embarrassment and to avoid creating negative attention when labeling a student for individual counseling. This applies to all students, especially to students with diverse learning needs.

Group Counseling

Group counseling can be a supportive counseling approach for students with diverse learning needs. Meeting others who share the same or similar difficulties or issues can lessen their feelings of isolation; it provides them an opportunity to assess their own condition in relation to others.

Family Counseling

In most cases, students with educational or special needs affect their families. Parents and siblings are integral participants in the counseling process. For example, Chinese parents of gifted children in Hong Kong have formed their own group to share their expectations and concerns for their gifted children, as well as to petition the government for support services. The dynamics of the group process is both therapeutic and empowering. However, the Confucian tradition sometimes prevents parents from communicating with schools because communication may be seen as a challenge to the authority of teachers. Parents may lack understanding of their children's educational needs, and they may feel a sense of shame and guilt for their children's perceived disabilities. In such situations, counselors may find it helpful to conduct home visits and initiate communication with the families of students.

Peer Counseling

Peer counseling may be effective in helping students with diverse needs, particularly those with physical or medical conditions. Peers are sometimes viewed as more supportive and less threatening than adults. Peer counselors, in turn, receive an opportunity to become caregivers and leaders. However, a well-organized peer training program must first be established and closely monitored to ensure the effectiveness of peer counseling.

Cross-Cultural Counseling for Asian Countries

Many Asian countries, after having emerged from experiences of colonization, have maintained international and diverse multinational societies; as such, they should consider a cross-cultural approach to counseling. Hong Kong Chinese are said to possess plural identities and cultures. Some have referred to this as a "hybrid self" (Yee & Brennan, 2004), which evolved from the "East meets West" Hong Kong context. Leung (2002), focusing on career counseling, proposed a cross-cultural research collaboration between Hong Kong and the US to "determine aspects of theories that are universal and aspects that are specific to a particular culture or group of cultures" (p. 244). A cross-cultural approach that explores the diverse needs of Chinese learners is beneficial to our holistic understanding of culturally specific learning needs, as well as to the creation of culturally relevant counseling theories and practices.

CONCLUDING REMARKS

The experiences of Ah Fai and other NISs apprise educators of the needs of immigrants and the nature of their needed support, particularly in terms of counseling. Hong Kong's traditions, along with its international and multinational community, highlight the complexity and diversity of its people. This study invites readers to develop an awareness of culture—as an embedded element of society—in constructing counseling theories and practices. Although contextualized within Hong Kong, this study presents implications and possibilities for the benefit of all immigrants worldwide.

NOTES

1. The work described in this chapter was partially supported by a grant from the Research Grants Council of the Hong Kong Special Administrative Region, China (project #141908).

REFERENCES

Anderson, L. E. (1994). A new look at an old construct: Cross-cultural adaptation. *International Journal of Intercultural Relations, 18*(3), 293–328.

Atkinson, D. R., & Wampold, B. E. (1982). A comparison of the counselor rating form and counselor effectiveness rating scale. *Counselor Education and Supervision, 22,* 25–36.

Census and Statistics of Hong Kong. (2001). *2001 Population census, thematic report—Ethnic minorities.* Hong Kong: Hong Kong Government.

Clandinin, D. J., & Connelly, F. M. (2000). *Narrative inquiry: Experience and story in qualitative research.* San Francisco: Jossey-Bass.

Dewey, J. (1938). *Experience and education.* New York: Simon & Schuster.

Elksnin, L. K., & Elksnin, N. (1995). *Assessment and instruction of social skills.* London: Singular.

Eng, B. C. (2007). A Chinese perspective on guidance and counseling for diverse learners. In S. Phillipson (Ed.), *Learning diversity in the Chinese classroom: Contexts and practice for students with special needs* (pp. 431–457). Hong Kong: Hong Kong University Press.

Hannigan, T. P. (1990). Traits, attitudes, and skills that are related to intercultural effectiveness and their implications for cross-cultural training: A review of the literature. *International Journal of Intercultural Relations, 14,* 89–111.

Hong Kong Curriculum Development Council. (2001). *Learning to learn—The way forward in curriculum development.* Hong Kong: Hong Kong Special Administrative Region of the People's Republic of China.

Hong Kong Curriculum Development Council. (2002). *Basic education curriculum guide: Building on strengths.* Hong Kong: Hong Kong Special Administrative Region of the People's Republic of China.

Hong Kong Education Commission. (1990). *Education Commission Report No. 4.* Hong Kong: Hong Kong Government.

Hong Kong Education Commission. (2002). *Progress report on the education reform: Learning for life, learning through life.* Hong Kong: Hong Kong Government.

Hong Kong Federation of Youth Groups. (1995). *A study of new arrivals from the mainland.* Hong Kong: Author.

Hui, E. K. P. (1998). Guidance in Hong Kong schools: Students' and teachers' beliefs. *British Journal of Guidance & Counseling, 26*(3), 435–449.

International Social Service–Hong Kong Branch. (1997). *A study on the Chinese new immigrants in Hong Kong.* Hong Kong: International Social Service, Hong Kong Branch.

Leung, S. A. (2002). Career counseling in Hong Kong: Meeting the social challenges. *Career Development Quarterly, 50*(3), 237–245.

McLeod, J. (1997). *Narrative and psychotherapy.* Thousand Oaks, CA: Sage.

Postiglione, G. A., & Lee, W. O. (Eds.). (1995). *Social change and educational development.* Hong Kong: University of Hong Kong Press.

Rogers, C. (1951). *Client-centered therapy.* Boston: Houghton Mifflin.

Sue, D. W., & Torino, G. C. (2005). Awareness, knowledge, and skills. In R. T. Carter (Ed.), *Handbook of racial-cultural psychology and counseling* (pp. 3–18). Hoboken, NJ: Wiley.

Sun, S., Fung, W. W., & Kwong, K. (2000). *A study on mental health of new arrival children for their first two years of settlement in Hong Kong.* Hong Kong: City University of Hong Kong & Christian Action, Hong Kong.

White, M., & Epston, D. (1990). *Narrative means to therapeutic ends.* New York: W.W. Norton.

Wong, D. F. K., Yan, P., Lo, E., & Hung, M. (2003). Mental health and social competence of mainland Chinese immigrants and local youth in Hong Kong:

A comparison. *Journal of Ethnic & Cultural Diversity in Social Work, 12*(1), 85–110.

Yee, Y. L. F. P., & Brennan, M. (2004). In search of a guidance curriculum for Hong Kong schools. *Journal of Educational Enquiry, 5*(1), 55–83.

Yuen, C. Y. (2004). The early experience of intercultural teacher education in Hong Kong. *Intercultural Education, 15*(2), 151–166.

9 Building a Culturally Responsive School

Cross-Cultural Experiences of Ethnic Minority Students in Hong Kong Schools

Ming Tak Hue

INTRODUCTION

Since 2006, the researcher has been aware of the diverse needs of ethnic minority students (Emss) enrolled in Hong Kong schools. A research project aimed at examining educational provisions for EMSs at various levels of schooling offered the researcher an opportunity to meet EMSs and their teachers, and to listen to their stories and struggles. The research project made the researcher realize that various school participants, the government, and nongovernmental organizations must work more closely to meet the diverse needs of EMSs (i.e., to support their learning and to promote their welfare). The most recent Hong Kong census (2007) indicates that only 2% of the school-age population comes from diverse ethnic backgrounds, suggesting that Hong Kong remains predominantly a Chinese society. Most EMSs are Pakistanis, Indians, Nepalese, Indonesians, Filipinos, and Thais. All students should be valued equally in schools, and Hong Kong schools should cater to the diverse needs of students, regardless of their ethnic backgrounds (Education & Manpower Bureau, 2004a, 2004b; Education Commission, 2000). Hence, there is a need to collaborate with Hong Kong schools to explore various ways of promoting multicultural education.

Understanding the school experiences of EMSs is a way of helping school practitioners contemplate the promotion of cultural responsiveness to diversity and the role of teachers in achieving the objectives of EMS schooling. This chapter examines how teachers, students, and parents construct the diverse needs of EMSs from India, Pakistan, Philippines, Nepal, and Thailand. First, this chapter examines relevant studies on the learning difficulties of EMSs. Second, based on such examination, a theoretical framework is established to examine the cross-cultural experiences and diverse needs of EMSs. Third, the research methods and findings are reported. Finally, implications on educational provisions for EMSs are discussed.

LITERATURE REVIEW

According to Hong Kong population census statistics, the number of EMSs is growing; however, their needs and rights are not being properly addressed. In 2001, 11,204 EMSs under 15 years of age were legally enrolled in schools and received free education. In 2006, the number grew by 20% (13,472 EMSs), and in 2007, there were 28,722 full-time EMSs in Hong Kong's educational institutions (Census and Statistics Department, 2007). Compared with local Chinese students, the school attendance of EMSs aged above 15 is relatively low, particularly for those enrolled in post-secondary educational programs. In 2007, the attendance rates of local Chinese students for age groups 17–18 and 19–24 were 82.8% and 37.3%, respectively; for EMSs, the corresponding rates were 74.3% and 6.7%, respectively (Census and Statistics Department, 2007).

With the growing EMS population in Hong Kong, there is a developing body of literature on EMS education. Loper (2004) found that many EMSs, such as Indians, Pakistanis, Nepalese, and Filipinos, are excluded from Hong Kong schools (Loper, 2004; Yang Memorial Methodist Social Service, 2000, 2002). Public concern about the education of EMSs is reflected in the experiences, difficulties, and struggles of these students in Hong Kong schools and communities, as reported in Hong Kong newspapers (Ku, Chan, & Sandhu, 2005; *South China Morning Post,* 2006a, 2006b). There are also some positive experiences reported by EMS classroom teachers. According to Kennedy, Hue, and Tsui (2008), teachers report higher levels of self-efficacy when teaching non-Chinese students compared with Chinese students, and both groups can equally engage in learning.

In Western societies, the education of EMSs is also an issue of great concern. Without doubt, they bring diversity to schools. The diverse needs of these students have been highlighted in studies on their cross-cultural experiences in mainstream schools (Codjoe, 2001; Haque, 2000; He, Phillion, Chan, & Xu, 2008; Mansouri & Trembath, 2005; Rassool, 1999). In general, EMSs meet difficulties in learning the local language, and their families struggle with economic insecurity or poverty (Cummins, 1989, 2000; Cuypers, 2001; Rutter, 1994; Stevenson & Willott, 2007). It is evident that the personal growth of these students is affected by economic insecurity, which is further compounded by language barriers, migration, and problems associated with acculturation processes (Ruiz-de-Velasco, Fix, & Clewell, 2000; Rutter, 1994).

Previous studies have examined the diverse needs of EMSs, and extensive research has also been conducted on multiculturalism and other diversity issues that are central to mainstream schooling. Studies have explored support mechanisms for EMSs (Caballero, Haynes, & Tikly, 2007; Cheminais, 2001; Dentler & Hafner, 1997; Ladson-Billings, 1994; Phillion, 2002), the management of student behavioral problems (Atzaba-Poria, Pike, & Deater-Deckard, 2004; Fuligni, 1998), and the learning styles of students from different ethnic groups and in different school subjects (Ali, 2003; Nabobo & Teasdale, 1994; Paku, Zegwaard, & Coll, 2003; Taylor & Coll, 2002). Some studies had even raised concerns for teacher education in the context of multiculturalism (Arora, 2005; Garcia & Lopez, 2005; Santoro, 2009; Solomon, Portelli, Daniel, & Campbell, 2005; Thomas & Kearney, 2008).

METHODOLOGY

Theoretical Framework

The sociological framework of the social construction of reality is adopted to help explain the social construction of EMS school experiences and how knowledge of social realities is constructed in everyday school life (Berger & Luckmann, 1973; Holzner, 1968). To explore this knowledge, narrative analyses and personal experiences were utilized (Anderson, 1991; Clandinin & Connelly, 1995; Denzin, 1998; Geertz, 1973; Holstein & Gubrium, 1995). Specifically, the approach suggested by Clandinin and Connelly (1995) was used to explore what constructs teachers, students, and parents use when talking about the cross-cultural experiences of EMSs across three dimensions: (a) changes in "space" from the school to the home of EMSs; (b) changes in the "place" of the Hong Kong schools where EMSs participate; and (c) changes throughout the "time" when EMSs are in school and at home, and changes in how they interact with others. Furthermore, the analytical framework of moving "inward," "outward," "backward," and "forward" was adopted. Moving "inward" was used to discover the inner feelings of EMSs toward others' cross-cultural experiences. By moving "outward," the constructs of the host society (i.e., Hong Kong) and the community of EMSs were explored. Moving "backward" and "forward" was used to narrate how teachers relate the "past" experience of EMSs to "the present" and how these experiences shape the "future" aspirations of EMSs.

Research Methods

This study is qualitative in nature. Unstructured interviews were conducted in three secondary schools where large numbers of EMSs were enrolled. After having received school permissions, 32 teachers and 32 students were invited to attend one-on-one interviews. Each interview lasted for about 60 minutes, and all interviews were tape recorded. Four focus-group interviews were also conducted; 15 parents were involved. Interviewees were provided with substantial freedom to talk about their issues of concern. The unstructured interview method adopted for this study, in which the parents and the interviewer played significant roles in constructing conversations, can be considered as an active interview (Holstein & Gubrium, 1995).

This study gathered information on individuals or individual situations, as suggested by the literature (Alderson, 1995; Ball, 1981; Economic and Social Commission for Asia and the Pacific, 1999; Hargreaves, 1967; Hill, Laybourn, & Borland, 1996; Lacey, 1974). Some important ethical considerations were also taken into account. For example, participation was voluntary, and it did not harm participants and other school members. Furthermore, potential confidentiality issues were checked by ensuring that participants had a clear understanding of how their contributions would be reported (Bentley, Oakley, Gibson, & Kilgour, 1999).

RESEARCH FINDINGS

Teachers construct diversity as a challenge. Whereas EMSs enjoy studying in Hong Kong schools, teachers experience cultural differences and struggle with disparities in school systems and academic programs. Furthermore, teachers have developed a sense of intercultural sensitivity. They struggle to fulfill the diverse needs of students through the streaming policy, to build partnerships with parents, and to work on broadening the educational and career aspirations of students. These themes are discussed below.

Developing a Sense of Intercultural Sensitivity

To satisfy the diverse needs of students, teachers incorporate knowledge of cultural differences into their work. When interacting with EMSs, they engage in an intercultural process that enriches their understanding of the differences, similarities, and uniqueness of students. One teacher highlights this point of view and further insists that the understanding of cultural differences between majority and minority groups should be adjusted to ensure that EMSs are not understood only in relation to the culture of the dominant group, that is, the Chinese:

> We don't see them [EMSs] as non-Chinese students. It is very wrong for you to put EMS as a single category of students, especially compared to Chinese. If you look at them closely, you would understand that they are all so different. The differences are so vast, much different than you could imagine. They occur because the students come from different countries, with different religions. They have different family backgrounds and different characters. Even students with the same ethnic background can be so different. It is just like Chinese students. There are so vastly different. In my eyes, there is no distinction between Chinese students and non-Chinese students. Rather, I try to see them all individually. Race is one of the differences between them.

The insistence on intercultural sensitivity is reflected in the strong sense of empathy among teachers, which ensures that teachers understand the social behaviors of EMSs from the perspective of ethnic minority groups. Teachers reflect on their interpretations of social signs related to EMSs and avoid stereotyping ethnic minorities. For example, one teacher explains why some EMSs like to sit with their peers on the ground in parks and on the floor of MTR (underground train) compartments while chatting loudly. This behavior is a way of expressing friendship and togetherness. Some teachers consider it inappropriate and perceive such behavior as "selfish," "noisy," or "the result of poor parenting."

Teachers assert that care should be offered based on an understanding of the culture and traditions of EMSs. One example is how a teacher helped his Pakistani student examine his viewpoint on the September 11 incident. The teacher engaged in an intercultural process, reflecting a frame of reference based on his interpretation of the student's behavior and needs:

> After the incident of 9–11, a Pakistani student just felt very happy about what happened in New York. He laughed and in the classroom said loudly how happy he was. "How could he be so happy?" I was surprised at first. Certainly, I realized it was something I really needed to handle carefully. It would not be good if I told the student directly that his view was wrong, as I assumed that not only his family members, but also most of his relatives and mosque tutors might also feel happy and hold the same view as he did. Therefore, I remained calm and had a long talk with him, and tried to encourage him to examine the incident from different angles. I asked him many questions, like "If something like this happened in your country or in Hong Kong, how would you feel?"

Fulfilling the Needs of Students through the Streaming Policy

When talking about the diverse needs of EMS, four categories of students are discussed: Hong Kong Chinese students, EMSs born in Hong Kong, new immigrant EMSs, and new immigrant students from mainland China. Different combinations of these students bring numerous unique characteristics to schools. One example is the learning behavior of Hong Kong–born EMSs. As teachers narrate, compared with Hong Kong Chinese students, Hong Kong–born EMSs are more likely to enjoy learning activities. They respond quickly to teachers' requests in the classroom, and they raise hands when questions are posed by teachers. However, they have relatively short concentration spans, and they dislike the "chalk-and-talk" teaching approach, which they usually find boring. Understanding this, teachers intend to promote student-centered and activity-based learning.

In addition to learning behavior, the presence of language differences among students is very prominent, especially between new immigrant EMSs and new immigrant students from mainland China. As highlighted by the narratives of both teachers and students, there is a wide range of student abilities in English and Chinese; hence, the streaming policy was adopted. Under the policy, students are streamed into different classes according to their language abilities. The three types of classes include "Chinese classes," "ethnic minority classes," and "mixed classes." Basically, students who cannot be taught in Chinese are streamed into Chinese classes, whereas students who cannot speak and read Chinese are streamed into one of the other classes. Chinese classes are mainly for local Hong Kong students and immigrant students from mainland China, whereas ethnic minority classes are for the other two categories of EMSs: new EMS immigrants and Hong Kong–born EMSs. Some Chinese students who have exceptional abilities in learning English are placed in mixed classes for them to learn with EMSs.

Teachers find that this streaming policy is "a relatively good strategy" for schools to adopt. They also describe it as "the no-other-alternative way," "the only way," and "the relatively good way" of managing the diverse learning needs of students, especially in schools where the proportions of Chinese students and EMSs are almost the same. However, this policy segregates Chinese students from EMSs. In both Chinese and ethnic minority classes, Chinese students and EMSs have no opportunity to interact with one another, except when brought together in other school contexts beyond the classroom. In mixed classes, segregation is also seen. Although Chinese students and EMSs are in the same class, the interaction between these groups tends to be limited. They seem to interact only when they engage in teacher-requested learning activities. Most of the time, Chinese students stay together, and EMSs do the same.

Collaborating with EMS Parents

To make the school culturally responsive, teachers have realized that it is crucial to collaborate with parents. However, in practice, teachers experience difficulties in realizing their expectations. This is partly because, compared with Chinese parents, EMS parents have different expectations of their parental roles, as well as different aspirations for their children's education and future careers. According to teachers, EMS parents, especially Pakistanis and Indians, make sense of their parental roles only in terms of complying with the law, which requires them to send their children, under age 15, to school. Most parents are not keen on helping teachers improve their children's classroom behavior, and very few work with teachers to supervise their children's learning at home. As estimated by teachers, almost 70% of EMSs do not submit their homework on time. Although parents acknowledge that they have to take responsibility and work with teachers, they do not have sufficient knowledge on how to support their children's success in school, especially parents who do not speak and read Chinese and English. These parents are overwhelmed by a sense of powerlessness, which is intensified when teachers attempt to "pull" them to collaborate with the school. Consequently, they "push" teachers away.

Teachers have realized that cultural and religious perspectives should be taken into account when making sense of parental roles and parental expectations of children's education. From a cultural perspective, gender roles among EMS families are culturally stereotyped. This is particularly the case for Pakistani and Indian families. Mothers are expected to stay at home and do housework and cooking, whereas fathers should earn money and refrain from all housework. In general, a wife is not supposed to leave the home or to get in touch with males without the permission of her husband. No exception is made, even when male teachers need to discuss the education of students. Hence, teachers find it difficult to work with EMS parents:

If the males [in a student's family] work outside, they definitely do not have any holidays and have to stay at home. For the females, it may be their natural character. They keep "the self" from the outside world. Ever since they arrived in Hong Kong, they have rarely gone outside. More often, they are subordinated to their husbands. They even feel shy when they participate in school activities, even in the company of their husbands. It may be related to their religious beliefs.

In contrast to Chinese students, most EMSs are devoted to their religions (e.g., Islam, Sikhism, and Hinduism). Many students have to attend afterschool classes to learn holy texts in mosques or Sikh temples, and these activities end at approximately 7:00 PM. When students go home, they feel too tired to study or complete their homework. Religion plays a very important role in the everyday life of most EMSs; hence, religion should be taken into account when care or guidance is offered:

The Muslim church puts a very strong emphasis on children's religious education. The first priority is to pray and participate in religious activities. It is completely different from what our school emphasizes, that is, academic achievement. If the schedule of their religious activities clashes with the schedule organized by school, especially religious activities not relevant to academic matters, it goes without saying that they will certainly choose praying and chanting.

The narratives of students and teachers show that religion is regarded as the first priority, especially for Pakistanis and Indians. Academic matters come next. However, as teachers insist, in the school setting, this religious priority should be put aside, and academic matters should always come first.

Given the differences between the home and school priorities of EMSs, any school practice that goes against the religion of these students is abandoned or ignored at home. For example, as students have explained, "Fai Chun" cannot be displayed at home, as it is in school, because it is considered violative of Islamic teachings. "Fai Chun" is the poster displayed on walls and doors during Chinese New Year; it has blessings printed on it. Parents of EMSs cannot also understand why it is inappropriate to encourage their children to be absent from school during some religious or cultural festivals, which are not included in the school calendar. In summary, the differences in religious values between the school and EMS families, as well as between teachers and EMS parents, sometimes become factors that make guidance teachers feel they are being "pushed" away from working with EMS parents.

Broadening the Educational and Career Aspirations of EMSs

In addition to building connections with EMS parents, teachers find it challenging to broaden the views of EMSs regarding their education and future careers. Most students do not have plans to pursue post-secondary education. Moreover, they do not have plans for career development in Hong Kong. Even if they have visions of becoming professionals, they do not know how such visions can be realized or which local university programs they should enroll in. What they envisage is completing the HKCEE public examination, equivalent to GCSE in the UK, although very few declare plans for further studies either aboard or in their home countries. Most EMSs are not confident of getting good results in the public examination and of being able to master the local Chinese language; hence, they plan to pursue the same careers that their parents have (e.g., musicians, chefs, and construction workers).

When talking about their educational and career aspirations, EMSs and their parents compare the opportunities offered by the host society, Hong Kong, with likely opportunities in their home countries. They believe that they would have more and better opportunities in Hong Kong. The frame of reference that allows them to maintain an optimistic view of their future possibilities comes from the idea that "life in Hong Kong will be a lot better than in their home country; at least they will be able to find jobs and earn a living in this city." To hold on to this belief, once they complete their secondary education, girls are encouraged to assume women's domestic roles and marry at a very young age (e.g., 15 years). They are not expected to achieve high levels of education. Boys are expected to start working and earning money to support their families. They are normally introduced and encouraged to get involved in the careers or businesses run by their families, relatives, and friends. Most are blue-collar jobs, such as working in construction sites, loading and unloading goods, and working in restaurants as waiters or waitresses:

I have discussed it with many colleagues. We think that they do not have any sense of belongingness [to the society of Hong Kong]. What they want to do is to earn more money and transfer it to their family [in their own country]. They hold the belief that education is not important. Even without education, they can easily access the careers of their parents or relatives, such as chefs, construction site workers, waiters, and so on. Most EMS[s] in this area rely on the social welfare subsidy from the government. In their mind, there is not such a strong sense of "future." If they can live today, it's fine for them; and they do not think it is necessary to think about tomorrow. Probably it is their religious belief too, so it is easy for them to feel satisfied. They know they have not yet been accepted by the [local] society, so they think they are merely "visitors." Even if their children do well in education, they will still find it hard to get a job.

When talking about their school lives, students tend to make sense of their social reality through a frame of reference—their perceptions of social realities in their home countries, rather than of social realities in Hong Kong. It allows them to compare their present situations with their former situations or with their "back-home" experiences. Although such a frame of reference enables them to develop and maintain an optimistic view of their school lives and diverts their thoughts to positive aspects of their school experiences, their teachers also intend to broaden the way they think of their futures. Teachers transmit the belief that education is a means of integration into the host society and a way toward occupational and social mobility. For these students, deciding to stay in Hong Kong appears the most likely way to break the cycle of poverty and to create lives that are different from the lives of their parents.

When teachers encourage EMSs to think about their futures in more expanded ways, teachers have to simultaneously work against the values of two cultures, that is, the examination-oriented culture of Hong Kong and the traditional cultures of these students. On one hand, they intend to help EMSs deal with the examination-oriented culture; hence, they teach according to the examination syllabus, rather than according to the academic abilities of students, while encouraging EMSs to think about possible careers and offering them information on post-secondary educational programs. On the other hand, they stress gender equality, which is lacking in most EMS homes, and they intentionally encourage girls to develop their full potentials and to create a vision of their own future.

CONCLUSION

The views of teachers, students, and parents regarding EMSs are expressed through stories. Their views vividly show the diversity of students' pastoral needs and cross-cultural experiences in school and at home, and how EMSs undergo the process of cultural integration into the host society, which is totally different from their own countries. This study has shown that teachers satisfy the diverse needs of students by (a) developing intercultural sensitivity, (b) adjusting their teaching strategies under the streaming policy, (c) dealing with the segregation between Chinese students and EMSs, (d) establishing partnerships with parents, and (e) helping students broaden their educational and career aspirations. This study argues that culturally responsive schools face two challenges: caring in the classroom, school, and home, and enhancing the intercultural sensitivity of school practitioners.

Regarding the first challenge, teachers attempt to connect caring across various subsystems within the school organization (i.e., classroom, school, and home). Teachers are aware that the home life and values of EMSs remarkably influence their academic success and their ability to deal with the difficulties associated with acculturation. The weak connections among the three subsystems are partially caused by differences in academic expectations, as well as in educational and career aspirations, between the minority and the majority (i.e., between the Chinese and the non-Chinese, and between the school and the home). These differences are linked to weak connections among the subsystems, preventing the school organization from functioning effectively as a system that cares for the pastoral needs of students. This is evident from the fact that within the classroom and school subsystems, teachers are not connected in appropriate ways to care for students (e.g., when Chinese students and EMSs are segregated). Furthermore, when promoting positive peer relationships between Chinese students and EMSs, and when broadening the educational and career aspirations of students, teachers feel that they are working against the benefits of the examination-oriented culture, the effects of the streaming policy, and some traditional values of students' families. With the weak connections among the subsystems, there is a need for a school environment where the classroom, school, and home are connected in dynamic ways to promote culturally responsive approaches to caring, teaching, and learning, and to ensure that every individual student is treated equitably.

Furthermore, this study argues that the promotion of cultural responsiveness to diversity is implemented based on school practitioners' mutual understanding of the differences, similarities, and uniqueness of students. It should also be built on an understanding of EMSs—from the point of view of the minorities themselves, rather than from an evaluation or interpretation made from the perspective of the dominant group or from local people's narratives about their social reality. To achieve this, the school should enhance the intercultural sensitivity of school practitioners and broaden the frame of reference they adopt in making sense of the cultural backgrounds of others.

When interacting with ethnic minority groups, school practitioners should be aware that they are engaged in a cross-cultural process. In this process, they should learn each other's culture, re-learn their own culture, and re-examine the rationales underlying cultural responsiveness. This should apply not only to teachers but to all other school practitioners, such as students, parents, and professional parties who work closely with teachers.

Caring for EMSs is an educational challenge for all school practitioners. Schooling also aims to ensure that caring is connected across the classroom, school, and home, and to enhance the intercultural sensitivity of all school practitioners. The foregoing points may not be the only ways to make schools culturally responsive. By identifying the unique organizational features of schools in terms of the combinations of different ethnic groups of students and the relationships between the majority and the minority groups of students, it would be easier for schools to identify the diverse needs of all students and to work out effective strategies to actualize caring. This is one of the ways to create a just and fair society. As such, all school practitioners (i.e., teachers, students, and parents) have an important role to play if this important goal is to be achieved.

REFERENCES

Alderson, P. (1995). *Listening to children: Children, ethics, and social research.* Essex, UK: Barnardos.

Ali, S. (2003). *Mixed-race, post-race: Gender, new ethnicities, and cultural practices.* Oxford, UK: Berg.

Anderson, B. (1991). *Imagined communities: Reflections on the origin and spread of nationalism.* London: Verso.

Arora, R. K. (2005). *Race and ethnicity in education: Monitoring change in education.* Aldershot, Hants, UK: Ashgate.

Atzaba-Poria, N., Pike, A., & Deater-Deckard, K. (2004). Do risk factors for problem behavior act in a cumulative manner? An examination of ethnic minority and majority children through an ecological perspective. *Journal of Child Psychology and Psychiatry, 45*(5), 707–718.

Ball, S. (1981). *Beachside Comprehensive: A case-study of secondary schooling.* Cambridge, UK: Cambridge University Press.

Bentley, T., Oakley, K., Gibson, S., & Kilgour, K. (1999). *The real deal: What young people really think about government, politics and social exclusion.* London: Demos.

Berger, P. L., & Luckmann, T. (1973). *The social construction of reality: A treatise in the sociology of knowledge* (3rd ed.). London: Penguin.

Caballero, C., Haynes, J., & Tikly, L. (2007). Researching mixed race in education: Perceptions, policies and practices. *Race, Ethnicity and Education, 10*(3), 345–362.

Census and Statistics Department. (2007). *Hong Kong 2006 population by-census thematic report: Ethnic minorities.* Hong Kong: Author.

Cheminais, R. (2001). *Developing inclusive school practice: A practical guide.* London: David Fulton.

Clandinin, J., & Connelly, M. (1995). *Teachers' professional knowledge land-scapes.* New York: Teachers College Press.

Codjoe, H. M. (2001). Fighting a "public enemy" of black academic achievement—The persistence of racism and the schooling experiences of Black students in Canada. *Race, Ethnicity and Education, 4*(4), 343–375.

Cummins, J. (1989). *Empowering minority students.* Sacramento: California Association for Bilingual Education.

Cummins, J. (2000). *Language, power, and pedagogy: Bilingual children in the crossfire.* Clevedon, UK: Multilingual Matters.

Cuypers, S. (2001). *Self-identity and personal autonomy: An analytical anthropology.* Aldershot, UK: Ashgate.

Dentler, R., & Hafner, A. (1997). *Hosting newcomers: Structuring educational opportunities for immigrant children.* New York: Teachers College Press.

Denzin, N. (1998). The art and politics of interpretation. In N. K. Denzin & Y. S Lincoln (Eds.), *Collecting and interpreting qualitative materials* (pp. 150–178). Thousand Oaks, CA: Sage.

Economic and Social Commission for Asia and the Pacific. (1999). *Youth participation manual.* New York: United Nations.

Education & Manpower Bureau. (2004a). *Guideline on student discipline: Principles and policy on student discipline.* Retrieved from http://www.edb. gov.hk/index.aspx?nodeID=944&langno=1 on 7th February 2011.

Education & Manpower Bureau. (2004b). *Student guidance in secondary schools: What is school guidance?* Retrieved from http://www.edb.gov.hk/ index.aspx?langno=1&nodeID=2234 on 7th February 2011.

Education Commission. (2000). *Learning for life Learning through life—Reform proposals for the education system in Hong Kong.* Hong Kong: Education Commission. Retrieved from http://www.e-c.edu.hk/eng/reform/annex/ Edu-reform-eng.pdf

Fuligni, A. J. (1998). The adjustment of children from immigrant families. *Current Directions in Psychological Science, 7*(4), 99–103.

Garcia, O. M., & Lopez, R. G. (2005). Teachers' initial training in cultural diversity in Spain: Attitudes and pedagogical strategies. *Intercultural Education, 16*(5), 433–442.

Geertz, C. (1973). Thick description: Toward an interpretive theory of culture. In C. Geertz (Ed.), *The interpretation of cultures: Selected essays* (pp. 3–32). New York: Basic Books.

Haque, Z. (2000). The ethnic minority "underachieving" group? Investigating the claims of "underachievement" amongst Bangladeshi pupils in British secondary schools. *Race, Ethnicity, and Education, 3*(2), 145–168.

Hargreaves, D. H. (1967). *Social relations in a secondary school.* London: Routledge & Kegan Paul.

He, M. F., Phillion, J., Chan, E., & Xu, S. J. (2008). Immigrant students' experience of curriculum. In F. M. Connelly, M. F. He, & J. Phillion (Eds.), *Handbook of curriculum and instruction* (pp. 1–32). Thousand Oaks, CA: Sage.

Hill, M., Laybourn, A., & Borland, M. (1996). Engaging with primary-aged children about their emotions and well-being: Methodological considerations. *Children and Society, 10*, 129–144.

Holstein, J., & Gubrium, J. (1995). *The active interview.* Thousand Oaks, CA: Sage.

Holzner, B. (1968). *Reality construction in society.* Cambridge, MA: Schenkman.

Kennedy, K., Hue, M. T., & Tsui, K. T. (2008, February 23). *Comparing Hong Kong teachers' sense of efficacy for teaching Chinese and non-Chinese students.* Paper presented at the annual conference of Comparative Education Society of Hong Kong, Hong Kong Institute of Education, Hong Kong.

Ku, H. B., Chan, K. W., & Sandhu, K. K. (2005). *A research report on the education of South Asian ethnic minority groups in Hong Kong.* Hong Kong: Center for Social Policy Studies, Department of Applied Social Sciences, Hong Kong Polytechnic University and Unison Hong Kong.

Lacey, C. (1974). *Hightown grammar: The school as a social system.* Manchester, UK: Manchester University Press.

Ladson-Billings, G. (1994). *The dream keepers: Successful teachers of African American children.* San Francisco: Jossey-Bass.

Loper, K. (2004). *Race and equality: A study of ethnic minorities in Hong Kong's education system: Project report and analysis.* Hong Kong: Center for Comparative and Public Law, Hong Kong University. Retrieved from http://www.legco.gov.hk/yr03-04/english/panels/ha/papers/ha0611cb2-2559-1e.pdf on 7th February 2011.

Mansouri, F., & Trembath, A. (2005). Multicultural education and racism: The case of Arab-Australian students in contemporary Australia. *International Education Journal, 6*(4), 516–529.

Nabobo, U., & Teasdale, J. (1994). Teacher education for cultural identity in Fiji. *Directions: Journal of Educational Studies, 16*(2), 3–13.

Paku, L., Zegwaard, K., & Coll, R. K. (2003, August). *Enculturation of indigenous people into science and technology: An investigation from a sociocultural perspective.* Paper presented at the World Association for Cooperative Education, biennial conference in Rotterdam, The Netherlands.

Phillion, J. (2002). *Narrative inquiry in a multicultural landscape: Multicultural teaching and learning, issues in curriculum theory, policy, and research.* Westport, CT: Ablex.

Rassool, N. (1999). Flexible identities: Exploring race and gender issues among a group of immigrant pupils in an inner-city comprehensive school. *British Journal of Sociology of Education, 20*(1), 23–36.

Ruiz-de-Velasco, J., Fix, M., & Clewell, B. (2000). *Overlooked & underserved: Immigration students in U.S. secondary schools.* Washington DC: Urban Institute Press.

Rutter, J. (1994). *Refugee children in the classroom: Including a comprehensive information briefing on refugees in Britain.* London: Trentham Books.

Santoro, N. (2009). Teaching in culturally diverse contexts: What knowledge about "self" and "others" do teachers need? *Journal of Education for Teaching, 35*(1), 33–45.

Solomon, P., Portelli, J., Daniel, B., & Campbell, A. (2005). The discourse of denial: How white teacher candidates construct race, racism and "white privilege." *Race, Ethnicity, and Education, 8*(2), 147–169.

South China Morning Post. (2006a, October 5). Minority interest.

South China Morning Post. (2006b, December 16). EMB put on notice to assist switch into Chinese.

Stevenson, J., & Willott, J. (2007). The aspiration and access to higher education of teenage refugees in the UK. *Compare, 37*(5), 671–688.

Taylor, N., & Coll, R. K. (2002). Constructivist-informed pedagogy in teacher education: An overview of a year-long study in Fiji. *Asia-Pacific Journal of Teacher Education and Development, 5*(1), 47–76.

Thomas, S., & Kearney, J. (2008). Teachers working in culturally diverse classrooms: Implications for the development of professional standards and for teacher education. *Asia-Pacific Journal of Teacher Education, 36*(2), 105–120.

Yang Memorial Methodist Social Service. (2000). *Educational needs and social adaptation of ethnic minority youth in Hong Kong.* Hong Kong: Author.

Yang Memorial Methodist Social Service. (2002). *A study on outlets of the South Asian ethnic minority youth in Hong Kong.* Hong Kong: Author.

10 The "Long March" toward Multiculturalism in Hong Kong

Supporting Ethnic Minority Students in a Confucian State[1]

Kerry J. Kennedy

INTRODUCTION

Joppke (2004) asserted that liberal democratic states support opposing responses to cultural diversity:

> Abolish it by means of "antidiscrimination" policy, and protect or promote it by means of "multiculturalism" policy. In other words, liberal-democratic norms require the simultaneous rendering of invisible *and* visible ethnic diversities. (p. 451)

This formulation raises interesting questions about the relationship between antidiscrimination and multiculturalist policies, and the extent of their dependence on each other. The distinction is particularly relevant to the current Hong Kong context—Hong Kong is grappling with its first Racial Discrimination Ordinance. Joppke's "antidiscrimination" element characterizes the bill that was introduced to the Legislative Council in December 2006 and passed into law in July 2008. Clause 8 of the bill regards "race" as "the race, color, descent, or national or ethnic origin of a person" (Home Affairs Bureau, 2006). The objectives of the bill are as follows (Legislative Council, 2006c, pp. 1–2):

- to make racial discrimination and harassment in prescribed areas and vilification on the ground of race unlawful and to prohibit serious vilification on that ground; and
- to extend the jurisdiction of the Equal Opportunities Commission to cover racial discrimination.

However, there is no attempt in the proposed legislation—or in any other legislation—to promote multiculturalism, the second dimension of policymaking advocated by Joppke. This is easily explained by the fact that Hong Kong is not a liberal democracy. It is a Special Administrative Region of the People's Republic of China. Its government is executive-led, with only the Chief Executive's position subject to what is called a "small circle election."[2] The other positions in the Executive Council are nonelective. These characteristics that fit well under Chinese sovereignty were inherited from the British colonial period. The important point to note for purposes of this chapter, however, is that concerns for ethnic diversity are not always embedded within the framework of liberal democracy. Other reasons behind the introduction of the antidiscrimination law must be explored.

Hong Kong's current policymaking context reflects its historical development, as well as its new political environment. As a Special Administrative Region of the People's Republic of China and a former British colony, Hong Kong has a legal system—a system from its colonial past—characterized by the "rule of law," a political system aligned to, but not subsumed by, mainland China and a cultural history that links the present day to an ancient civilization. The Hong Kong government must navigate these multiple influences while trying to resolve competing public interests. It was in this context that the Hong Kong government, over a two-year period, grappled with an antidiscrimination law for ethnic minorities.

While this extended period of policymaking resulted in a successful outcome, it has also raised numerous issues that require further analysis:

1. Given that this policy process took place outside a liberal democratic theoretical framework as described by Joppke (2004), what motivated the enactment of the antidiscrimination law in Hong Kong?
2. Second, how is cultural diversity constructed in the unique Hong Kong context?

These two questions are addressed in the remainder of this chapter. The purpose is to re-frame concerns for cultural diversity and to account for a context that is very different from that which often dominates Western experiences. This chapter seeks to identify alternative analytical tools that can expand the understanding of social processes in societies whose values and histories do not reflect mainstream Western development. However, this is not to underplay the importance of such development; rather, this chapter recognizes that other development processes operate for a large proportion of the world's people. These processes must be understood if we are to have a broader appreciation of diversity in the global community.

DIVERSITY IN THE INTERNATIONAL SCENE: FROM INCLUSION TO EXCLUSION

Joppke's (2004) view of multiculturalism highlights liberal democratic ways of dealing with issues of diversity within nations. This position considers either of two perspectives: (a) liberal democracies are the only sites where issues of diversity are addressed, or (b) liberal democratic solutions are the best ways to address issues of diversity. Western politicians, policymakers, and scholars often take the latter perspective; hence, liberal multicultural-ism has been put forward as a universal prescription in dealing with cul-tural diversity (Kymlicka, 1995). Yet, even the main protagonist of liberal multiculturalism has some reservations about the ability of communities to fully realize primary multicultural principles (Kymlicka, 2007).

According to Kymlicka, "specific models of multiculturalism [cannot] be transported directly from one country to another, particularly not the Canadian model, which is a product of a very unique history" (Klymlicka, cited in Peonidis, 2008, paragraph 13). In considering transnational justice, Chwaszcza (2008) asserted that "we lack a clear understanding of what the rights and duties of individuals are (or ought to be) outside the socio-polit-ical background institution of the liberal paradigm of the (national) legal state" (p. 121). Yet, the realities of multiculturalism confront many states, both liberal and authoritarian. If liberal versions of multiculturalism are "context dependent" (Chwaszcza, 2008, p. 119), how about states that can-not draw on liberal political values to address issues of cultural diversity? If history, politics, and culture do not conspire to create values and struc-tures that are conducive to multiculturalism (i.e., multiculturalism that val-ues differences, supports equality, and actively champions equity), how do such states and their communities respond to the needs of multiple groups within their boundaries? The answers to these questions are important in framing ethnic diversity outside the context of liberal multiculturalism and as a point of comparison for an analysis of the Hong Kong context.

There is a growing literature on the realities of cultural diversity in non-Western states. Kymlicka and He (2005) provided an Asian perspective:

> Western models are often not well understood in the region and may not suit the specific historical, cultural, demographic, and geopolitical circumstances of the region. Moreover, many Asian societies have their own traditions of peaceful coexistence among linguistic and religious groups, often dating to pre-colonial times. All the major ethical and religious traditions in the region—from Confucian and Buddhist to Islamic and Hindu—have their own conceptions of the value of toler-ance, and their own recipes for sustaining unity amid diversity. (p. 1)

From this context, it is possible to identify non-Western policies and the-oretical variants that seek to consider the interests of minority groups. Saravanamuttu (2005, p. 204) argued that both liberal multiculturalism in the West and communitarian multiculturalism in places like Singapore and Malaysia are based on consensus and conformity, which are inimical to the real spirit of multiculturalism. He sought for "unforced consensus multiculturalism" from local traditions of tolerance. McCarthy (2009), focusing on ethnic minorities in China's Yunnan Province, explored the tension between nation building and specific policies that support ethnic minorities. This tension is serious not only in China but also in many parts of Asia. McCarthy showed that when the twin objectives of supporting ethnic minorities and nation building are pursued, nation building always wins over minority rights. This is why she refers to "communist multiculturalism" as a policy controlled by, and subject to, the Chinese Communist Party. Although communist multiculturalism recognizes the need to provide for ethnic minorities, it does not view this response as a threat to the hegemony of the state.

The restrictions that can be imposed when it comes to cultural diversity within the context of an authoritarian state are worth highlighting. Gladney (2005) outlined the processes used in mainland China:

> For ethnic identification in China, the state defines what traditions qualify as language, locality, and culture, regardless of the group's belief in its existence as a people, or in the legitimacy of these cultural traditions. The state of China imagines what qualifies as cultural tradition for the communities in question, and the communities respond to that depiction in terms of their own traditional notions and imaginations of identity. These often conflicting imagined identities are then negotiated in each socioeconomic setting, according to symbolic representations of state, self, and others. (p. 213)

The Chinese context is as far from liberal multiculturalism as can be imagined. From a somewhat different perspective, van der Walle and Gunewardena (2000), in relation to ethnic minorities in Vietnam, showed that without an appreciation of and respect for local traditions, interventions may fail. Furthermore, they argued that "when policies are additionally imbued with prejudice and majority group ethnocentrism, they further result in a fraying of indigenous customs and identity, and can lead to greater marginalization" (p. 1). The state's role in this context is supportive, but community attitudes are not. Thus, even a hegemonic state cannot control the contexts within which ethnic minority policies are implemented. This may be called "authoritarian multiculturalism." In this form of multiculturalism, the impetus and support are found in the state, perhaps for reasons of nation building, for ensuring social cohesion, or for economic advantages. However, this form of multiculturalism does not necessarily signal the recognition of diversity as a value for either the state or for individuals. Authoritarian multiculturalism is instrumental in nature, designed to serve the interests of the state and only indirectly the interests of ethnic minorities themselves.

Instrumentalism may not be the optimal driver of multiculturalism, but it moderates what may be called "naked authoritarianism." When unchecked, authoritarianism can produce catastrophic results for ethnic minorities. Ang (2007), for example, showed that in the case of Myanmar, ethnic minorities provide the key to any future political settlement, but the current government has not paved the way for such a settlement. The paralysis caused by the authoritarian regime is summarized in a report from the International Crisis Group (2003, paragraph 6):

> While many ethnic groups originally fought for independence, today almost all have accepted the Union of Myanmar as a fact and merely seek increased local authority and equality within a new federal state structure. The military government, however, still suspects them of scheming to split the country and sees this as justification for its repressive, often brutal policies in minority areas.

At its worst, this kind of approach to ethnic minorities can lead to "ethnic cleansing" (Bell-Fialkoff, 1999) where ethnic groups are systematically and intentionally eliminated, either by forced removal from an area or by genocide, usually by a dominant group. There is a long and sad history of such actions; unfortunately, they are evident in recent times in places such as Darfur, Kosovo, Chechnya, and Rwanda. The ability of ethnic minorities to evoke this kind of response is a testimony to the power of differences and the threat that differences can pose even to politically and economically dominant groups.

Approaches to cultural diversity, therefore, can range from a refocusing of local traditions of tolerance to the apparent need for authoritarian states to include ethnic minorities in a broader nation-building project, to the total exclusion of ethnic minorities, even to the point of extermination. These approaches nearly represent a continuum, and they offer powerful contrasts to Western-oriented liberal multiculturalism. They indicate that cultural diversity is treated as a threat. However, none of these scenarios adequately explains the Hong Kong context. The ethnic minority population in Hong Kong is not large enough to warrant the kind of authoritarianism that is found in mainland China. Moreover, the economic motivation for improving the conditions of ethnic minorities in Hong Kong is not the same as that in Vietnam, and—in contrast to how minorities are perceived in Myanmar—Hong Kong's minorities are not viewed as threats. Therefore, the question remains, what motivated the enactment of the antidiscrimination law in Hong Kong?

HONG KONG CONTEXT: INTERNATIONAL LAW, THE RULE OF LAW, AND THE CONFUCIAN HERITAGE

To understand the Hong Kong context, it is first necessary to appreciate the impetus behind the enactment of the antidiscrimination law and the progress of the law's implementation. This appreciation provides insights into the uniqueness of Hong Kong's situation as an Asian society with a Western history, and a long and continuous commitment to traditional Chinese values.

Given the variety of ways by which national governments respond to ethnic minorities, it is not surprising that much effort has been invested in the development of international laws regarding minority rights (Hernard, 2000). The presence of international laws is a recognition that respect for differences and diversity does not come naturally and that the powerful arguments of liberal multiculturalism are not universally tenable. International laws seek to influence the legal systems of sovereign states that do not specifically promote the necessary respect and support for cultural diversity. However, the function of such laws can often be contested, and their application in sovereign states may be problematic (Macklem, 2008). Nevertheless, international laws seem to have influenced the enactment of the Racial Discrimination Ordinance, but the presence of these laws is not the only influencing factor. The initial consultation paper on the proposed ordinance indicates broad social purposes (Home Affairs Bureau, 2004):

> All of us are equal before the law and are entitled to equal protection of the law against all forms of racial discrimination and incitement to racial hatred. Discrimination against individuals and groups by other individuals and groups on the grounds of race, color, descent, and national or ethnic origin is an obstacle to the development of a just and harmonious society. There is a need to introduce legislation to prevent and combat all forms of racial discrimination in Hong Kong. (p. 1)

One purpose of the ordinance rests in international law, that is, to fulfill Hong Kong's obligations under the International Convention on the Elimination of All Forms of Racial Discrimination.

These principles—the development of a just and harmonious society, and the necessity to meet international obligations—were made more salient by reports on discriminatory practices in housing, employment, and education from ethnic community members and nongovernmental organizations. "Harmony" is an important Chinese value; hence, the antidiscrimination law can be understood as a move to ensure such in Hong Kong. At the same time, the need to conform to international standards can be seen as an appropriate policy lever that the government can use, especially to convince a community that is not used to thinking about diversity. This was a particularly important issue for the government because less than 5% of Hong Kong's total population is classified as "ethnic minorities," and the dominance of Han Chinese is taken for granted in Hong Kong. This point necessitates further elaboration.

When Hong Kong's ethnic minority population is broken down, the majority are Filipinas who work in Hong Kong largely as domestic helpers (32.9%, around 112,583), followed by the Indonesians (25.7%, around 87,945). The third largest group is composed of Indians, Pakistanis, and Nepalese (6%, 3.2%, and 4.7%, respectively, making up 13.9%, around 47,566). Westerners comprise an even smaller group (10.6%, around 36,273) (Census and

Statistics Department 2007, p. 5). For certain, these numbers represent the multicultural nature of Hong Kong, which is reflected in Hong Kong's school population (about 2.9% of students under the age of 15 are ethnic minorities) (Census and Statistics Department 2007, p. 51). However, the numbers render these minority groups almost invisible. In addition, because of the geographic concentration of these groups, it is entirely possible to live in Hong Kong without being aware of Hong Kong's diverse population.

The numbers suggest that within Hong Kong, issues of diversity and even racism may not have a great deal of salience. The government could ignore them without fear of serious community backlash. Thus, although the Hong Kong government does not have a constituency in the sense that Western democratic governments do, it must nevertheless convince the community of the necessity of any action that it takes. The extent to which the enactment of the Racial Discrimination Ordinance was enmeshed in local politics cannot be overstated. Hong Kong's non-democratic, executive-led government has the capacity to initiate legislation, but all legislations are reviewed by the partially democratically elected Legislative Council.[3] Normally, the government has the "numbers" to ensure the approval of its legislative programs but not before such programs have been tested through the committee system of the Legislative Council and through public consultation. Legislative Council Committees hold public hearings and take public submissions, and the committees are composed of members from different parties. This ensures that the government's agenda is well tested. Such hearings attract a great deal of public and media attention; hence, governmental initiatives must be well planned and presented. The appeal to international law, therefore, may have helped the government bolster its case for a racial discrimination ordinance within a community that has little awareness of the need for such an ordinance.

The appeal to international law appears as a somewhat pragmatic use of international conventions, and such pragmatism often characterizes policy-making in Hong Kong. However, Hong Kong's attitude toward the law is not entirely pragmatic. From its colonial past, Hong Kong has inherited the "rule of law" as understood from the English legal tradition. As asserted by Tsang (2001):

> What sets it (i.e., Hong Kong) apart from the People's Republic of China (PRC) is the existence of the rule of law and an independent judiciary. They are generally accepted in Hong Kong as the most important legacy of 156 years of British imperial rule. (p. 1)

Hills (1994, Section 13) asserted that "although the Rule of Law does not necessarily require a liberal society, it is a hallmark of all liberal societies. The Rule of Law respects the dignity and autonomy of the individual." Cullen (2005) also highlighted the key features of the rule of law in his discussion of Hong Kong:

- Governments must always be subject to the law and never above it.
- Regardless of their status, all persons must be treated equally before the law.
- Laws must be fairly and transparently enacted.
- Everyone subject to the application of the law is entitled to due process, that is, the fair and proper application of the law.

In this commitment to the rule of law, there is therefore a commitment to individuals and to equality—the key values of antidiscrimination laws. However, Hills (1994, Section 13) argued that in Hong Kong, these values are overlaid by "Confucian and Communist ideologies [that] also allow for the dignity of the individual; however, they do not allow for the concept of individual autonomy . . . There is an irreconcilable conflict between the 'egotism' of liberalism and the 'communitarianism' of socialism." This is an important comment, especially in relation to the impact of Confucianism on the modern society of Hong Kong.

Numerous writers have acknowledged that overlaying the legal and political systems of Hong Kong is a connection to Confucianism that transcends modern politics and even modern life. King (1996) averred that it is not "imperial Confucianism or institutional Confucianism" but rather "social Confucianism or the Confucianism of everyday life" (p. 275). Liu (1996) referred to Confucianism as a "storehouse of popular values" (p. 111). Hue (2008), for example, has recently shown how teachers' beliefs about school counseling in Hong Kong are influenced by Confucian principles. At the heart of Confucianism is obedience to the family and to the state, and a very fixed order for social and personal relationships. It is not clear how Confucian values are disseminated or maintained because Confucianism is not an organized religion, but commentators agree that such values continue to play an important role in the lives of Hong Kong's people. The statement of Hills (1994), as presented above, may be better phrased with reference to "Confucian communitarianism" rather than "socialist communitarianism" because it is the former rather than the latter that is more likely to influence modern-day Hong Kong. This point is discussed in the next section, along with an examination of the aspects of the implementation of the Racial Discrimination Ordinance. The focus of the next section is on the issues raised by one aspect of the bill, educational provision for ethnic minority students, and how this aspect became enmeshed in local politics.

POLICY AND ACTION: CATERING TO THE NEEDS OF ETHNIC MINORITY STUDENTS IN HONG KONG SCHOOLS

In Hong Kong schools, 2.9% of students under the age of 15 belong to ethnic minorities (Census and Statistics Department, 2007, p. 51). Both before and after the formal promulgation of the ordinance, the government's

Education and Manpower Bureau, now Education Bureau (EDB), sought to address a range of issues affecting ethnic minority students. These measures are outlined below.

Initiation Program

Since 2000, EDB has been supporting a six-month full-time initiation program as an alternative support service for newly arrived children before they join mainstream schools in Hong Kong. The integrated program aims to enhance the Chinese and English language abilities of the children, to help them adapt to the new learning and classroom environment in Hong Kong, and to facilitate their personal development and social adaptation. The program is operated in a school setting, and schools can use the program's grant to design their own curricula that meet their students' needs (Education and Manpower Bureau, 2004b). Since 2004, five schools have joined the program: one in Hong Kong Island, three in Kowloon, and one in the New Territories. Three schools provide primary schooling, and two offer secondary schooling for newly arrived children from the mainland. Only two offer primary schooling, and one provides secondary schooling for newly arrived non-Chinese speaking children and returnee children (Education and Manpower Bureau, 2004a).

New Admission Scheme

Prior to SY 2004–2005, ethnic minority children had suffered from a limited choice of schools. There were only four public sector schools (two primary and two secondary schools) providing non-Chinese curricula (Ku, Chan, & Sandhu, 2005). Under a new school placement policy, children of ethnic minority families can approach schools by themselves, as long as the schools can provide them support in learning Chinese.

Induction Program

EDB has been providing a 60-hour induction program for newly arrived Chinese and non-Chinese speaking children since 2005. The program aims to assist students in adapting to their new social and school environments. With subsidies from the EDB, the program strengthens children's personal development, social adaptation, and basic learning skills. The program is operated by nongovernmental organizations (Education and Manpower Bureau, 2004b).

Designated Schools for Ethnic Minority Students

In SY 2006–2007, the EDB designated ten primary and five secondary schools as recipients of intensive on-site support to enhance the teaching of ethnic minority students. The support includes regular visits by professional officers, as well as assistance in the development of school-based Chinese language curricula, teaching and learning strategies, and other school-based teaching resources (Education and Manpower Bureau, 2007).

Teaching Chinese to Non-Chinese Speaking Students

The teaching of Chinese to non-Chinese speaking students emerged as a significant issue following the introduction of the antidiscrimination bill in the Legislative Council. Ethnic minority groups wanted an alternative Chinese curriculum for non-Chinese speaking students. The EDB insisted that the standard Chinese curriculum, together with suitable school-based adaptations, is appropriate. A resolution from the Legislative Council forced the resolution of the issue (Legislative Council, 2007):

> That this Panel urges the Government to immediately formulate an alternative Chinese Language curriculum for non-Chinese speaking students and establish another open examination which is recognized by local universities as a channel for non-Chinese speaking students to enter universities and receive post-secondary education in Hong Kong. (p. 5)

Some 12 months later, the Curriculum Development Council released an "alternative curriculum" for consultation. However, the supposed curriculum was not an alternative curriculum but a "Supplementary Guide to the Chinese Language Curriculum for Non-Chinese Speaking (NCS) Students" (Curriculum Development Council, 2008). It proposed a range of teaching strategies and organizational arrangements for the teaching of Chinese, but it did not establish a new curriculum for second language learners. Ironically, the supposed curriculum was originally produced in Chinese and not in English, much to the consternation of ethnic minority groups (Clem, 2008, EDU1).

The various support schemes and resources offered by the EDB are clearly designed to improve learning opportunities for ethnic minority students while ensuring that the government is not accused of any form of discrimination.[4] It is important to note that all these support schemes were instituted prior to the final approval of the antidiscrimination bill. However, community advocates have constantly challenged the EDB's prescriptions and have sought for further improvements. It is of some interest to note that ethnic community advocacy groups use and avow political processes in securing their ends. Thus, on October 9, 2006, Hong Kong Christian Service, a nongovernmental organization that supports ethnic minority families, wrote to the Chair of the Legislative Panel on Education to further clarify the following issues, which, in their view, have not been adequately addressed by the EDB (Legislative Council, 2006a):

- additional designated schools in areas of need;
- additional ethnic minority staff for designated schools, especially to support after-school tutorials;
- lengthening of the summer bridge program; and
- a "standardized alternative Chinese language curriculum," as well as a "tailor-made public examination."

The EDB responded to these issues through the Legislative Council Panel on Education (Legislative Council, 2006b). It denied the ethnic minority group's requests and asserted rationales for maintaining the status quo. The issue was consistently on the extent of educational provisions and whether "special conditions" could be created for ethnic minority students. For example, on the issue of a "tailor-made examination," the EDB replied:

We are of the view that the standards referenced language paper under Hong Kong Certificate of Education and the future Hong Kong Diploma of Secondary Education will illustrate different proficiency levels that are suitable for both native and non-native speakers aspiring to get a qualification in Chinese language . . . In the longer term, we shall continue to explore the need for bringing in additional qualifications and deploying a local-based examination for non-native speakers (p. 3).

On the surface, it is not clear why EDB officials always appear reluctant to grant ethnic community groups their requests. It is certainly not funding, which is generally abundant in Hong Kong. It is not also because the government is unwilling to acknowledge the needs of ethnic minority students. The EDB works on a broad front with schools, vocational educational institutions, and universities to make extra provisions. However, there is clear reluctance on the part of government officials to meet the full demands of ethnic minority students. Consistent media reports and Legislative Council debates are witnesses to this reluctance. The final section of this chapter addresses this issue. It seeks to explain the issue in cultural and theoretical terms.

CULTURE AND THEORY: RECONSTRUCTING EQUITY IN EASTERN TERMS

States have different responses to cultural diversity. In the West, many states have adopted policies to recognize and even celebrate the diversity of their populations, although motives for doing so are often mixed (Legislative Council, 2006a). Bokhorst-Heng (2007), for example, referred to the ideologies and political constructions made by states to support their version of multiculturalism as "statal multicultural narratives" (p. 631). She examined specific Singaporean and Canadian narratives to show how contexts, ideologies, and politics dictate the form that multiculturalism assumes in different jurisdictions. A "statal narrative" assumes that a state recognizes diversity within its borders and seeks to construct narratives that will accommodate such diversity in ways that do not threaten the existence of the state. Drawing on earlier examples in this chapter, it is possible to identify just such a "statal multicultural narrative" in mainland China or Vietnam because in both cases, although the state has not opted for a liberal version of multiculturalism, it has seen the necessity for such a narrative for nation building or economic growth. However, there is no such narrative in Hong Kong; there is no acknowledgment of the value of diversity. Without such a rationale, it seems that antidiscrimination is pursued as a pragmatic policy objective; hence, only concessions that are deemed reasonable by the bureaucracy and the government are granted. This may be one explanation for the reluctance of officials to agree with the persistent demands of ethnic minority groups. This, however, is not the only possible explanation.

Concepts of social justice are central to liberal democratic theory and practice. There is some evidence, however, suggesting that Western concepts of social justice are not the same as those in Confucian societies, such as Hong Kong (Chan, 2001; Chiu & Hong, 1997). For example, it has been argued that "when it comes to matters about people's well being, material welfare, and life chances, Confucian justice seeks to promote sufficiency for all and not equality [among] individuals" (Chan, 2001). This concept of social justice is expressed through the idea of impartiality (Chan, 2001, Section 3):

> Political rule should be impartial or fair (*gong* in Chinese) to everyone—by that, it means political rule should promote the good of everyone without prejudice or favoritism. In other words, it would be a violation of fairness or justice (*gong*) if the ruler were selectively concerned about some people only.

This view may be seen as the communitarian aspect of Confucianism. Individuals are not more important than the society; therefore, no individual should benefit more than another. This view is supported by Fan's (2003) discussion on the Confucian conception of social justice:

> Confucians would agree with Rawlsians that there ought to be fundamental principles to direct institutions, laws, and policies of the society. I would argue that Confucians could not affirm that such principles concern *distribution* of primary social goods. For Confucians, the first subject of fundamental social principles should not be distribution. (p. 145)

Yung (2007), who explored different approaches to housing policies in Hong Kong, drew on Fan's views to show how the Confucian conception of social justice differs from the Western conception developed by John Rawls. She identified four ways in which Confucian attitudes differ from traditional liberal views of social justice (Table 10.1).

Table 10.1   Comparison of Western and Confucian Views of Social Justice (Yung, 2007)

Concept	Western	Confucian
Equality	All individuals are treated equally.	"The Confucian generalconcept of social justice is to treat people harmoniously, not equally." (p. 115)
Needs	Governments may have a major responsibility to address the needs of all citizens.	"The family is the mostbasic and important tier to distribute [goods] according to needs. The village or thecommune is the second tier of help. It is under the circumstances that the first two tiers of help fail, that assistance from the government is sought as the last resort." (p. 115) .
Rights	There are individual rights.	There are no individual rights, but families are responsible for all of their members.
Deserts	In determining deserts, talent and effort count most.	"In a Confucian society, what counts as merit is one's effort in the exercise of virtues, not talent and effort in doing something." (p.115)
Equality of opportunity	All individuals should have the same opportunities to live fulfilling and rewarding lives. At times, governments may need to ensure that equal opportunities are available for all individuals, especially for those who are disadvantaged in some ways.	"Families can give children special advantages, which may improve their chances of finding offices and high positions in society" (Fan 2003, p. 151). This is considered appropriate or "just" in a Confucian society. State intervention provides equal opportunities (as suggested by Rawls) by attenuating the autonomy of families that are seen as "unjust" (p. 116).

Combining the views of Fan (2003) and Yung (2007) on Confucian approaches to justice and social justice provides some insight into the way the EDB has dealt with ethnic minority issues. The concept of impartiality, as explained by Chan, can account for the EDB's insistence on a common curriculum, a common examination, limited support for induction programs, and a reluctance to expand the number of designated schools for ethnic minorities. In terms of the theory outlined in this chapter, the principle being used by the EDB can be described as *sufficient* provision rather than *equitable* provision. This interpretation is further supported by Yung's (2007) description of Confucian attitudes toward social justice. The role of the government should be limited and not overly interventionist, and the role of the family should be emphasized more because the family is where the basic responsibility should rest. In addition, as long as harmony exists, there is no need to strive for equality or to guarantee equal opportunities for all.

If the foregoing analysis is correct, then multiculturalism in Hong Kong is constructed in an environment that is very different from that where Western liberalism drives its multicultural agenda. Of course, more work is needed to explore the impact of Confucian thinking on educational policies regarding ethnic minority students in Hong Kong. Yet as an explanation, the analysis has certain face validity because it helps explain the current attitude of Hong Kong's government officials toward ethnic minority students. If they see these students within the framework outlined above, then the minimal levels of provision are understandable and their unwillingness to move toward more egalitarian provisions can be understood (if not sanctioned). Nevertheless, what does this mean for multiculturalism in Hong Kong? Where, in the "long march," can local efforts be located?

PATHWAYS TO MULTICULTURALISM: WHAT ARE THE OPTIONS?

As has already been pointed out, Hong Kong's current policy approach to ethnic minority students is not conceived as an exercise of multicultural policy development. Rather, it arose directly from the politico-legal processes that were earlier described in this chapter. These processes aim to develop a legal framework that will protect ethnic minorities in Hong Kong from exploitation, especially in employment-related areas. Little thought is given to schools and education. Furthermore, because the government itself is excluded from the ambit of the proposed antidiscrimination bill, it is even less likely that the treatment of ethnic minority students will ever surface as an issue under the Racial Discrimination Ordinance. Thus, the enactment of the antidiscrimination ordinance was not a deliberate attempt on the part of the Hong Kong government to create a policy on the treatment of ethnic minority students; rather, as public discussion on the Racial Discrimination Bill was under way, ethnic minority students and their treatment emerged as an issue. This was largely caused by the advocacy of numerous nongovernmental organizations on behalf of ethnic minorities and by numerous reports that documented the disadvantages being suffered by ethnic minority students. It is against this background that Hong Kong's educational orientation to diversity can best be understood.

Skerrett and Hargreaves (2008, pp. 914–915) provided a broader framework by which to understand Hong Kong's particular orientation toward cultural diversity. Drawing on a significant range of literature in the field, they identified three main educational orientations toward diversity, each with distinctive characteristics. Table 10.2 describes these orientations that, in themselves, can represent the deliberate policy choices of governments.

Table 10. 2   Educational Orientations to Diversity (Skerrett and Hargreaves, 2008)

Orientation	Description	Proponents
Monocultural education	All students benefit from the same curriculum, instructional strategies, and assessment practices.	Edmonds, 1979; Gilborn, 2004
Multicultural education	Schools and the school curricula reflect the knowledge, values, skills, pedagogies, assessment practices, and policies, among others, that recognize, support, and celebrate the contributions of all groups in the school community.	Banks, 1986
Critical multiculturalism	Teaching against all forms of racism is explicit, and eliminating all forms of discrimination is a key goal.	Troyna and Carrington, 1990

In Hong Kong's case, the choice is not deliberate but *de facto*. It is not difficult to identify Hong Kong's approach to diversity as monocultural. This approach is consistent with the cultural explanation of social justice offered in the previous section. Enhancing educational provisions for ethnic minority students was an almost unintended issue that emerged from the Racial Discrimination Bill. Besides, the Han Chinese dominate Hong Kong's population (about 95%), making ethnic diversity almost invisible. Hong Kong is still far from a fully developed form of liberal multiculturalism. The "long march" in Hong Kong has just begun.

CONCLUSION

A monocultural approach to diversity in Hong Kong means that the needs of ethnic minority students are being recognized through new policies and increased resource provision. This results in positive outcomes for students. At the same time, such an approach does not signal a commitment to celebrating cultural diversity or to adapting the curriculum to meet the special needs of ethnic minority students. Thus, monocultural multiculturalism in Hong Kong has its limitations. The extent to which Hong Kong may transcend these limitations is an important issue. It is important for the society as a whole because it involves not only the recognition of differences but also the recognition of the positive contributions of these differences to social development. However, this is clearly not an issue to be resolved quickly because it involves the adoption of liberal political values and a reorientation of long-held cultural values. Going beyond monocultural multiculturalism to embrace multicultural and anti-racist education may currently be outside the cultural reach of the Hong Kong community, but it remains a worthwhile objective if ethnic minority students are to be valued as citizens and contributors to Hong Kong's welfare.

NOTES

1. This research was supported by a public policy research grant (HKIEd8001-PPR-2) from the Hong Kong Research Grants Council. The views expressed are those of the author.
2. The Chief Executive is elected by an Election Committee of 800 people who themselves are also elected by representatives of functional constituencies in the Legislative Council. The successful candidate must then be confirmed by the national government in Beijing.
3. The Legislative Council is composed of members who are democratically elected from residential/population-based electorates across Hong Kong, as well as members elected from functional constituencies that represent the interests of business, industry, and education. Some, although not all, people in Hong Kong have two votes—one for their residential electorate and the other for their functional constituency, if their occupation happens to be so represented.
4. The extent to which government agencies come under the provisions of the antidiscrimination bill is not clear. For example, Peterson (2007) commented that "Clause 3 of the RDB [Racial Discrimination Bill] . . . provides for very limited application of the bill to governmental acts and policies (far more limited than provided in the SDO and DDO). As drafted, the RDB only applies to government acts that are similar in nature to acts by private persons, such as when the government is an employer. The RDB does not bind the government in its truly 'governmental' responsibilities, such as policing, correctional services, taxation, licensing, and most regulatory responsibilities" (p. 3). If educational provision falls into the category of "governmental responsibilities," then it seems that the EDB will not be liable for discriminatory practices as long as it is exercising its role as a government agency. However, this can only be tested in law.

REFERENCES

Ang, C. (2007). Political legitimacy in Myanmar: The ethnic minority dimension. *Asian Security*, 3(2), 121–140.

Banks, J. (1986). Multicultural education: Development, paradigms and goals. In J. Banks & J. Lynch (Eds.), *Multicultural education in Western societies* (pp. 2–28). New York: Praeger.

Bell-Fialkoff, A. (1999). *Ethnic cleansing*. New York: St Martin's Press.

Bokhorst-Heng, W. (2007). Multiculturalism's narratives in Singapore and Canada: Exploring a model for comparative multiculturalism and multicultural education. *Journal of Curriculum Studies*, 36(9), 629–658.

Census and Statistics Department. (2007, December 28). *2006 Population by-census. Thematic report: Ethnic minorities*. Retrieved from http://www.censtatd.gov.hk/freedownload.jsp?file=publication/stat_report/population/B11200502006XXXXB0100.pdf&title=Hong+Kong+2006+Population+By cens us+Thematic+Report+%3a+Ethnic+Minorities&issue=-&lang=1&c=1 19 February 2011.

Chan, J. (2001). *Making sense of Confucian justice*. Retrieved from http://them.polylog.org/3/fcj-en.htm 19 February 2011.

Chui, C., & Hong, Y. (1997). Justice in Chinese societies. In H. Kao & D. Sinha (Eds.), *Asian perspectives on psychology* (pp. 165–184). Thousand Oaks, CA: Sage.

Chwaszcza, C. (2008). Beyond cosmopolitanism: Towards a non-ideal account of transnational justice. *Ethics & Global Politics, 1*(3), 115–138.

Clem, W. (2008, January 26). Minorities allege indirect racism in language row. *South China Morning Post*, p. EDU1.

Cullen, R. (2005). *Protecting and advancing the rule of law in Hong Kong*. Retrieved from http://www.civic-exchange.org/eng/upload/fi les/200511_RuleofLaw.pdf 19 February 2011.

Curriculum Development Council. (2008). Supplementary guide to the Chinese language curriculum for non-Chinese speaking students. Retrieved from http://www.edb.gov.hk/index.aspx?nodeID=7261&langno=1 19 February 2011.

Edmonds, R. (1979). Effective schools for the urban poor. *Educational Leadership, 37*(1), 15–27.

Education and Manpower Bureau. (2004a). *Full-time initiation programme for newly arrived children*. Retrieved from http://www.edb.gov.hk/index.aspx?nodeid=635&langno=1 19 February 2011.

Education and Manpower Bureau. (2004b). *Induction programme for newly arrived children*. Retrieved from http://www.edb.gov.hk/index.aspx?nodeid=634&langno=1 19 February 2011.

Education and Manpower Bureau. (2007). EMB attaches importance to providing education support for ethnic minorities. Retrieved from http://www.edb.gov.hk/index.aspx?nodeID=5845&langno=1 19 February 2011.

Fan, R. (2003). Social justice: Rawlsian or Confucian . In B. Mou (Ed.), *Comparative approaches to Chinese philosophy* (pp. 144–168). Aldershot, UK: Ashgate.

Gilborn, D. (2004). Antiracism: From policy to praxis. In G. Ladson Billings & D. Gilborn (Eds.), *The RoutledgeFalmer reader in multicultural education* (pp. 35–48). New York: RoutledgeFalmer.

Gladney, D. (2005). Relational identity and ethnic conflict resolution. In M. Intriligator, A. Nikitin, & M. Tehranian (Eds.), *Eurasia: A new peace agenda* (pp. 209–228). Amsterdam: Elsevier.

Hernard, K. (2000). *Devising an adequate system of minority protection: Individual human rights, minority rights, and the right to self-determination*. Leiden, Netherlands: Martinus Nijhoff.

Hills, M. (1994, May). *The rule of law and democracy in Hong Kong—Comparative analysis of British liberalism and Chinese socialism. Murdoch University Electronic Journal of Law, 1*(2). Retrieved from http://www.murdoch.edu.au/elaw/issues/v1n2/hills12.html 19 February 2011.

Home Affairs Bureau. (2004). *Legislating against racial discrimination—A consultation paper*. Retrieved from http://www.info.gov.hk/archive/consult/2005/lard-e.pdf 19 February 2011.

Home Affairs Bureau. (2006). *Race Discrimination Bill*. Retrieved from http://www.hkhrm.org.hk/racial%20discrimination/database/eng/RaceDiscriminationBill_e.pdf 19 February 2011.

Hue, M. (2008). The influence of Confucianism: A narrative study of Hong Kong teachers' understanding and practices of school guidance and counselling. *British Journal of Guidance & Counselling, 36*(3), 303–316.

International Crisis Group. (2003, May 7). *Myanmar backgrounder: Ethnic minority politics Asia Report No. 52*. Retrieved from http://www.crisisgroup.org/en/regions/asia/south-east-asia/burma-myanmar/052-myanmar-backgrounder-ethnic-minority-politics.aspx 19 February 2011.

Joppke, C. (2004). Ethnic diversity and the state. *British Journal of Sociology , 55*(3), 451–463.

King, A. (1996). The transformation of Confucianism in the post-Confucianism era: The emergence of rationalistc traditionalism in Hong Kong. In W. M. Tu (Ed.), *Confucian traditions in East Asian modernity: Moral education and economic culture in Japan and the four mini-dragons* (pp. 265–276). Cambridge, MA: Harvard University Press.

Ku, H. B., Chan, K. W., & Sandhu, K. K. (2005). *A research report on the education of South Asian ethnic minority groups in Hong Kong.* Hong Kong: Center for Social Policy Studies, Department of Applied Social Sciences, Hong Kong Polytechnic University.

Kymlicka, W. (1995). *Multicultural citizenship: A liberal theory of minority rights.* Oxford, UK: Oxford University Press.

Kymlicka, W. (2007). *Multicultural odysseys: Navigating the new international politics of diversity.* Oxford, UK: Oxford University Press.

Kymlicka, W., & He, B. (Eds.). (2005). Multiculturalism in Asia. Oxford, UK: Oxford University Press.

Legislative Council. (2006a). *Hong Kong Christian Service to Chairman of Education Panel, 9 October 2006. Opinion on designated schools for non-Chinese speaking (NCS) students* (LC Paper No. CB(2)77/06–07(01)). Retrieved from http://www.legco.hk/yr06–07/english/panels/ed/papers/edcb2–77–1-e.pdf 19 February, 2011.

Legislative Council. (2006b). *Education Bureau to Legislative Council Secretariat. 1 November 2006. Panel on Education-Designated Schools for Non-Chinese Speaking Students* (LC Paper No. CB (2)260/06–07(01)). Retrieved from http://www.legco.gov.hk/yr06–07/english/panels/ed/papers/ed1113cb2–260–1-e.pdf 19 February 2011.

Legislative Council. (2006c). *Race Discrimination Bill* (Briefing Paper No. HAB/CR/1/19/102). Retrieved from http://www.legco.gov.hk/yr06-07/english/bills/brief/b12_brf.pdf 19 February 2011.

Legislative Council. (2007, January 8). *Background brief prepared by the Legislative Council Secretariat—Provision of an alternative Chinese language curriculum for non-Chinese speaking students.* Retrieved from http://www.legco.hk/yr0607/english/panels/ed/papers/ed0108cb2–757–3-e.pdf 19 February 2011.

Liu, S. (1996). Confucian ideals and the real world: A critical review of neo-Confucian thought. In W. M. Tu (Ed.), *Confucian traditions in East Asian modernity: Moral education and economic culture in Japan and the four mini-dragons* (pp. 92–117). Cambridge, MA: Harvard University Press.

Macklem, P. (2008). *Minority rights in international law.* Retrieved from http://papers.ssrn.com/sol3/papers.cfm?abstract_id=1262967 19 February 2011.

McCarthy, S. (2009). *Communist multiculturalism: Ethnic revival in Southwest China.* Seattle: University of Washington Press.

Peonidis, F. (2008). *Multiculturalism and liberal democracy—Four questions to Will Kymlicka.* Retrieved from http://www.eurozine.com/articles/2008–07–25-kymlicka-en.html 19 February 2011.

Peterson, C. (2007, June). *Hong Kong's Race Discrimination Bill—A critique and comparison with the sex discrimination and disability discrimination ordinances.* Retrieved from http://www.hku.hk/ccpl/pub/conferences/documents/Paper-CarolePetersen-rev19June.pdf 19 February 2011.

Saravanamuttu, J. (2005). Multiculturalism in crisis: Liberal-conformity, Asian values or unforced conformity? In M. N. Intriligator, A. Nikitin, & M. Tehranian (Eds.), *Eurasia: A new peace agenda* (pp. 195–208). Amsterdam: Elsevier.

Skerrett A., & Hargreaves, A. (2008). Student diversity and secondary school change in a context of increasingly standardized reform. *American Educational Research Journal, 45*(4), 913–945.

Troyna, B., & Carrington, B. (1990). *Education, racism, and reform*. London: Routledge.

Tsang, S. (2001). *Judicial independence and the rule of law in Hong Kong*. Hong Kong: Hong Kong University Press.

van der Walle, D., & Gunewardena, D. (2000). *Sources of ethnic inequality to redress ethnic inequality in Vietnam* (Policy Research Working Paper No. 2297). Retrieved from http://www-wds.worldbank.org/external/default/WDS-ContentServer/IW3P/IB/2000/04/24/000094946_00040605325051/Rendered/PDF/multi_page.pdf 19 February 2011.

Yung, B. (2007). An interplay between Western and Confucian concepts of justice: Development of Hong Kong housing policy. *Housing, Theory, and Society, 24*(2), 111–132.

11 Cross-Boundary Students in Hong Kong Schools

Education Provisions and School Experiences

Celeste Y. M. Yuen

INTRODUCTION

In the last five years, the number of cross-boundary students (CBSs) from mainland China in Hong Kong has rapidly grown. In some cases, the cross-boundary schooling of CBSs only last for short periods following the decision of their families to move to Hong Kong or the success of their mainland mothers in obtaining visas to live in Hong Kong. This student group often faces the transitional challenge of forming new social networks, and they experience identity and acculturation problems as they move to new schools (Yuen, 2004a). Very few schools have established services to help these students cope with their transitional needs (i.e., adjusting to new schools and new environments). Their transitional needs, which are closely linked to their disadvantaged social and family backgrounds, are thus often unmet. To compound this problem, research on their social and cultural needs in the context of Hong Kong schooling is scarce.

The 1997 handover of Hong Kong to China, along with the "one country, two systems" rule, has accelerated the socioeconomic and physical inter-regional development between Hong Kong and Shenzhen. These two Chinese cities are at either side of the Shenzhen River; they are bridged by the Lo Wu immigration control point—the major land boundary control point. With the opening of southern cities along the boundary between the mainland and Hong Kong, and with excellent rail and road services, Lo Wu control point is expected to receive 90,000 and 120,000 vehicles by 2011 and 2016, respectively. Apart from promoting socioeconomic activities, these close boundary links also promote intercultural courtships and marriages between mainland Chinese and Hongkongers. Most Hongkongese men stay in the mainland primarily for employment opportunities and family affairs (So, 2003), and children born to these intercultural families raise many issues. Hence, in the last decade, Hong Kong was embroiled in debates over the status of mainland Chinese citizens in the city. However, now that the legal issues have been settled, the challenge begins. The mutation of the demographic structure of Hong Kong has many policy implications, especially in the provision of appropriate housing, employment opportunities, and assistance for immigrant families. The educational provision for immigrant children is another key area to be investigated because it represents a unique social phenomenon in Hong Kong.

CROSS-BOUNDARY STUDENTS

According to the latest statistics, the number of CBSs from China has increased by 68% over the past six years—from 3,490 in 2001–2002 to 6,768 in 2008–2009, with 1,780 pre-primary, 3,910 primary, and 1,078 secondary students in Hong Kong schools (Hong Kong Special Administrative Region Government, 2009) (Table 11.1). The needs of CBSs are quite different from those of newly arrived students (NASs) from mainland China, and these needs are even more different from those of Hong Kong–born students (HKBSs). However, because they are all ethnic Han Chinese, they are often treated in the same way (Yuen, 2008). Literally, CBSs live between two cultures, and they have to make frequent psychological adjustments to Hong Kong/mainland cultural differences every school day. Their bicultural identities are barriers that may potentially prevent them from identifying with either mainland or Hong Kong societies (Yuen, 2008). They have to sacrifice quality extracurricular time to commute to and from school (Wong, 2001). Often, their home environments are also found to be unfavorable to academic learning. Parents are largely unfamiliar with the Hong Kong educational system, and they often fall short of school expectations, especially in terms of homework supervision and in assisting their children's learning (Yuen, 2002a + b, 2004b, 2005).

POLICY CONTEXT

As previously indicated, the educational system does not agree that CBSs should be given any special attention because the system views them as

Table 11.1 Number of Cross-boundary Students (2004–2009)

School Year	Kindergarten	Primar School	Secondary School	Total (increase/decrease)
2004–2005	733	2,589	481	3083
2005–2006	962	2,998	538	4498 (+18.3%)
2006–2007	797	2,878	799	4474 (-0.5%)
2007–2008	1456	3,466	937	5859 (+31%)
2008–2009	1780	3,910	1078	6768 (+15.5%)

Sources: Hong Kong Special Administrative Government, 2008.

members of the "ordinary" Hong Kong school community. Aside from long travel time, another major educational challenge is the establishment of fixed school bus schedules, which also means high travel costs and less school time for learning and socialization (Yuen, 2004a). The families of CBSs are mainly distributed in the southern border towns of mainland China, such as Shenzhen and Sha Tau Kok. For a single school journey, most CBSs have to travel first to Lo Wu immigration control point and, after having their permits checked, they need to transfer to Hong Kong school buses.

Public concerns have been concentrated on logistical issues, such as travel subsidies for CBSs and security in crossing boundary control points (Christian Action, 2007). Hence, coordination between Hong Kong and Shenzhen on matters of transport and immigration is critical in facilitating CBS schooling. In 2008, in response to the aforementioned concerns, the Hong Kong government took several measures. For example, it issued 20 special quotas for service providers to operate cross-boundary school buses and to provide parents with more choices that match their own needs (*Sing Tao Daily*, 2008). In terms of pastoral care, schools may flexibly arrange counseling services and after-school activities in after-lunch or recess time slots (Hong Kong Special Administrative Region Government, 2008). In addition, education authorities in Shenzhen and Hong Kong have agreed on a trial-run cooperation that allows Hong Kong children who are studying in two Hong Kong–style primary schools in Shenzhen to join Hong Kong's Secondary 1 allocation system in 2010 (*Takungpao*, 2008). These measures are breakthroughs in inter-regional educational collaboration. However, the service gap in bridging intercultural family and school collaboration remains because Hong Kong social workers cannot provide necessary services to mainland residents.

Today, more secondary schools are admitting CBSs. However, the largest proportion of CBSs is under the age of 10, and they are clustered in kindergarten to junior primary school levels. Given their age and the concerns raised above, the role of the family-school-community cooperation becomes relatively more important. The biggest obstacle in home–school collaboration is the lack of effective communication channels. A majority of CBS mothers cannot commute to Hong Kong daily because of visa restrictions and costly transportation fees; hence, with their limited knowledge of Hong Kong's school system, they normally play only a very passive role in their children's education (Hong Kong Commercial Press, 2007).

As far as supporting the educational needs of CBSs is concerned, there are no official policy guides for schools receiving CBSs (Hong Kong Social Service Federation, 2006). At the pre-primary level, CBSs may be enrolled by their parents under the voucher scheme so they can pay for their children's fees in Hong Kong. At primary and secondary levels, for every CBS in his or her first year of Hong Kong schooling, his or her school may apply for and flexibly use the School-Based Support Grant to provide the student with necessary learning support, such as supplementary English language classes. Effective September 2008, the grant is HK$2,830 per child at the primary level and HK$4,198 at the secondary level (Education Bureau, 2009).

PRACTICAL CONTEXT

Teaching students with diverse cultural backgrounds has never been highly emphasized in the educational agenda of teachers. The one-size-for-all pedagogical practice is very common in schools with immigrant students, regardless of their ethnicity (Phillion, 2008; Yuen, 2002, 2004; Yuen & Grossman, 2009). Hence, in Hong Kong, NASs and South Asian students face difficulties in their academic, social, and psychoemotional adjustments. Every school that admits immigrant students is entitled to a subsidy of HK$2,720 per student at the primary level and HK$4,035 per student at the secondary level. However, in line with the school-based management initiative, the Education Bureau has adopted a laissez-faire nonintervention policy regarding the response of schools to the education of immigrant students. Under such policy and practice, some immigrants have obtained outstanding academic performance and have made the headlines of newspapers; however, many have failed to manage the challenges.

LITERATURE REVIEW

In Hong Kong schools, teachers provide inappropriate and inadequate curriculum and instruction that caters to individual differences (Lee & Yuen, 2003; Yuen 2002, 2003a, 2003b). There is no doubt that educating diverse learners has created additional stress for Hong Kong teachers. Most teachers are trained in a predominantly monocultural program, and they largely undergo monocultural socialization; hence, they are either insufficiently prepared for, or are lacking in, personal intercultural awareness to foster appropriate classroom environments and to practice high pedagogical standards necessary in the promotion of effective learning.

Academic achievement is the predominant focus of schooling, especially in Chinese societies, such as Hong Kong, Taiwan, Singapore, and mainland China. Research indicates that minority students are disproportionately represented at the two ends of the achievement spectrum (National Research Council, 2002). Research also shows that academic achievement is influenced by the home context of children, including the educational levels, occupations, income, and social networks of their parents (Rumbaut, 2000).

Geographically, most CBS families reside in mainland border towns along the Shenzhen River. Most CBSs typically come from disadvantaged low-income families, and usually, their Hong Kong fathers are employed in semi-skilled or low-skilled jobs while their mainland mothers are engaged in full-time housework (Lo, 2006; Yuen, 2004b, 2005). These families have little social capital, and father absence is always a matter of concern among them. Mainland mothers normally stop working after bearing children, and they have to shoulder the home management responsibilities of their husbands. They usually have higher expectations for, and are more involved in, their children's education than their husbands (Yuen, 2005).

With the education voucher policy and the newly opened West Corridor, the number of CBSs is expected to soar in the coming years. About 80% of CBSs are under the age of 10, and they are clustered in kindergarten to junior primary school levels. The role of the family-school-community cooperation thus becomes important, especially in homework supervision. The biggest obstacle to home–school collaboration is the very passive role that most CBS mothers play in their children's education (Hong Kong Commercial Press, 2007). In addition, there is little knowledge of the social and cultural needs of CBSs in the context of Hong Kong schooling. The involvement of mainland mothers in their children's education is a determining factor that affects the successful academic achievement of CBSs. Furthermore, many CBSs have diverse learning needs, and they do not receive much support from their schools and families.

In a culturally diverse environment, the role of friendship among children is crucial in understanding their behaviors and their coping responses to new educational systems. Children with positive friendships and peer acceptance tend to have better self-control and school adjustment outcomes (Betts & Rotenberg, 2007), and friendship experiences and school adjustment are closely linked (Kutnick & Kington, 2005). Among children, peer acceptance is particularly important in preventing negative socioemotional outcomes, such as loneliness and depression (Erdley, Nangle, Newman, & Carpenter, 2001). Several Hong Kong studies concluded that friendship is critical for new arrival adolescents; it helps them build social identity, and it increases their physical and psychological proximity with their Hong Kong counterparts (Yuen, 2008, 2010). To many CBSs, the school is not simply the first place to learn about Hong Kong, it is also the only avenue for them to establish new friendships. Hence, how young CBSs feel about their friendship experiences in Hong Kong schools is worth studying.

Deegan (1996) argued that sociometry is an important instrument in studying young children's social choices. The picture-sociometric technique has been widely employed in studies related to immigrant children who encounter difficulties in understanding verbal protocols.

The literature on the curricular and social experiences of CBSs in Hong Kong is limited. Previous studies were conducted primarily from the perspectives of teachers and policies, and student voices were almost neglected; moreover, these studies mainly focused on mainland immigrant students (Bauhinia Foundation Research Center, 2009; Yuen, 2004). This study builds on the extant literature and widens the research focus to the major curricular and social experiences of target students from their own perspectives. It hopes to contribute to research efforts on CBSs in Hong Kong and to spark further research and discussions on the situation of these students. This study also hopes to see whether student views on their schools and families are likely to be ignored.

METHODS

A case study approach was employed to compare the different curricular and social experiences of target students from their own perspectives. The case study method is a narrative approach that explores new meanings of phenomena (Ford, 1998). The relational and experiential aspects of a narrative approach open a window for viewing personal experiences in societies and schools (Hoffman, 1989). Phillion (2002) found that a narrative approach provides studies with insider views regarding the language, culture, and identity of immigrant students. Data were collected through field-based observations and interviews with target informants. Based on naturalistic observation, student behaviors were tracked, and the nature and occurrence of their responses to a range of situations were categorized. More importantly, studying the school experiences of students responds to our research questions because it provides fluid descriptions of their main academic and social concerns, including interactions between their home and school cultures.

RESEARCH QUESTIONS

Specifically, this study aims to answer the following questions:

1. What are the major school-based educational provisions for CBSs?
2. What are the major curricular experiences of CBSs?
3. What are their social/friendship experiences?

This study adopted a systematic observation method, which involved student tracking and interviews. Student tracking helped build a detailed inventory of the behavior of target students. Formal parental consent was first obtained before the tracking. The field research involved case studies on the school experiences (both curricular and social aspects) of nine students from three schools with significant numbers of CBSs. All three schools are located in the boundary towns of Hong Kong. Two of them have large CBS populations (>60 %) and one has a small CBS population (<30%). Three students were selected from each school. Of these three students, one has been with the school for less than a year, one for two years, and one for at least three years.

Prior to data collection, a preparatory school visit was conducted to explain the nature of the research to participating schools. In addition to the pre- and post-fieldwork visits, the actual data collection involved four days in each school. The two-day tracking (Days 2 and 3) helped minimize student reactivity and self-correction in providing data. Day 4 involved follow-up interviews to clarify questions and observations related to the tracking. To study the academic and social experiences of target students, cliques were detected by sociometry. In culturally diverse classrooms, young children's friendship choices are linked with their academic achievements, and sociometry is an important instrument in studying these social choices (Deegan, 1996). In addition, the picture-sociometric technique is widely used for immigrant children who may have difficulties in understanding verbal protocols. Sociometric data also help satisfy research questions on social/friendship experiences.

THE STUDY

This case study tackles the school experiences of nine students from three primary schools with significant CBS populations. It aims to examine the school experiences of CBSs in Hong Kong from the perspective of students. Specifically, the study aims to find out their curricular and social experiences in schools, as well as their coping strategies in adapting to Hong Kong schooling.

FINDINGS

The study produced interesting results. The CBSs are principally enrolled in schools in the northern New Territories. The age range of the nine students included in this research is 7 to 11 years old. Five were born in mainland China and four in Hong Kong. Among them, four are males and five are females. Eight attended pre-primary schools in Hong Kong. The majority of their mainland mothers (seven) are not engaged in full-time work. These students spend an average of 1.5 hours a day traveling to and from their schools.

School-Based Provisions

Regarding school-based policies and provisions for CBSs, the school with the highest CBS enrollment (>90%), STK School, operates an after-school support scheme, which aims to provide extra homework to help CBSs. According to the principal, "a lot of CBSs are actually from families receiving full grants from the Textbook Assistance Scheme and Comprehensive Social Security Assistance." To cater for the perceived needs of CBSs, the school offers a range of activities for them and their families, such as free English classes for parents, parental education seminars, and homework assistance workshops. To cut travel time and expenses, most of the activities are held in the mainland, thereby encouraging parental participation.

In terms of the curriculum design, extra efforts are exerted only in terms of the English language. According to one teacher, because CBSs have relatively lower levels of English proficiency, they try to reduce the amount and the level of difficulty of homework; they also focus on basic concepts. Peer tutoring and study groups are also arranged to boost the English proficiency of low performers. Teachers "ask students with higher abilities to assist one or two classmates with lower performance. Classroom seating is arranged to this effect." When it comes to learning complex Chinese characters, teachers "give them a grace period without deducting marks for wrong Chinese writing." The school arranges many outdoor activities and trips for CBSs to get to know Hong Kong better. Furthermore, they "encourage [CBSs] to subscribe to newspapers from Primary 4 so that [they] can bring them home and acquire more information about Hong Kong." All of these measures are direct responses to the transitional educational needs of CBSs.

In the second school, YY School, more than 60% of the students are CBSs. In the last few years, the school has actively recruited CBSs to fill up the admission gap. According to the principal, they "are very sensitive to the needs of parents; for example, [they] have been holding regular parents' meetings in Shenzhen." Similar to STK, learning English is the biggest challenge for CBSs at YY. The school offers after-school and Saturday English programs for CBSs. In addition, the school has a policy to help all students complete their homework during the last period of each school day. Additional learning support for homework and complex Chinese characters are also provided. With school-based support grants, YY School has organized a range of special visits to famous Hong Kong landmarks for CBSs and their families. For instance, the school has already "[brought] them to the Peak, Bauhinia Square, Space Museum, and Science Museum." Teachers arrange one-day trips around Hong Kong; hence, "children's getting to know Hong Kong is mainly through schools." Through these trips, CBSs have seen the newest theme park, Noah's Ark, in Ma Wan.

English teachers at YY School also arrange outings for CBSs, giving them opportunities to practice simple conversational English with English-speaking tourists. As far as the school curriculum is concerned, the English teacher "gives them easier assignments and designs worksheets that are relatively simpler to increase their confidence in English." However, according to the Chinese teacher:

> There are more and more CBSs in our school. I can't see any difference between CBSs and HKBSs. I use the same method to teach them. Some of them are very motivated to learn. They are especially active

in Putonghua lessons. But the new CBSs admitted to Primary 1 are more misbehaved. They swear, although the situation has [already] been improved.

The general studies teacher shares the same view: "In terms of learning needs, all students are the same, not much different. But the CBSs would swear. I guess that's because of family background and upbringing."

The third school, CW School, is much larger in terms of student population than STK and YY schools. This school is regarded as a performing school in the local district. Many CBS parents aspire to enroll their children in this school because of its good reputation. Attaining good academic results is the top priority of CW School. In this school, teachers tend to downplay differences between the learning needs of CBSs and HKBSs. Interviews with teachers prove this observation:

Mathematics teacher: I personally don't see any differences between CBSs and HKBSs. I treat them the same.
English teacher: I would think that family support is the only difference. Most CBS parents cannot offer help in their [children's] English homework.
Chinese teacher: Most CBSs are good at Chinese. Some of them are even better than HKBS, especially in speaking Putonghua.

The school gives CBSs a grace period (one term) for adjustment, mainly for switching from simplified Chinese characters to complex Chinese characters. According to the principal, their school accepts the differences between these two groups of students, but they hope that CBSs will be able to adapt to the school system:

> We usually give them half a year to adjust; if they write simplified Chinese, we will circle the script without deducting [from] scores. Teachers remind CBSs to write complex Chinese characters. But we [are not] too strict in Chinese dictation either. After half a year, we set the same requirements as those for local students.

Apart from this, there are no other specific support measures given to CBSs. The school only provides limited support to CBSs compared with the two other schools, and the school has not adopted any special policy for the education of CBSs.

Curricular Experiences

Despite some studies showing that CBSs have to face many challenges in Hong Kong schools, findings from both student interviews and student tracking reveal that most CBSs have adjusted well to their school lives. In both STK and YY, where relatively high concentrations of CBSs are found, teachers are generally friendlier and more supportive compared to teachers at CW. The six CBSs in the first two schools (i.e., STK and YY) have not shown any signs of reservations in classroom participation. On the contrary, four of them were appointed class prefects. Among other things, they often offer solutions to questions and assist teachers in helping other classmates who have poor learning abilities. They are academically confident. Among these four active and outstanding CBSs, one enjoys the privilege of being both class representative and head boy at STK. The principal and teachers have proudly introduced him to the researcher, referring to him as a well-rounded CBS. The boy is in his final year of primary schooling, and he has been with the school for more than three years. Another outstanding girl has stayed at YY for three years. She is regarded as a model student by her teachers and as a good girl by her parents. She is very comfortable with her learning and with her fellow classmates, regardless of their places of origin. Many CBSs have problems in comprehending English and in writing complex Chinese characters, among others; however, subject to individual learning abilities, these problems are also shared by their Hong Kong counterparts. Below highlights the key themes of the school experiences of CBSs.

Formal Curriculum—Subject Learning

Nearly all the CBSs have expressed that Chinese and mathematics are generally simpler and more manageable compared with English. Only Jim who is in his first year of Hong Kong schooling hates Chinese because complex Chinese characters are difficult to master. Based on the interviews, English is the most challenging subject for CBSs, especially during their first year of schooling when they have little knowledge of the English language.

Difficult Subjects

Three male CBSs, Jim, Lee, and Szeto, claim that English is a difficult subject. Szeto claims that English is the most difficult (although his lowest score is 70+) because his mother does not teach him the subject, and "she [Szeto's mother] doesn't know any English at all." One student asserts that English is difficult because of spelling. Learning new vocabulary is also considered difficult. It is worth noting that these three CBSs, who are claiming that English is a difficult subject, are all in their first year of schooling in Hong Kong. They attended mainland kindergartens in Shenzhen, and they have little readiness to learn English.

Favorite Subjects in School

Liking school subjects seems to be a personal rather than a collective choice. Although some boys (Jim and Lee) consider English a difficult subject, two girls (Lai and Chan) indicate that English is actually their favorite subject. Lai claims that "learning English is fun," and Chan asserts that she "scored high in English dictation as she worked hard for it." Three boys (Yau, Jim, and Lee) like physical education the most because they enjoy sports and exercises. Two other boys (Yau and Szeto) like computer, and one girl (Lam) has music as her favorite subject.

Least Favorite Subjects in School

Interestingly, while the nine CBSs are very sure about their favorite subjects, four of them do not have any least favorite subject in school. Chan is alone in pointing out that Chinese is her least favorite subject because "the complex Chinese characters are really hard. [She does not] know a lot of words." Two boys (Jim and Lee) say that mathematics is their least favorite subject. Jim claims that when he was in kindergarten, his math teacher would always punish them physically regardless of their ages, and "there was dictation in mathematics class. If [they] got good scores in dictation, [they will] get some rewards." Learning for rewards has become the primary aim of most students and their parents.

Formal Curriculum—Language Adaptation

In terms of mastering spoken Cantonese, the common dialect in Hong Kong, all of the nine CBSs do not seem to encounter many problems. However, Jim, Chan, and Cheung still struggle with complex Chinese characters, and the rest report that they needed time to adjust during their first semesters in school. In fact, Jim has fears in writing Chinese characters, and he often gets them wrong. Chan is left-handed; hence, she also struggles with Chinese writing. The three schools use Putonghua (the official Chinese language) to teach Chinese; hence, most CBSs outperform their Hong Kong counterparts in this subject.

Language Used in School and Family Communication

The findings show that spoken Cantonese is not a barrier to the academic learning of CBSs, except that some still have mainland accents and some still prefer to use their dialects in personal conversations. Szeto, Chan, Lai, and Jim speak Mandarin/dialects at home. Nevertheless, six of the students prefer Cantonese to Mandarin/dialects because they are most familiar with the language. For family communication, four of the nine CBSs use Putonghua or their regional dialects; the other three use Cantonese. Meanwhile, the majority of CBSs claim that Cantonese, Mandarin, and other dialects are sometimes used in family communication, but in general, Cantonese is used. According to the interviewed parents, their children use the local dialect in family conversations, but their children can also use Cantonese in school or outside the house.

Adaptation to Complex Chinese Characters

According to the findings, CBSs can easily adapt to complex Chinese characters. Very few students find the characters as obstacles to their studies. Only two CBSs have asserted that they experience difficulties with complex Chinese characters. For CBSs, these difficulties mostly appear during the first few years of Hong Kong schooling. As they move to higher forms, they become more accustomed to complex Chinese characters. It is worth noting that schools generally allow CBSs a transition/grace period for adaptation. During the period, no demerits are given when simplified characters are used in homework or exams. Based on the foregoing findings, there seems to be a personal issue, instead of an ability issue, in considering which subjects are more welcomed by CBSs.

Informal Curriculum—Teachers and School Environments

In general, CBSs view teachers positively, thinking that they are very friendly, kind, patient, and helpful. For example, Yau, Lai, Szeto, Lam, and Chan are very pleased with their good relationships with teachers. They cannot recall unpleasant experiences, except Chan, who claims that the spaces between school tables are too narrow. Interestingly, they tend to like all teachers, and they have no least favorite teachers. Their favorite teachers are usually the ones who teach their favorite subjects.

Although both STK and YY schools are relatively small and are located in the suburbs, most CBSs like their school environments very much. They associate their pleasant experiences with the activities they have in school (e.g., sports and playing computer games in the cases of Lee, Yau, and Jim).

Informal Curriculum—Extracurricular Activities

Generally, CBSs have rigid daily timetables for traveling to and from their schools; hence, the majority of CBSs are unable to take part in extracurricular activities in schools. In interviews, most CBSs do not give details of their extracurricular activities in school. However, their parents arrange various activities in mainland China. These CBSs participate in extracurricular activities with neighboring classmates/friends. Parents describe the extracurricular activities of their daughters:

Lai's parent: She sometimes goes to classmates' homes to play.
Ng's parent: If she doesn't go to study these things, she would be very bored
and have no one to play with. Taking part in these activities

means she chats with friends of around the same age. On Saturdays, she learns dancing and piano.

Yau, Szeto, and Cheung engage in activities with those outside their circles of classmates/friends. Their parents reveal the following: "after school, he plays Ping-Pong and does sports"; "on Sundays we take him to play Ping-Pong"; "she loves to paint (watercolors)"; and "I would like her to learn something else but there isn't time."

Informal Curriculum—English Tuition

Generally, CBSs are new to the Hong Kong educational system; hence, in one way or another, they experience difficulties in learning English and in adjusting to the school system. Schools have arranged remedial classes and after-school free English classes to help CBSs with their English learning. Parents also arrange English tuition for their children.

After-School Remedial Classes

The three schools in this study provide remedial English classes to support students with unsatisfactory academic performance. One school provides remedial classes for CBSs from 3:30 PM to about 5:00 PM. The school invites those from the Hong Kong Institute of Education to help with the students' homework and review lessons.

Additional After-School Free English Classes Catering to Primary 1 CBSs

Free English classes are provided to help CBSs, and this kind of support is conducted throughout the entire school year. The participants are placed in two different classes according to their academic needs, and they receive weekly one-hour after-class lessons. One school provides English tutorial classes from Mondays to Thursdays (one hour per session), and most of the participants are Primary 1 and Primary 2 students (about 50 of them). The school employs a retired English teacher to coach the students.

English Tuition Arranged by Parents

Aside from the free English classes being provided by schools, four CBS parents mention that they arrange private English tuition to help their children learn English.

Lai's parent: I can't help with her English; I hired an English teacher to teach her on a one-on-one basis once a week.

Chan's parent: [There] is no progress made, even with private English tuition.

Cheung's parent: She goes to private tuition class every Monday to Friday evening. The main focus is on English.

Szeto's parent: He has private English tuition classes.

Social Experiences

In the whole process of acculturation, friendship is a mediating factor in one's identity development. The nine CBSs in this study have adjusted well to their school lives. Most of them think they get along well with all kinds of Hong Kong students (whether HKBS or not). Only a few of them have unpleasant experiences in schools.

The nine CBSs are actively involved in school activities, both within and outside their classrooms. Yau, Lai, and Jim are more socially active than Ng, Chan, and Lee in school. Yau, Szeto, and Lai are more attentive and active in learning than the rest, and they outperform their classmates. They are happy, and they have adapted well to their school lives. Those who are in their second (Chan, Ng, and Cheung) and third years (Yau, Lai, and Lam) of Hong Kong schooling are more competent in their social interaction with peers than those in their first year of schooling. This seems to echo previous studies (e.g., Erdley et al., 2001) stating that friendship experiences are closely linked with psychological adjustment and confidence.

Only Chan and Jim complain that it is difficult to get along with some of their classmates. Most CBSs have very positive pictures of friendship building in schools. The following remarks characterize the social experiences of CBSs in schools: "He treats me things to eat, and I reciprocate"; "A few days after school started, she took the initiative to come over and make friends with me . . . it was the same with Zhang Jiamin"; "They often skip rope with me"; "I have a lot [of good friends], for example . . . [one of them] is in my class and lives in the same building"; "She helps me with my homework, and I help her with hers"; "[We play together] 'hawks and chickens' and 'traffic lights'"; "We play badminton, hide and seek, and tag"; "[I like playing with them] because they play with me every day"; and "[I play] 'cat and mouse' and sometimes go for walks [with my friends]."

DISCUSSION

In terms of school-based policies and the provision of support for CBSs, the three schools mainly provide free and extra remedial lessons in English and complex Chinese characters, especially for students in their first year of schooling. The delivery of English learning opportunities seems to be one of the most common provisions for immigrant or ethnic minority students by host societies (Equality Unit, Department of Education, UK, n.d.). However, whether the acquisition of English skills is tantamount to a big step in new immigrant societies needs to be studied further. Some immigrants have special learning needs, which extra English tuition may not sufficiently address. For example, Jim lags far behind in his class. He often fails in English dictation. In addition, he receives few points in his Chinese homework assignments. Although his mother is keen to provide extra help to encourage him to work harder in his homework, he does not seem bothered. Clearly there is a gap to be filled in addressing the learning struggles of ethnic students.

All of the studied CBSs are fluent in both Cantonese and Putonghua, although some teachers mention that younger students may initially find Cantonese a problem. Nevertheless, it is very common for these CBSs to speak Mandarin/dialects at home, especially when they communicate with their mothers. Five of them prefer Cantonese to Mandarin/dialects. In fact, being the medium of communication in Hong Kong, Cantonese is also very popular among Chinese populations in southern China (e.g., Shenzhen). This is an advantage for them in establishing social circles in Hong Kong schools.

Generally, the curricular experiences of the nine CBSs are positive and encouraging. Among the nine CBSs, Yau, Lai, and Cheung have been with the educational system for at least three years. They not only outperform most HKBSs but they also are very optimistic about their academic learning. All of them have been with their schools for more than three years, and they show no problems in learning English or in writing complex Chinese characters. They have successfully assimilated into the school system (Yuen, 2008). They have established good social networks, although most of their best friends are also CBSs. This confirms that friendship is a key factor in school adjustment (Betts & Rotenberg, 2007; Kutnick & Kington, 2005) and is linked with academic achievement (Deegan, 1996).

Lam, Ng, and Chan, who are already in their second year of schooling, had at least one year of school experiences under the Hong Kong curriculum; they have already been accustomed to the school routine. Their academic results vary, and the differences are connected with their learning motivation, strengths, and needs. Both Ng and Chan are at the middle range of school results, while Lam is relatively doing better. This is partly because Lam has higher achievement motivation, and she spends more time on homework revisions. However, for these girls, English remains the most challenging subject. Although getting familiar with the school system is an advantage in school adjustment, individual learning differences must be addressed. Suppressing learning strengths hinders both the progress and motivation of the CBSs.

Finally, Szeto, Jim, and Lee have formed social circles, although they are only in their first year of schooling in Hong Kong. To reiterate, they play mostly with students with whom they share the same school buses and/or ethnic backgrounds. Aside from learning English as their common challenge, Jim also fears learning complex Chinese characters. Moreover, they have relatively little homework support from their parents. All their mothers have high expectations, but they cannot offer concrete help in English learning. All three share their mothers' anxieties in getting good results. Evidently, they are very afraid of failing. Some of their mothers hire private tutors to compensate for their own inadequacies in homework supervision, and extra tuitions are normally held at home. However, for families that cannot afford to pay for extra fees, they just have to rely on school provisions.

CONCLUSION

The nine CBSs reported in this study have given rather positive and encouraging pictures of school adjustment—not negative and discouraging as common knowledge dictates—especially in terms of curricular and social experiences. Overall, the findings reveal that the nine CBSs have no major adjustment problems in the academic and social fields. This finding deviates from the results of other studies and provides an alternative view of the situation of some CBSs in Hong Kong. To these young CBSs, their relationships with teachers play a more important role than their actual academic performance. All nine CBSs prefer Hong Kong schooling to that of schooling in mainland China because teachers in Hong Kong are more considerate, kind, and patient, and these teachers do not resort to corporal punishment in dealing with children.

Friendship is another key factor contributing to their positive perceptions of Hong Kong schooling. Paradoxically, it is friendship with their CBS peers that is the key factor. All three schools have a number of CBSs, and the nine students have consequently forged stronger friendships with those they commute with rather than with their Hong Kong counterparts. Friends in their home neighborhoods are also important to them.

The stories of the nine CBSs underscore the fact that home factors and school experiences are closely linked. Although they are not educated enough to help their children, parents are generally very concerned about their children's school performance, and they have high expectations. Meanwhile, these students are highly aware of their parents' expectations regarding their studies. Consequently, they are more motivated in subjects that they think are more important in the satisfaction of their parents' expectations than in other subjects.

Finally, the length of Hong Kong schooling is a key mediating factor in the self-reported school experiences and aspirations of CBSs. There is a marked difference between those with at least three years of school experiences in Hong Kong and those with at most two years of experiences. During the first two years of Hong Kong schooling, CBSs tend to focus more on friendships; friendship becomes less important after they gain more confidence in their academics. These findings provide insights into the situation of CBSs. However, this study is only the first step, and more work must be done to reveal the situation of CBSs fully.

REFERENCES

Bauhinia Foundation Research Center. (2009). Hong Kong-Shenzhen Education Cooperation. Retrieved November 30, 2009, from http://www.bauhinia.org/publications/tchi_HK-SZ_EducationCooperation_SubReportMain.pdf

Betts, L., & Rotenberg, K. (2007). Trustworthiness, friendships, and self-control: Factors that contribute to young children's school adjustment. *Infant and Child Development, 16,* 491–508.

Cheung, F. (2007). Invisible cross-border policy. Oriental Daily, 2007–03–15.

Ching, S.T. (2007). Hidden Hong Kong babies- Challenging the Education and Manpower Bureau. Sing Tao Daily, 2007–01–12, F02.

Christian Action, (2007). Concerns about cross-border students and family needs seminar booklet. Hong Kong: Christian Action.

Curriculum Development Council. (2008). *Developing a supplementary guide to the Chinese language curriculum for non-Chinese speaking students* (Consultation paper). Retrieved from http://www.legco.gov.hk/yr08–09/english/panels/ed/papers/ed0112cb2–615–1-e.pdf

Deegan, J. (1996). *Children's friendships in culturally diverse classrooms.* London: Falmer Press.

Equality Unit, Department of Education, UK. (n.d.). *Summary of main issues for policy on supporting ethnic-minority children and young people who have English as an additional language.* Bangor, UK: Author. Retrieved January 10, 2011, from http://www.deni.gov.uk/eal_summary.pdf

Erdley, C., Nangle, D., & Newman, J., & Carpenter, E. M. (2001, Spring). Children's friendship experiences are a unique aspect of peer relations with important implications for psychological adjustment. *New Directions for Child and Adolescent Development, 91,* 5–24.

Ford, M. G. (1998). *A multi-site case study: Total quality management within a Texas school district.* Unpublished doctoral dissertation, Texas A&M University–Commerce.

Hoffman, E. (1989). *Lost in translation: A life in a new language.* New York: E. P. Dutton.

Hong Kong Commercial Press, 2007. Unauthored (2007). Organizations advocate more subsidy for the cross-border students. Hong Kong Commercial Press, 2007–04–22, A03.

Hong Kong SAR Press Releases (2007). LCQ8: Cross-boundary students. Retrieved December 23, 2007 from http://www.info.gov.hk/gia/general/200710/17/P200710170142.htm

Hong Kong Social Service Federation (2006). *Responding to cross-border social and livelihood development, raising the living standard of quality and support. Hong Kong Vision 2012: towards sustainable and integrated society.* Hong Kong: Hong Kong Social Services Federation.

Kutnick, P., & Kington, A. (2005). Children's friendships and learning in school: Cognitive enhancement through social interaction. *British Journal of Educational Psychology, 75,* 521–538.

Lee, W.O. & Yuen, Y.M.C. (2003). *Multicultural Education and Education for the Newly Arrived Children: Training, Practice and Reflection,* (in Chinese), Hong Kong, The Commercial Press (Hong Kong) Ltd.

Legislative Council. (2009). *Education for non-Chinese speaking students* (Paper No. CB(2)579/08–09(06)). Retrieved from http://www.legco.gov.hk/yr08–09/english/panels/ed/papers/ed0112cb2–579–6-e.pdf.

Lo, K. H. (2006). *Cross-boundary students between Hong Kong and Shenzhen: A case study of Shan Tsui Public School*. Unpublished master's thesis, University of Hong Kong, Hong Kong.

National Research Council. (2002). *Minority students in special and gifted education*. Washington, DC: National Academy Press.

Phillion, J. (2002). *Narrative inquiry in a multicultural landscape: Multicultural teaching and learning*. Westport, CT: Ablex.

Phillion, J. (2008). Multicultural and cross-cultural narrative inquiry into understanding immigrant students' educational experience in Hong Kong. *Compare: A Journal of Comparative Education*, 38 (3), 281–293.

Rumbaut, R. G. (2000). *Children of immigrants and their achievement: The role of family, acculturation, social class, gender, ethnicity, and school contexts*. Available online at: http://www.ksg.harvard.edu/inequality/Seminar/Papers/Rumbaut2.pdf (accessed 18 June 2009).

Sing Tao Daily. (2008, August 29). Government granted 20 quotas for cross-boundary school coach (in Chinese). Retrieved September 23, 2008 from http://www.singtao.com/yesterday/edu/0829go02.html.

So, A. (2003). Cross-border families in Hong Kong. *Critical Asian Studies*, 35(4), 515–534.

Takungpao. (2008, September 2). Trial-run on Hong Kongers' children joining Secondary One allocation system in 2010 (in Chinese). Retrieved September 3, 2008 from http://www.takungpao.com.hk/news/08/09/02/JX-955235.htm.

Wong, M. S. (2001). *Crossing the world's busiest border for knowledge*. Unpublished master's thesis, University of Hong Kong, Hong Kong.

Yuen, C. Y. M. (Ed.). (2005). *Border-crossing education and parent support services: A review*. Hong Kong: Christian Action.

Yuen, C. Y. M. (2008). The cultural and civic identity of cross-boundary and newly arrived students from mainland China. *Journal of Basic Education*, 17(2), 159–174.

Yuen, Y.M.C. (2002), Education for new arrivals and multicultural teacher education in Hong Kong. *New Horizons in Education*, No.45, May, 12–21.

Yuen, Y. M. C. (2002a, May). Education for new arrivals and multicultural teacher education in Hong Kong. *New Horizons in Education*, 45, 12–21.

Yuen, Y. M. C. (2002b). Initial exploration of border-crossing education. In C. Yuen, *Border-crossing education and parent support services: A review* (pp. 5–8). Hong Kong: Christian Action.

Yuen, Y. M. C. (2003a). *One classroom two systems: Education for the newly arrived children from the mainland and teacher professional development*. Hong Kong: Commercial Press (Hong Kong).

Yuen, Y.M.C. (2003b). *Multicultural Education: Hong Kong – Mainland Curriculum and Instruction* (in Chinese), Yunnan, Yunnan Technology Publication.

Yuen, Y.M.C. (2004). Home school collaboration for border-crossing students: challenges and opportunities. *Hong Kong Journal of Early Childhood*. Vol.3 (1), pp.30–34.

Yuen, Y. M. C. (2004a). Border-crossing education: Marginalization and accommodation. In C. Y. M. Yuen (Ed.), *Education for the newly arrived students from the mainland: Research and development* (pp. 53–66). Taipei: Shih Ta Book.

Yuen, Y. M. C. (2004b). Home school collaboration for border-crossing students: Challenges and opportunities. *Hong Kong Journal of Early Childhood*, 3(1), 30–34.

Yuen, Y.M.C. (2008). The Cultural and Civic Identity of Cross-Boundary and Newly Arrived Students From Mainland China, *Journal of Basic Education*, 17 (2), 159–174.

Yuen, Y.M.C. (2010). Assimilation, Integration and the Construction of Identity: The experience of Chinese cross-boundary and newly arrived students in Hong Kong schools. *Multicultural Education Review*. 2(2), 1–32.

Yuen, Y.M.C. & Grossman, D., (2009). The intercultural sensitivity of student teachers in three cities. *Compare*. Vol.39, No.3, May 2009, 349–365.

Part III

Minority Students in Japan, South Korea, and Taiwan

12 Language Learning Experiences of International Students in Japan
Facilitating Access to Communities of Practice

Tae Umino

INTRODUCTION

Learning to communicate effectively in a new language is a common challenge faced by those living in a foreign country, whether they are immigrants, families of resident employees, or students. Without effective communicative skills, they have limited access to the necessary material and symbolic resources needed to succeed in their new environments. To gain access to such resources, they need to learn the new language and to participate in sociocultural practices using the new language. Unfortunately, however, it is often difficult for linguistic/cultural minority students to gain access to opportunities to participate in such practices.

My interest in the problems of linguistic/cultural minority students stems from my personal experience as the the child of a Japanese government employee stationed in the United States. I was placed in a local school where I was the only English as a Second Language (ESL) student. Through this experience, I have realized how not having the linguistic channel of communication affects one's opportunities to participate in various activities, and how developing the skills to communicate in the new language is connected to the development of one's identity and empowerment. This experience eventually led me to enter the language teaching profession. As an adult student, I was given the chance to live in an English-speaking country. During that time, I had sufficient ability to communicate in English. Still, it was by no means easy to gain access to various sociocultural practices that are taking place in the everyday lives of native speakers.

Through these experiences, I have recognized that classroom language instruction is limited in nature, and I have become aware of language teaching for linguistic minorities. Ozaki (2001) asserts that language teaching has two perspectives. In a narrow sense, it refers to systematic and deliberate classroom activities that involve teachers and learners. In a broad sense, it refers to unsystematic and unintentional everyday life activities that take place outside the classroom between learners and their various supporters. To acquire the communicative ability to participate in sociocultural practices in the new language, language teaching in the broad sense is vital.

However, often, linguistic minorities do not have access to opportunities for participation.

Since I entered the profession of Japanese language teaching 18 years ago, I have been involved in the education of international university students and have studied their second language (L2) learning process.[1] I have therefore developed an interest in understanding the opportunities for participation that are available to international students outside the classroom, and how these students develop language proficiency through such opportunities. Envisioning the active involvement of international students in Japanese society during and after their university schooling, this study aims to consider the educational steps that can be undertaken to provide them opportunities to become actively involved in language-mediated sociocultural practices.

MINORITY POPULATION AND CONTEXT

This chapter focuses on international linguistic minority students in Japanese universities. The group consists of students from China, Korea, Taiwan, Mongolia, and Burma. Following the Japanese government's policy of "internationalization" to increase the number of international students, there has been a rapid growth in the number of international students in Japanese higher educational institutions (HEIs), particularly over the past two decades. In 1983, the plan to increase the number of international students to 100,000 by around the beginning of the 21st century was implemented. It was accomplished in 2003. In 2008, the government implemented a new policy to increase the number of international students to 300,000 by 2020.[2] This policy not only aims to promote the acceptance of study-abroad students but also envisages the organization of a system for promoting the residence and employment of these students in Japan after graduation. These policies accelerated the growth in the number of regular international students, particularly in the number of Asian students. According to the 2009 White Paper on Education, Culture, Sports, Science, and Technology, the total number of international students in HEIs as of May 1, 2008 was 123,829, accounting for 3.5% of the overall registered student population.[3]

Contrary to the government's expectations, however, international students are often isolated and have few opportunities to mingle and become involved with members of the local community (DuFon & Churchill, 2006; Miyo, 2008). From a situated learning perspective, participation in Japanese social practices is vital to the development of Japanese language skills and cultural understanding. If they are to eventually settle in Japan, they need to share not just the language but also the discourse in use—what Gee (1996, p. 127) has termed "ways of being in the world, or forms of life," without which there can be no collaboration or negotiation.

Using life-story interviews (Atkinson, 1998), this study presents the perspectives of 26 Japanese-major international students on their study-abroad experiences, especially on their Japanese language learning experiences. The narratives indicate that international students have limited opportunities to participate in the language-mediated social practices of communities of practice (COPs) outside the school, particularly at the preparatory stage. Furthermore, even if such opportunities are available to them, mere participation does not always improve their communicative abilities. The study further examines cases of students who have succeeded in developing their Japanese communicative skills through participation in COPs. Some of the conditions under which participation in COPs improves target language skills are examined, the importance of social participation as a learning opportunity is discussed, and implications for educational practice are drawn.

LITERATURE REVIEW

Learning a New Language through Participation in COPs

To understand the process by which international students learn Japanese, the situated learning theory is employed (Lave & Wenger, 1991; Wenger, 1998). The theory views learning as participation in social practices within COPs. On the basis of their anthropological study on apprenticeship, Lave and Wenger (1991) assume that the learning of a skill or knowledge occurs as a result of participation in situations where such skill or knowledge is required. From their perspective, social contexts consist of many complex and overlapping communities in which variously positioned participants learn specific, local, historically constructed, and changing practices. Wenger (1998) terms such a community a COP (pp. 6–7), a notion proposed as a way of theorizing and investigating social contexts. According to Wenger, a COP is "a set of relations among persons, activities, and the world" (Lave & Wenger, 1991, p. 98). The members of a COP have mutual engagement, joint enterprise, and shared repertoire. People learn by participating in the social practices of the communities as novices or apprentices, and they gradually learn to function as full participants. This process, which constitutes the core of the learning process, is called legitimate peripheral participation (LPP) (Lave & Wenger, 1991). "Participation" refers not just to local events of engagement in certain activities with certain people, but to a more encompassing process of active participation in the practices of social communities and in the construction of identities in relation to these communities (p. 4). Lave and Wenger further suggest that the key to becoming a full member of a COP is access to learning resources in the COP, such as "a wide range of ongoing activities, old-timers, and other members of the community, and to information, resources, and opportunities for participation" (p. 100).

In the past decade, the situated learning perspective has been gaining ground in the fields of education (e.g., Anderson, Greeno, Reder, & Simon, 2000; Anderson, Reder, & Simon, 1996, 1997; Cobb & Bowers, 1999) and applied linguistics. Moreover, a number of studies have examined language learning from this perspective (e.g., Belcher, 1994; Casanave, 1998; Kanno, 2003; Kanno & Norton, 2003; Miller, 2003; Norton, 2000, 2001; Norton & Toohey, 2001; Norton Peirce, 1995; Sharkey & Layzer, 2000; Toohey, 1998, 2000; Umino, 2008, 2009; Willet, 1995). From the perspective of this theory, learning a new language is not just about the acquisition of language structure but is more about developing, or failing to develop, (a) new ways of mediating between ourselves and (b) our relationships with others and with ourselves (Lantolf & Pavlenko, 2001, p. 145), as well as about acquiring various patterns of social participation. To do so, learners must have opportunities to participate in COPs using multiple aspects of the new language (i.e., social, cognitive, cultural, linguistic, and paralinguistic features) (Johnson, 1995).

Opportunities for Participation

In understanding language learning within the situated learning framework, we need to consider that learners do not possess sufficient linguistic skills that serve as means of gaining access to practices in the target language. This makes it even more difficult for newcomer language learners to have access to COPs. On the basis of her study on immigrant high school students in Australia, Miller (2003) stresses the importance of "speaking" in gaining access to social practices in the target language. The acquisition of speaking skills in a target language is vital in establishing new networks and in finding a place and a voice in new settings (p. 2). However, as Johnson (1995, p. 52) asserts, language learners are trapped in a paradox: they must participate in interpersonal interaction in the language to acquire the multiple aspects of language use, but without this knowledge, they have limited opportunities for such interactions.

Studies on second language acquisition (SLA) based on the above framework report that language learners have limited access to opportunities for participation in both naturalistic environments (Norton, 2000) and classrooms (Sharkey & Layzer, 2000). Norton notes that often, there are unequal power relations between language learners and target language speakers, which hinder learners' access to COPs and learning resources in COPs. Wenger (1998, p. 216) distinguishes "peripherality," which refers to areas of overlap, connections, and possibilities for participation offered to outsiders and newcomers, from "marginality," which refers to the exclusion of the competencies or experiences of certain members. If language learners cannot engage with other members of COPs, they may easily be marginalized and may withdraw from COPs before they develop into skilled participants.

Acquiring participation skills in social practices in the target language is also important in gaining access to various resources necessary for living and succeeding in the target language society. In a study on immigrant women in Canada, Norton Peirce (1995) argues that language learners invest in L2s with the understanding that through this investment, they will be able to acquire a wider range of symbolic resources (e.g., language, education, and friendship) and material resources (e.g., capital goods, real estate, and money), which will in turn alleviate their social status. Similarly, Sharkey and Layzer (2000) assert that ESL high school students need access to academic resources (i.e., people, practices, and physical items that facilitate their academic success) to gain access to higher education that will enable them to achieve success in society.

For newcomer learners, the above studies indicate the importance of gaining access to opportunities for participation. However, these studies mostly focus on immigrant adults and children, and there is less focus on international students (Umino, 2009). Furthermore, little is known about the process by which novice L2 learners become full participants in COPs as they develop higher L2 proficiency. Norton and Toohey (2001) suggest that mere access to COPs does not guarantee that L2 learners can obtain opportunities for LPP, and propose that to understand this process, we need to pay attention to both the social practices in COPs in which individuals learn L2s and the ways by which learners exercise their agencies in gaining access to the social networks of their communities. By exercising their human agencies, learners actively engage in constructing the terms and conditions of their own learning. To understand how international students access opportunities for participation and eventually become full participants in COPs, this chapter describes the process by which they develop Japanese communicative skills through their participation in language-mediated social practices.

RESEARCH STUDY

This section presents the results of the attempt to understand the L2 learning process of adult learners in a naturalistic environment (Spolsky, 1989). Two groups of learners were interviewed: Japanese university students who have studied abroad and international students studying at a Japanese university. This chapter focuses on the latter group. Data were gathered through life-story interviews with 26 Japanese-major international students. The specific research questions addressed in this study are as follows:

1. What opportunities for participation in the target language do international students in Japan have outside the classroom?
2. What pattern(s) of COP participation can lead to the development of communicative skills in the target language?

Prior to the semi-structured interviews, students filled out a questionnaire on their demographics, learning histories before and after studying in Japan, and their self-perceived developmental stages of language learning. On the basis of this information, the students were interviewed about their language learning histories. The interviews were conducted in Japanese (the extracts presented below are translations by the author). Data were recorded and later transcribed for analysis.

The interviewees belonged to different nationalities: 12 Chinese, 1 Taiwanese, 11 Korean, 1 Mongolian, and 1 Burmese. There were 19 females and 7 males, and ages ranged from 19 to 29 (mean age = 24 years). At the time of the interviews, all the students were in their first year at the university, and they were enrolled in a university course for less than one year. They all passed Level 1 of the Japanese Language Proficiency Test (JLPT) prior to entering the university. Of the students, 10 arrived in Japan with little or no knowledge of Japanese, while 16 had previously received instruction in Japanese for 4 months to 7 years. Except for 1 student who arrived in Japan just before entering the university, all of them attended a language school or a technical school for preparatory education in Japanese (mean period = 2.1 years) in Japan before entering the university.

RESEARCH FINDINGS

Access to Target Language-Mediated COPs

First, I describe the types of COPs that may be accessed by international students. The narratives reveal that all but one student had little or no contact or involvement with Japanese native speakers during their preparatory education. International students in Japan, particularly at the preparatory stage, have very limited opportunities to participate in language-mediated social practices outside the school. This is not only due to the individual characteristics of learners but also due to the characteristics of Japanese educational institutions and their places of residence.

Typically, Japanese language schools only have international students, and the only Japanese native speakers in the school are the administrative staff, teachers, and volunteer assistants:

KKY, Chinese: The teacher was the only person to whom I could speak in Japanese. So, I could not tell if I was making any progress in my speaking ability. Although I spoke in Japanese while shopping or at the ward office, I hardly ever made any other contact with whom I could speak in authentic Japanese. It was no different from being in China. I was anxious about whether this would continue to be the case. (Extract 1)

It is evident from this narrative that students have limited opportunities to speak in Japanese. In schools where students of certain nationalities are concentrated, this problem is even more acute, and some students report avoiding contact with students of the same nationality or L1:

KYM, Korean: There were many Koreans at the school, so I spoke in Korean, except during lessons. The teacher was the only Japanese around. I did not speak a word of Japanese outside the class during my one-year preparatory education. I did not mingle with my classmates because I thought I could not go on to university if I did. (Extract 2)

As for places of residence, most students live by themselves in international students–only dormitories or apartments, and they engage in limited interaction in Japanese or with Japanese people. This observation is even more prominent among those who live in or go to schools within ethnic communities:

LSG, Chinese (Korean): I had no Japanese friends and had no opportunity to speak Japanese. The school was in Shinookubo (a Korean ethnic community) in Tokyo, and I went to church there. There were Koreans everywhere, so I spoke in Korean. Most students of the school were Korean or Chinese. I could not speak Japanese until after I finished school. (Extract 3)

OK, Chinese: Since I had a part-time job in Chinatown (a Chinese ethnic community) in Yokohama, 90% of the interaction I was involved in was Chinese. I only memorized simple expressions like "Irasshaimase" (Welcome). Although my listening skills improved a little, my speaking skills did not. Moreover, while I could use Japanese words, I could not compose sentences during my first year. (Extract 4)

Furthermore, students from kanji regions can understand Chinese characters; hence, they get along without speaking Japanese:

KYM, Korean: In shops, everything is written in kanji (Chinese characters), so I looked at the kanji words and said "Kore kudasai" (Give me this) as I pointed to them. I didn't need to talk. I could live without talking. So, I tried to learn more kanji. If I needed something more complicated like mobile phones, I went to Shinookubo in Tokyo (Korean ethnic community), so that I could speak in Korean. (Extract 5)

It is extremely difficult for international students to access Japanese-mediated COPs or to have any contact with Japanese native speakers if they simply attend Japanese language schools. As such, what opportunities for interacting with native Japanese speakers do international students have? Most students cite "part-time work" as the only opportunity to interact with Japanese people (Table 12.1)[4]. In many cases, students choose to engage in part-time work in an attempt to speak authentic Japanese or to interact with Japanese speakers.

Apart from part-time work, hobby circles and events hosted by dormitories are opportunities for participation (Table 12.1). In the former case, the use of the Internet is a means of access to people with whom students share common interests (Extract 6). Moreover, there are cases in which particular teachers, volunteers, or classmates help learners access various activities by serving as "mediators." As seen in Extract 7, YSM contacts Japanese volunteer S almost every day either directly or through the Web, even when she temporarily returned to Korea. Encounters with mediators, such as S, lead to opportunities for language learning:

CCK, Chinese: For the first three months after arrival in Japan, I could not speak a word in Japanese. My classmates were not interested in music, so I listened to music by myself. In the fourth month,

Table 12.1 Activities and People Mediating Learners' Participation in Japanese-Mediated COPs Outside the Classroom Before and After Entering Universities[4]

	Before university (counts)	After entering university (counts)
Activities		
Part-time work	21	20
Internet SNS	2	1
Events at fans club of a singer	1	1
Events at place of residence	0	1
Club activities	0	2
People		
Japanese language teacher	2	0
Japanese volunteer	2	0
Japanese spouse/ partner	1	3
International classmates	1	0
Japanese classmates	0	2
Japanese tutor	0	1

Note: Numbers indicate the frequency by which these activities and people were mentioned by the interviewees.

I found out that the Japanese teacher liked Japanese pop music, so I started talking with him. Later, I started to contribute to an electronic bulletin board run by the fans club of M (a Japanese pop singer). I then became friends with a Japanese man who was also a fan of M. Although it was not easy for me to engage in a normal social network service (SNS), it became easier to do so through the network of M's fans club because we shared something in common. (Extract 6)

YSM, Korean: About ten days after I started going to the Japanese language school, I met S (a Japanese woman in her 50s), who was a volunteer Japanese teacher. She treated me like her daughter. She was a housewife and was not too busy, so she talked to me every day and helped me with my homework. When I was injured, she looked after me. I observed how she did things in Japanese, like calling a taxi and talking over the telephone, and I tried to imitate her. (Extract 7)

Access to Target Language-Mediated Patterns of Participation within COPs

In the previous subsection, we saw how learners accessed COPs outside the school. However, simply gaining entry into COPs does not immediately lead to target language development. For learners to improve their target language proficiency through participation in COPs, they need to use the target language and to become full COP participants as users of the target language. The interviewees cite part-time work as the most frequently accessed COP. In this section, we focus on part-time work as a COP and investigate how learners learn to become full participants using Japanese through participation in part-time work.

Table 12.2 shows the part-time work of the interviewees before and after entering the university. The types of workplaces that are frequently mentioned are restaurants (23), shops (8), supermarkets (5), and factories

Table 12.2 Part-Time Work of Students

Name	Nationality (L1)	Sex	Age	Before university	After entering university
KKY	Chinese (Chinese)	F	28	factory, Japanese bar	none
YG	Chinese (Chinese)	F	27	family restaurant	family restaurant
CM	Korean (Korean)	M	19	fast-food shop	fast-food shop

Continued

Table 12.2 Continued

Name	Nationality (L1)	Sex	Age	Before university	After entering university
SSM	Burma (Burmese)	F	24	fast-food shop	fast-food shop
LEJ	Chinese (Chinese)	F	21	supermarket	none
KYJ	Korean (Korean)	F	26	Korean restaurant, Spanish restaurant	none
SKA	Korean (Korean)	F	22	Western restaurant	Western restaurant
SSY	Korean (Korean)	F	29	private lessons in Korean	private lessons in Korean
LSG	Chinese (Korean)	F	25	fast-food shop, laundry, data input, public bath	supermarket
SJA	Korean (Korean)	F	19	none	none
IJH	Korean (Korean)	F	25	family restaurant	none
GT	Chinese (Chinese)	F	25	factory, construction, fast-food shop, convenience store	Korean restaurant
CKK	Chinese (Chinese)	M	24	supermarket, sushi shop, café	café
YSM	Korean (Korean)	F	25	none	supermarket
TCD	Mongolia (Mongolian)	F	28	NGO, bakery	NGO, teaching Mongolian
JML	Korean (Korean)	F	21	convenience store	family restaurant
CJK	Chinese (Korean)	F	25	supermarket	supermarket
OK	Chinese (Chinese)	F	26	Chinese restaurant	Japanese restaurant
HMK	Chinese (Chinese)	M	24	factory, Korean restaurant, Japanese restaurant	Japanese restaurant
LKG	Chinese (Chinese)	M	25	convenience store	Japanese bar, various short-term work

Continued

Table 12.2   Continued

Name	Nationality (L1)	Sex	Age	Before university	After entering university
KYM	Korean (Korean)	M	27	none	family restaurant
IJI	Korean (Korean)	F	19	not applicable	Japanese restaurant
GTK	Chinese (Chinese)	M	21	Japanese inn	Japanese restaurant
HK	Chinese (Chinese)	F	25	karaoke, convenience store, noodle shop	convenience store
NL	Chinese (Chinese)	F	21	duty free shop	children's hall
YHJ	Korean (Korean)	M	27	public bath	public bath

(4). In terms of target language development, the number of opportunities available to learners seems to vary depending on the type of workplace and occupation, time of work, and characteristics of other employees and customers. When learners start studying abroad—at a time when their oral proficiency in Japanese is still low—they often have access only to work, such as factory labor, which involves minimal use of the target language. Because this pattern of participation does not lead to target language development, learners quit such work in a short time (Extract 8). Work at a fast-food shop or a family restaurant requires only a set of routines and patterns and is not perceived as requiring more creative language use (Extract 19). Even if the work requires language use, it may not involve the use of the target language. Working in a place where most employees and customers are Chinese speakers leads to few opportunities for participation in the target language (Extract 9). Furthermore, access to practices using the target language varies depending on the type of occupation, shop size, and time of work. SSM in Extract (10) has succeeded in accessing the language-mediated pattern of participation by changing her occupation type within the same workplace.

HMK, Chinese: I worked in a factory where vegetables were processed. I did not need to use Japanese. I had no opportunity to speak. The work was simple and depressing. There were some Chinese people, but I did not talk with them. We were busy with our work and could not express ourselves in Japanese. I quit the place after three months. (Extract 8)

NL, Chinese: I worked in a duty-free shop, but the customers were mostly Chinese, and I spoke to them in Chinese. I did not have many opportunities to speak Japanese. (Extract 9)

SSM, Burmese: I worked in a kitchen in a fast-food shop, but I hardly spoke much . . . Six months later, I started working as a cashier. I began to speak more. Initially, I used a set of phrases, but soon customers asked me questions, and I responded. Later, I worked in a different shop. This shop was small and I did not need to go to the hall, so I had fewer opportunities to speak, whereas in the previous shop, I had more opportunities because it was bigger. (Extract 10)

To sum up, part-time work can be a COP in which learners can participate and improve their ability to communicate in the target language if they succeed in accessing a target language-mediated pattern of participation within the given COP. Norton and Toohey (2001) assert that learners do not necessarily gain opportunities for LPP simply by entering COPs. We need to examine the characteristics of both community practices and learner agencies in understanding conditions for LPP. The next section examines two cases of learners who have succeeded in becoming full participants in their given COP of part-time work, and considers conditions for L2 development through LPP by focusing on community practices and learner agencies.

Path to Becoming Full Participants Using the Target Language

Characteristics of COP as a Learning Resource

In this subsection, I examine the case of GTK, a male Chinese student, 21 years of age, through his narrative of learning experiences in Japan.

GTK, Chinese: I came to Kyoto, Japan, with almost no knowledge of Japanese. The students in the Japanese language school I attended were all Chinese. Apart from talking with the teacher in Japanese, I mostly spoke in Chinese. As I had no opportunity to try out my Japanese, I took a part-time job at a Japanese inn. I went to work three to five times a week. The job involved assisting in room service. (a) *I went to the guests' rooms with a waitress and helped her serve food.* (b) *The employees of the inn were all very nice, and they asked me questions and taught me how to do things.* I developed greater interest in Japanese through this work. (c) *It allowed me to immediately apply what I studied in school. If I learned a new word, I tried to use it at work.* If any person has such an environment, I think they can progress quickly. (d) *I was not ashamed of making mistakes because people were tolerant.* For example, when I first attempted to use the word "tonikaku" (anyway), it did not make sense, and my colleagues asked me to repeat what I had said. I had been confused with the word "toriaezu" (for the time being). By trying out new words in this manner, I continued to learn more. (e) *I became friends with a Japanese man who was also a part-timer there. He taught me things, and we even went to a karaoke place after work.* We had a lot in common, so we naturally talked a lot. I was making progress on a daily basis. After one month, I could understand simple conversations. After two or three months, I could talk about myself. I also started to talk to guests. They asked me questions like "Arashiyama wa doko ni arimasuka?" (Where is Arashiyama?) and "Yasaka-jinja wa?" (Where is Yasaka-jinja Shrine?), and I could respond appropriately. (Extract 11)

GTK acquired an opportunity for LPP in a target language-mediated COP in his part-time workplace, and he eventually learned to function in his given role. We can make the following observations about the contextual factors that made this possible, as evidenced by lines in the extract:

1. An experienced waitress provided GTK a model to imitate (a).
2. Old-timers were "nice" to GTK, and they "taught him things" (b).
3. GTK had a chance to try out the new words and expressions he learned in school (c).
4. GTK was not ashamed of making mistakes when he tried out new words and expressions (d).
5. There was a Japanese man who helped GTK mediate activities within and outside work (e).

Lave and Wenger (1991) assert that the "observation stage" and "practice stage" are levels of institutionalization in the learning process in apprenticeship. Points 1 through 5 above indicate that GTK was given an opportunity for observation and practice. Furthermore, the Japanese man indicated in Point 5 mediated GTK's access to activities within and outside work. The presence of such a mediator has particular significance in deepening and expanding the participation of beginning L2 learners who do not have sufficient language skills to gain access to learning resources within COPs. Having participated in this COP for two years, GTK was eventually able to function as a full participant by using Japanese and by acquiring a new Japanese identity:

GTK, Chinese: In the second year, my personality began to change. My parents pointed out to me that I had changed. I greet people more often. When I speak in Japanese, I follow the Japanese customs and ways of life. I ask the elderly "How is your health?" I pay more attention to others. The Japanese always greet each other by saying "How are you?" "Have you eaten lunch?" etc. I never get angry when speaking in Japanese. I do not express my feelings. I act like a person speaking Japanese, a "good" person, an "ambiguous" person. When conversing in Chinese, I tend to get angry or express myself in a more straightforward manner. (Extract 12)

As seen in the preceding extract, access to learning resources within a COP is an important contextual factor for successful LPP in L2 learning. In particular, the presence of a mediator, who facilitates access to learning resources, is an important factor in the process. The same is observed in the narratives of other students:

YG, *Chinese:* There are more young people at work. It is easier to talk with high school students. We can find common topics, and they do not care about grammar as long as they get what I say. They helped me compose sentences, so I spoke in short sentences, such as "It's cheap," "I want these clothes," and "Do you have a girlfriend?" (Extract 13)

SSM, *Burmese:* There are many foreigners at work, so the manager is used to talking to foreigners. He easily understands what I want to say. (Extract 14)

In contrast, if access to learning resources within COPs is low, learners are only allowed a fixed pattern of participation, and they may be hindered from becoming full participants. CM notes that he could only use fixed routines, and he had no access to creative language use (Extract 15). HK reports that another Chinese student blocked her access to other members and activities mediated by the target language (Extract 16). These cases indicate that limited access to learning resources in COPs hinders the language development of newcomers.

CM, *Korean:* At work, I use a set of fixed phrases, but I don't talk about myself. There were people of the same age, of older age, and a manager. We worked at midnight and so everyone was tired and busy and couldn't be bothered to talk to me. (Extract 15)

HK, *Chinese:* When I was working at a convenience store, the Japanese people were nice to me, but a Chinese girl was very strict with me. There were only three people in the shop, and she was one of them. She had been in Japan for three years and was fluent in Japanese. I was not and did not have much experience. She complained to me in Chinese, but as I could not speak Japanese, I could not tell anybody about it. It was hard. I quit after three months. (Extract 16)

GTK, who moved to Tokyo from Kyoto upon entering a university, comments on differences in accessibility depending on COPs (Extract 17). Kyoto is a city with many universities, and it has a tradition of hospitality toward students. GTK worked part-time at a restaurant in Tokyo, but he did not get as much assistance as he did in Kyoto. Even his Japanese classmates at the university did not act as mediators. He was not treated specially as a "foreigner," and he could not get the necessary assistance. This indicates that participation (or nonparticipation) in COPs is not only attributable to learners—it is also dependent on the nature of COPs.

GTK, Chinese: In Kyoto, people are sympathetic and kind, but things are different in Tokyo. I feel lonely in Tokyo. In Kyoto I could both study and play. Now, there is nothing. I don't share anything in common with my classmates. We live far away from each other, so we are not close. I have no Japanese friends. I chat with my friends in Kyoto via the Internet. My Japanese classmates talk with each other in young people's language, but I can only talk in polite Japanese. I cannot mingle with them. At work, half of the part-time workers are high school students, and I don't get along with them. The manager doesn't provide me any special treatment as a foreigner, but sometimes I cannot understand him and I get into trouble. People talk about "pachinko," but I have never been there. They make jokes, but I don't get what is funny. Sometimes I go out with them to a bar, but I only listen to them, and I cannot speak. Somehow, I want to get over this. (Extract 17)

Human Agency of Learners

How do learners cope with situations where learning resources in a given COP are not easily accessible, and there is not enough assistance from other members? In this section, I focus on the case of a learner, SKA, who negotiated her situation and who eventually succeeded in becoming a full participant.

SKA, Korean: My father was transferred to Tokyo from Korea, and I followed him. Having no knowledge of Japanese, I started to learn Japanese at a language school. The first nine months were smooth. I learned the hiragana, greetings, and formulas for the first three months, and I finished basic grammar in six months. (a) *I made friends with some classmates* and (b) *tried to use what I had learned on a given day. I made rapid progress.* I skipped two grades and got into the highest class in nine months. However, I began to stagnate. I did not feel I was making any progress. If I said anything in class, I felt I was getting in the way of other lower-level students. I was beginning to lose interest. (c) *I felt I had limited opportunities to use Japanese. I needed more opportunities to use Japanese. So, I decided to take a part-time work.* Normally, a Korean student would work at a Korean restaurant, but (d) *I deliberately chose a private restaurant that had only Japanese employees.* (e) *I also avoided fast-food shops and family restaurants because I heard that they only require simple Japanese.* (f) *I also avoided Shinookubo (Korean ethnic community) because then, I would only speak Korean. Hence, I chose a restaurant in Azabu, Tokyo.* The first two months were difficult. There were four part-time employees working at the same hours, but I was the only foreigner. They spoke very fast and used lots of new words, so I could not understand them. We were busy, and I had no chance to ask questions. I realized that my Japanese was not good enough. I could not follow them and was silenced when we were talking in a group of four. (g) *I felt I would not make any progress this way so I decided to request a change in the working hours.* Between 17:00 and 22:00, the restaurant was not very busy, and there were younger employees. Although the hourly wages were lower, I could be alone with another employee and had a greater chance to speak. After three months, I was able to follow conversations among the four of us. (Extract 18)

SKA is a 21-year-old Korean female who succeeded in developing her Japanese by working part-time at a restaurant. SKA intentionally acquired access to a target language-mediated pattern of participation in her given COP in the following manner:

1. SKA made friends to create a need for communication in the target language (a).
2. SKA attempted to use what she learned outside the school (b).
3. When she felt she was not making much progress, she placed herself in a situation that required higher skills in the target language (c).
4. In choosing part-time work, she intentionally chose the appropriate type of occupation, employees, customers, and region to increase her chances of using the target language (d, e, and f).
5. When she felt she was not getting enough opportunities to speak at work, she changed her working hours to gain more opportunities to speak Japanese (g).

At SKA's workplace, there were only Japanese native speakers, and she did not receive any special treatment as a foreigner, nor did she immediately gain access to a target language-mediated participation pattern. However, by changing her working hours, she gained more chances to speak Japanese, and she succeeded in developing her speaking skills. This case indicates that it is possible for learners to negotiate their environment to create appropriate conditions for successful LPP.

In the narratives of other students, we see that at times, students leave their workplaces if they decide that there is no room for negotiation, and they search for other COPs to gain opportunities for LPP:

LSG, Chinese: I worked in the kitchen of a fast-food shop. I only needed to memorize a set of expressions like "Kyuukei hairimasu" (I take a break now), "Otsukaresama" (Good-bye, literally "you must be tired"), and "Mizu kudasai" (Give me water). There was not much to say. I could get by easily. So, next, I worked as a receptionist at a laundry. Here as well, I only used simple expressions, such as "Shatsu, tatami desu ka?" (Would you like your shirt folded?) and "Hangaa, kakemasu ka?" (Would you like to have it hung on a hanger?). The job did not involve much more interaction with customers, and this did not get me any further. I finally got a chance to speak when I started to work as a receptionist at a public bath. Here, 95% of the customers were Japanese, so I was speaking Japanese eight hours a day. I not only used fixed expressions, but I was talking in various ways to various people. On holidays, there were families, even children. I could not make any friends in school, but here, I could make friends. I called them and chatted with them through e-mail. (Extract 19)

CCK, Chinese: Two months after arrival, I started to work at a supermarket, where I had to prepare ready-made food. The work was simple and there were many elderly ladies. I could not talk to them; I quit after three months. I wanted to find a workplace where I would have to speak a lot of Japanese, so I got a job at a sushi restaurant. I had more opportunities to converse with the customers and to use my Japanese. Although it was not easy to learn all the names of the different types of fish and sushi, such as "makimono" (rolled sushi), "yakimono" (grilled fish), "nigirizushi" (sushi shaped by hand), and "chirashizushi" (scattered sushi), I learned a lot. I worked there for one year. At the end of the year, I could answer customers' questions. (Extract 20)

As shown in this section, if learners are not gaining enough access to the learning resources necessary for them to become full participants, it is important for them to negotiate with the COP to gain access to the necessary resources. If they find that this is not possible, they may need to seek another COP.

SUMMARY

The foregoing discussions highlight the process by which international students develop their Japanese abilities through participation in a workplace as a COP. In the first place, international students have limited opportunities to participate in language-mediated social practices. Therefore, their first task is to gain access to such an opportunity. Once they succeed in this task, the next step is to gain access to a target language-mediated pattern of participation in a given COP. It is desirable to have access to patterns involving creative language use rather than the use of routines and patterns. Furthermore, learners need to have constant access to learning resources in the COP (e.g., a wide range of activities, old-timers, information, shared repertoire, and opportunities for participation) to function as full participants. The presence of a mediator in the COP facilitates this access. If learners do not gain access to these learning resources, they need to negotiate with the COP to solve their problem, and if they find that it is not possible to do so, they may need to move to another COP. A summary of the steps involved in entering an LPP, which leads to language development, is provided here.

1. When learners have limited or no access to a target language-mediated COP, they need to gain access through mediators (e.g., teachers, volunteers, and classmates), places of residence, hobby circles, or part-time work.
2. When learners have access to a target language-mediated COP but do not have access to a target language-mediated pattern of participation in the COP, they need to negotiate with the COP or search for another COP that allows for the target language-mediated pattern of participation.
3. When learners have access to a target language-mediated pattern of participation in a target language-mediated COP, they follow a path toward becoming full participants by gaining further access to learning resources in the COP.

CONCLUSION AND IMPLICATIONS

This chapter, through student narratives, considered how international students in Japan learn how to communicate in Japanese through their participation in language-mediated social practices. The results of the study have implications not just for international students but for all those who continue their lifelong L2 learning through participation in various everyday social practices in target communities.

The students in the study observed that although they were receiving classroom instruction, their levels of Japanese proficiency were not improving; hence, they sought external opportunities. Participation in language-mediated social practices became essential in the development of their ability to communicate in Japanese. To gain access to opportunities for participation, they consciously exploited various resources to increase their opportunities for participation. Aside from strategies regarding the workplace, other strategies were used: using Internet SNS to connect with people with whom they share common interests, joining club activities, interacting with volunteers, and living in dormitories to increase contact with other students, among others. These strategies can also be effective for other students.

However, the study showed that international students find difficulties in accessing opportunities for participation in the target language, just as immigrants do. The limited availability of opportunities not only hinders language development and cultural understanding, but it also impedes access to various resources necessary for success in the target language society. Language learners, particularly those at the beginning stage, face a double bind: they do not have access to various opportunities for participation because of their inability to speak the language, and they cannot improve their speaking skills because they have no opportunities for participation. As Norton and Toohey (2001) assert, it should not be the sole responsibility of learners to find their way out of this double bind. It is important for educational institutions and teachers to provide appropriate assistance so that learners can gain initial access to participation in the target language.

Direct connections between educational practice and language-mediated social practices may not easily be drawn because such practices are found outside the classroom. However, as Kikuchi (2008) claims, the amount and range of resources to which learners have access varies greatly depending on the institutional effort made by schools, particularly at the preparatory stage. Institutions and schools can assist learners in their attempt to access social practices outside the classroom. Assistance may come in various forms as follows: (a) introduction to task-based activities that create opportunities for authentic language use; (b) organization of various extracurricular activities involving the use of the target language with target language speakers; (c) introduction to Japanese volunteer assistance programs to increase opportunities for interaction with native speakers; and (d) provision of information, networks, and resources for social participation using the target language. Moreover, preparatory schools and universities can foster the coeducation of Japanese and international students, instead of placing international students in particular classes or schools. Similarly, universities can provide mixed dormitories for both Japanese and international students.

Even if students are learning in a naturalistic environment, they can easily get along without speaking Japanese; hence, they need to create opportunities for using Japanese to increase their target language proficiency. Teachers should make learners aware of this fact; teachers should encourage them to mingle with learners with different L1s and to access the various available learning resources around them. If learners attempt to achieve higher target language proficiency through part-time work, teachers can encourage them to seek work involving the use of the target language or target language-mediated patterns of participation. Learners also need to carefully select the type of occupation and working hours. The workplace can be an important opportunity for international students to learn Japanese social practices. Educational institutions need to recognize the significance of this opportunity and should advise students to select their workplaces more strategically, so that they can have greater access to learning resources.

Finally, this study touched on two issues that deserve further consideration. First, the study used narratives as data to reveal language learning experiences from the emic views of learners (Pike, 1964). However, the transformation that learners experience when they interact with other members of a COP can cause changes in other participants. Such mutual aspects have not been investigated in the present study, and they must be considered in future research.

Second, while the use of life-story interviews provided an understanding of students' language learning experiences in the entire process from gaining access to becoming full participants in COPs, it does not allow us to capture the detailed process of students' linguistic development. In future studies, it is necessary to combine other data sources that would serve as records of their learning process, such as diaries and observations, to carry out a more multifaceted analysis.

This research was supported by the Global COE program 'Corpus-based Linguistics and Language Education' (Tokyo University of Foreign Studies). The views expressed are those of the author.

NOTES

1. In this chapter, the term second language (L2) is used to refer to a language learned in addition to the first language of learners. In many cases, this may be the third or fourth language studied by learners in addition to their mother tongue.
2. Ministry of Education, Culture, Sports, Science, and Technology, Japan (http://www.mext.go.jp/b_menu/houdou/20/07/08080109.htm)
3. There are 60,522 undergraduate and 32,666 graduate international students in Japan's universities (Statistical Abstract of Education, Culture, Sports, Science, and Technology, 2009).
4. International students with "ryuugaku" (study abroad) status are permitted to work part-time if they need to supplement their school and living expenses, and if they have obtained work permits that allow them to work 28 hours or less as full-time students and 14 hours or less as non-regular students (including research students). During long holidays, they are allowed to work for 8 hours or less a day.

REFERENCES

Anderson, J. R., Greeno, J. G., Reder, L. M., & Simon, H. A. (2000). Perspectives on learning, thinking, and activity. *Educational Researcher, 29*(4), 11–13.

Anderson, J. R., Reder, L. M., & Simon, H. A. (1996). Situated learning and education. *Educational Researcher, 25*(4), 5–11.

Anderson, J. R., Reder, L. M., & Simon, H. A. (1997). Situative versus cognitive perspectives: Form versus substance. *Educational Researcher, 26*(1), 18–21.

Atkinson, R. (1998). *The life story interview.* Thousand Oaks, CA: Sage.

Belcher, D. (1994). The apprenticeship approach to advanced academic literacy: Graduate students and their mentors. *English for Specific Purposes, 13*(1), 23–34.

Casanave, C. (1998). Transitions: The balancing act of bilingual academics. *Journal of Second Language Writing, 7*(2), 175–203.

Cobb, P., & Bowers, J. (1999). Cognitive and situated learning perspectives in theory and practice. *Educational Researcher, 28*(2), 4–15.

DuFon, M., & Churchill, E. (Eds.). (2006). *Language learners in study abroad contexts.* Clevedon, UK: Multilingual Matters.

Gee, J. P. (1996). *Social linguistics and literacies: Ideology in discourses* (2nd ed.). London: Taylor & Francis.

Johnson, K. E. (1995). *Understanding communication in second language classrooms.* Cambridge, UK: Cambridge University Press.

Kanno, Y. (2003). *Negotiating bilingual and bicultural identities.* Mahwah, NJ: Erlbaum.

Kanno, Y., & Norton, B. (2003). Imagined communities and educational possibilities: Introduction. *Journal of Language, Identity, and Education, 2*(4), 241–249.

Kikuchi, F. (2008). Gakushuu risoosu riyou wa kojinkan de donoyou ni kotonaru ka: Dai ni gengo kankyou ni okeru butteki risoosu riyou no "tayousei" o saguru. *Dai San Kai Nihongo Kyouiku Kokusai Kenkyuu Taikai Yokoushuu, 2,* 456–459.

Lantolf, J., & Pavlenko, A. (2001). (S)econd (L)anguage (A)ctivity theory: Understanding second language learners as people. In M. Breen (Ed.), *Learner contributions to language learning* (pp. 141–158). London: Longman.

Lave, J., & Wenger, E. (1991). *Situated learning: Legitimate peripheral participation.* Cambridge, UK: Cambridge University Press.

Miller, J. (2003). *Audible difference: ESL and social identity in schools.* Clevedon, UK: Multilingual Matters.

Miyo, J. (2008). Ryuugaku seikatsu ni okeru Nihongo no ichizuke to Nihongo shien no arikata: Kankokujin ryuugakusei ni taisuru raifu hisutorii chousa yori. *Dai San Kai Nihongo Kyouiku Kokusai Kenkyuu Taikai Yokoushuu, 1,* 270–273.

Norton, B. (2000). *Identity and language learning: Gender, ethnicity, and educational change.* Harlow, UK: Longman/Pearson Education.

Norton, B. (2001). Non-participation, imagined communities, and the language classroom. In M. Breen (Ed.), *Learner contributions to language learning: New directions in research* (pp. 159–171). Harlow, UK: Pearson Education.

Norton, B., & Toohey, K. (2001). Changing perspectives on good language learners. *TESOL Quarterly, 35*(2), 307–322.

Norton Peirce, B. (1995). Social identity, investment, and language learning. *TESOL Quarterly, 29*(1), 9–31.

Ozaki, A. (2001). Nihongokyouiku wa dare no mono ka. In N. Aoki, A. Ozaki, & S. Toki (Eds.), *Nihongokyouikugaku o manabu hito no tame ni* (pp. 3–14). Kyoto, Japan: Sekaishisousha.

Pike, K. L. (1964). *Language in relation to a unified theory of structures of human behavior.* The Hague, Netherlands: Mouton.

Sharkey, J., & Layzer, C. (2000). Whose definition of success? Identifying factors that affect English language learners' access to academic success and resources. *TESOL Quarterly, 34*(2), 352–368.

Spolsky, B. (1989). *Conditions for second language learning.* Oxford, UK: Oxford University Press.

Toohey, K. (1998). Breaking them up, taking them away: ESL students in Grade 1. *TESOL Quarterly, 32*(1), 61–84.

Toohey, K. (2000). *Learning English at school: Identity, social relations, and classroom practice.* Clevedon, UK: Multilingual Matters.

Umino, T. (2008). Gakushuu taiken to shite no guruupu intabyuu: Joukyouronteki kanten kara no kousatsu. In K. Murata & T. Harada (Eds.), Applied linguistics and language teaching in Japan—A Widdowsonian perspective: Explorations into the notion of communicative capacity *(pp. 79–101).* Tokyo: Hitsuji Shobo.

Umino, T. (2009). Daini gengo shuutoku ni okeru "chinmokuki": Joukyouronteki kanten kara no saikou. In M. Minegishi & Y. Kawaguchi (Eds.), Corpus-based linguistics and language education research report *(Vol. 3, pp. 265–284).* Tokyo: Graduate School of Tokyo University of Foreign Studies.

Wenger, E. (1998). Communities of practice: Learning, meaning, and identity. Cambridge, UK: Cambridge University Press.

Willet, J. (1995). Becoming first graders in an L2: An ethnographic study of L2 socialization. TESOL Quarterly, 29(3), 473–503.

13 Migrant Workers and International Marriage Minorities in South Korea

Jungmin Lee

INTRODUCTION

South Korea, traditionally classified as a single ethnic-group nation, is becoming an ethnically and racially diverse society due to the significant increase in foreign migrant workers and international marriages. In response to the emerging racial and ethnic diversity in South Korea, the educational issues resulting from the diversity have become of growing interest in the country's public education system. Specifically, in 2006, the Ministry of Education and local education offices took an interest in the ethnically and racially diverse student population, and began to develop policies and support plans to address the new needs. Educational researchers also became interested in the ethnic and racial minorities. In addition, some public schools located in areas with migrant workers and international marriage minority populations began to develop curricula according to their needs.

This chapter examines South Korean educational policies and school practices created in response to the educational challenges posed by migrant workers and international marriage minorities in South Korea. In-depth analysis of the educational policies and school practices, interviews with teachers, and site visits to schools with minority students were conducted. The author used narrative inquiry to describe the stories of the participants who interacted with ethnically and racially diverse students in multicultural situations (Phillion, 2008). Narrative inquiry is a methodological approach dealing with a narrative, which is a powerful tool for understanding the human condition (Connelly & Clandinin, 1990). In this study, participants were invited to share their stories through in-depth interviews (Clandinin & Connelly, 1994; He, 2002).

INCREASING ETHNIC AND RACIAL DIVERSITY

Foreign Migrant Workers

An increasing number of foreign laborers have migrated to South Korea. Foreign migrant workers numbered 6,409 in 1987. In 2005, the number was estimated at 345,679, of which 180,792 (52.3%) were undocumented (Korean Ministry of Education and Human Resources Development, 2006a). The Chinese, including Korean Chinese (35.4%), make up the majority of foreign laborers, followed by Filipinos (9.0%), Thais (4.8%), Vietnamese (4.3%), and Bangladeshis (4.0%) (Korean Ministry of Education and Human Resources Development, 2006a).

With the recent increase in foreign labor, the number of foreign children who are of school age residing in South Korea has increased. The number of undocumented children in South Korea has risen as well. The number of foreign children who were of school age in 2005 was estimated at 17,287. Among this number, 7,800 children attended foreign schools sponsored by their own countries, and 1,574 children (i.e., those who were mainly legal foreign children) attended Korean schools. About 95% of the undocumented children did not attend school. The number of undocumented children who were of school age in 2005 was estimated at 2,500, but only 148 of these children (5.9%) attended school. The foreign children enrolled in Korean elementary school numbered 995; in middle school, 352; and in high school, 227. Among them, the undocumented children enrolled in elementary school numbered 99; in middle school, 43; and in high school, 6 (Korean Ministry of Education and Human Resources Development, 2006a).

The South Korean Nationality Law is based on the personal nationality principle, which means that a child has the parents' nationality. That is, children born to foreign parents are considered foreign even if they are born in South Korea. However, under the *United Nations International Convention on the Protection of the Rights of All Migrant Workers and Members of Their Families,* children of foreign migrants are entitled to the same basic education rights as Korean children, whether they are documented or undocumented. This is based on the *United Nations Convention on the Rights of the Child* and the *Recommendations of the United Nations Committee on the Rights of the Child.* According to Clause 2, Article 6 of the Korean Constitution, the United Nations convention has the same legal force as domestic laws within South Korea (Korean Ministry of Education and Human Resources Development, 2006a).

In 2003, the Ministry of Education simplified regulations for children of foreign migrants so that they could enter elementary school to ensure basic education for them. For instance, these children can be admitted to school with either a certificate of fact on entry or a certificate of fact on foreigner's registration. Undocumented children without these certificates can present verification of their residence by submitting a copy of a housing rental contract or a neighbor's written guarantee of their residence (Korean Ministry of Education and Human Resources Development, 2006a). Even though undocumented children were able to gain admission more easily due to this relief admissions process, most of these children did not attend school. This low enrollment is caused by their insecure legal status, fear of a government crackdown and possible deportation, and poverty (Korean Ministry of Education and Human Resources Development, 2006a, 2006b). On April 4, 2006, one Sri Lankan mother, an undocumented migrant worker, was arrested by an immigration official from the Ministry of Justice near her six-year-old son's school while she was picking him up. This uncertain legal status has been recognized as one of the most serious problems that undocumented children face. After this event, the child and his parents were ordered to go back to their country, and the undocumented students who were planning to enter the school abandoned the idea because of fear of a crackdown. To respond to this problem, in May 2006, the Ministry of Education and the Ministry of Justice announced a new policy banning immigration officials from pursuing children around schools as a way to catch their parents; the ban was implemented so that these children could obtain an education (Korean Ministry of Education and Human Resources Development, 2006a, 2006b).

International Marriage Minorities

Recently, there has been an increase in the number of international marriages in South Korea. According to the data on international marriages from the Korean National Statistical Office (2006), international marriages numbered 43,121 in 2005, representing 13.6% of all marriages in South Korea. The numbers increased tenfold from 1990, and this trend is continuing. International marriages represented 1.2% of all marriages in 1990, 3.7% in 2000, and 11.4% in 2004. Figure 13.1 shows the recent increase in the number of international marriages.

In the past, the rate of international marriages between Korean women and foreign men was high, but the rate of the international marriages between Korean men and foreign women is now higher. Marriages between Korean men and foreign women represented 72% of international marriages in 2005 (Korean Ministry of Gender Equality and Family, 2007; Seol, 2005). The total number of married immigrant women between 1990 and 2005 was 159,942 (Korean Ministry of Gender Equality and Family, 2007). Table 13.1 shows the number of international and all marriages in South Korea, as well as the differences among native and foreign spouses.

Many internationally married couples consist of a Korean man and a foreign woman from another Asian country. In 2005, Chinese (66.2%), including Korean Chinese, made up the majority of foreign spouses, followed by Vietnamese (18.7%), Japanese (4.0%), Filipinos (3.2%), Mongolians (1.8%), Uzbeks (1.1%), Americans (0.9%), Thais (0.9%), and others (3.3%) (Korean National Statistical Office, 2006). The term "Kosian" reflects this phenomenon. This newly coined term is a compound word combining "Korean" and "Asian" and is used to identify interracial children with one Korean parent and another parent from a different Asian country (Korean Ministry of Education and Human Resources Development, 2006b).

220 *Jungmin Lee*

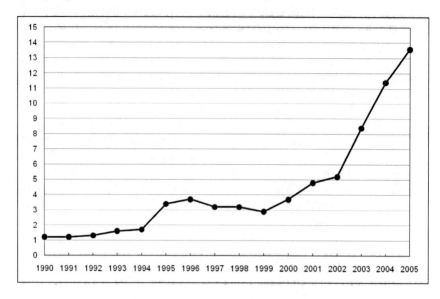

Figure 13.1   Increase in international marriages in South Korea (%, year).
Source: "Statistics on International Marriages," Korean National Statistical Office, 2006.

Table 13.1   The Composition of International Marriages in South Korea (number, %)

Year	All marriages	International marriages	International marriages with foreign female spouse	International marriages with foreign male spouse
1990	399,312	4,710 (1.2)	619 (0.2)	4,091 (1.0)
1995	398,494	13,494 (3.4)	10,367 (2.6)	3,129 (0.8)
2000	334,030	12,319 (3.7)	7,304 (2.2)	5,015 (1.5)
2003	304,932	25,658 (8.4)	19,214 (6.3)	6,444 (2.1)
2004	310,944	35,447 (11.4)	25,594 (8.2)	9,853 (3.2)
2005	316,375	43,121 (13.6)	31,180 (9.9)	11,941 (3.8)

Source: "Statistics on International Marriages," Korean National Statistical Office, 2006

Recently, international marriages have suddenly increased in number in fishing, mountain, and agrarian villages. Poor Korean fishermen or farmers who do not have good chances of marriage with Koreans have sought spouses from other Asian countries. International marriages often take place in rural areas (fishing and agrarian villages) and represented 35.9% of all international marriages in South Korea in 2005 (Korean National Statistical Office, 2006).

With this recent increase in the number of international marriages, the number of children from internationally married couples—mainly those whose father is Korean and mother is from another Asian country—has increased in South Korean schools. Children who attend school and have one Korean parent and one foreign parent numbered 13,445 in April 2007 (6,121 in 2005, 7,998 in 2006), representing an increase of 68.1% over the previous year (Korean Ministry of Education and Human Resources Development, 2008). Among these children, elementary school students numbered 11,444; middle school students, 1,588; and high school students, 413 (Korean Ministry of Education and Human Resources Development, 2008).

POLICY CONTEXT

Educational Support Plan for Children from Multicultural Families

As a result of these two new populations (i.e., children of foreign migrant workers and children of international marriages), students of different races, ethnicities, languages, or cultures are increasing in number in Korean schools. Therefore, education for them has received much attention from policymakers, educational researchers, and educators. In 2006, the Korean Ministry of Education and Human Resources Development (2006a, 2006b) established a comprehensive set of measures and policies on multicultural education, entitled *Educational Support Plan for Children from Multicultural Families.*

In the policies, the term "multicultural families" indicates a foreign migrant worker's family, an international marriage family, or a North Korean defector family, who have different ethnicities, races, or nationalities (Cho, 2006). Children of multicultural families are categorized into six groups: foreign children born in South Korea, foreign children born outside of South Korea but living in South Korea, children of international marriages between a male Korean and a female foreigner, children of international marriages between a female Korean and a male foreigner, children of North Korean defectors born in North Korea, and children of North Korean defectors born in South Korea (Cho, 2006).

The support policies of the Ministry of Education for multicultural family children were devised with three multifaceted purposes: (1) to foster an understanding of diversity, to improve the human rights of minority people, and to strengthen social integration; (2) to ensure educational equity for children of foreign migrant workers and children of international marriages through educational support; and (3) to educate students with diverse cultural and linguistic characteristics for the human resource requirements in a globally competitive world (Korean Ministry of Education and Human Resources Development, 2006a). Among these three purposes, the key goal is to support these children so that they will not be neglected or alienated from normal school education, and so they may receive the benefits of school education. Under this policy, multicultural family children are considered a disadvantaged class, which needs support through several measures prepared with respect to educational welfare (Korean Ministry of Education and Human Resources Development, 2007).

The main purposes of the Ministry's policies for the children of foreign migrant workers, one of the target groups, are to ensure that these children receive basic school education regardless of their legal status and to assist them as they adapt to Korean culture and life (Korean Ministry of Education and Human Resources Development, 2006a). To respond to the low enrollment of undocumented children due to their parents' fear of government crackdown, in May 2006, the Ministry of Education and the Ministry of Justice announced a policy banning immigration officials from chasing these children near schools as a way to catch their undocumented parents. This ban was implemented to ensure that these children obtain school education (Korean Ministry of Education and Human Resources Development, 2006a, 2006b).

The support plan of the Ministry of Education for children of international marriages, the other target group, emphasizes strengthening educational support for these children's Korean language, school studies learning, and school adaptation, and providing their immigrant mothers with support through Korean language and social adaptation programs. The Ministry's support for the children began with two assumptions about these children and their parents. One was that these children are more likely unskillful in their Korean language development and school learning because their immigrant mothers are not fluent in Korean and are unfamiliar with Korean culture and life. The other assumption was that these children, because their mothers are foreign, would be alienated from their Korean peers and would experience difficulties in shaping their cultural identity in the South Korean education system, which emphasizes ethnic and racial homogeneity (Korean Ministry of Education and Human Resources Development, 2006a).

To support children of foreign migrants and children of international marriages, called children of multicultural families, the May 2006 policy included some educational support plans. The Ministry of Education encouraged schools to implement programs to strengthen the school support for these children. These include the implementation of the following: after-school programs, in which additional instruction is given for Korean language learning and other school subjects; cultural experience programs, in which foreign mothers' cultures are shared; designating teachers specialized in communicating with these children; and the establishment of one-to-one relationships between the child and a Korean peer to help him or her get along with others. The Ministry provided parents who were not familiar with Korean school culture with information, translated into different languages, about the Korean school system and life. The Ministry encouraged a mentoring program where undergraduate students serve as mentors to such children. The Ministry also planned to enhance teachers' capacities for multicultural education by providing teacher training programs on multiculturalism and minority issues, and Korean language and culture. The Ministry revised and corrected some content emphasizing racial and ethnical homogeneity, containing national and cultural exclusionism, and implying racial discrimination in textbooks. It added multicultural education content that would help Korean students better understand cultural and racial diversity (Korean Ministry of Education and Human Resources Development, 2007). In response to the Ministry's policies and measures, in 2006, most local offices of education began to implement multicultural education projects that were appropriate for individual provinces with ethnically and racially diverse student populations. Some schools that were selected as model schools by each provincial education office began to implement the curriculum for multicultural education (Korean Ministry of Education and Human Resources Development, 2007).

Aid Plans for Multicultural Families Supported by Government Departments

Responding to the newly emerging ethnic and racial diversity in South Korea, in 2006, government departments raised awareness about multicultural families and devised diverse support policies (Korean Ministry of Education and Human Resources Development, 2006a). The multicultural policies of the Ministry of Education were interrelated with those of other government departments but sometimes were in conflict with others. For example, the Ministry of Justice helped multicultural families settle by deregulating requirements for married immigrants; in doing so, families can apply for naturalization in Korea. It also protected their human rights by banning immigration officials from chasing undocumented children near schools as a way to catch their parents. The Ministry of Gender Equality and Family founded the Care Center for Married Immigrants to help married women adapt to South Korean life by providing family counseling and mentoring, developing Korean language textbooks that contain information about Korean life and culture, offering Korean language classes, and developing guidelines with information on how to raise a child in South Korea. The Ministry of Health and Welfare supported multicultural families of low socioeconomic status through providing living expenses and school tuition for interracial people and providing health insurance guidelines in different languages. The Ministry of Labor provided migrant workers with employment support. The Ministry of Culture and Tourism offered culture and arts programs, Korean language, and culture education, to protect such children from cultural alienation (Korean Ministry of Education and Human Resources Development, 2006a).

SCHOOL PRACTICES AND TEACHER RESPONSES ON MINORITY STUDENTS

This section consists of the narratives of two teachers, Ms. Hong and Ms. Cha[1].Ms. Hong interacts with foreign students, especially children of undocumented foreign migrant workers, at Ansan Elementary School near an industrial complex, and Ms. Cha teaches children of international marriages and married immigrant women at Jeollabuk Elementary School. (The larger study on which this chapter is based has additional cases.[2])

Students from Migrant Workers

To respond to the Ministry's policy and to encourage undocumented children to obtain elementary school education, in March 2006, Ms. Hong's school began a special class for children of foreign workers and recruited foreign children, especially children of undocumented foreign workers, who had been isolated from school education as a result of their parents' uncertain legal status. At the time of the data collection, Ms. Hong's special class consisted of 12 foreign students of different nationalities, whose ages ranged from 7 to 16. Their parents came from Mongolia, India, Japan, China, Sri Lanka, Uzbekistan, and Russia. Students older than their Korean elementary peers, whose education had been neglected both in their own country and in South Korea, entered this class. All of the students had a minimum low level of communication skills in the Korean language when they were admitted. Furthermore, these students differed in their language and learning progress based on their different ages.

Language Issues

The most important goal of Ms. Hong's class was to improve her foreign students' Korean language ability. She believed that knowing the Korean language is a prerequisite for living in South Korea. Her students, however, had serious problems with the Korean language when they entered her class, as most of them had not learned Korean in their home country. They also could not get help from their parents, as they were not fluent in Korean. She said:

> When my children entered this class, they were not able to say or even ask, "What is this?" They didn't even know the words "yes" and "no" and they could not understand the appropriate context when they could say "yes" or "no." It took a month for them to get used to the

appropriate uses of "yes" and "no." It took a whole month to teach this simple thing. You can guess how difficult other things would be."

Ms. Hong was concerned about her students keeping their own cultures and languages. However, in practice, she focused only on teaching Korean language and culture. As for the language issue, she believed these students should first learn the core values, language, and culture of South Korea, which she considered indispensable, and adapt themselves to live and survive as a minority in South Korean society. She also believed that Korean language education enabled them to participate in and not be alienated from cultural experiences. Thus, she focused on cultural adaptation in school, and she expected parents to teach their children the home culture, including the home language, to preserve their culture and language. She explained:

> Both of the cultures should be considered. We cannot eliminate all of their unique culture. However, radiating their colors too much may cause some trouble. Focusing on the adaptation itself is too much. Removing their colors is also not good for them. The best way is to find a balance between the two. We can focus more on Korean culture in school, and they can put more emphasis on their own culture at home. They need to learn a lot about their own culture at home. However, in school, it is important for them to follow the same rules applied to their Korean friends.

Legal Issues

The prevalent issues emerging from the experiences of Ms. Hong, who had been interacting with children of undocumented foreign migrants as a special class teacher, were the children's uncertain legal status and their educational neglect resulting from this uncertainty. Most children of undocumented foreign migrants had not attended school because of fear of government crackdown and possible deportation, as well as because of poverty resulting from their parents' uncertain legal status. Thus, the teachings and curriculum of Ms. Hong, who taught the children of undocumented foreign workers, were influenced by the children's and their parents' legal status, and by the policies of the Ministry of Education and the Provincial Office of Education as related to the legal issues and admission requirements.

International Marriage Minorities

Schools like Ms. Cha's Jeollabuk Elementary School are located in rural areas, such as in fishing, mountain, and agrarian villages, where international marriages have recently increased in number. International marriages represented 35.9% of all international marriages in South Korea in 2005 because Korean fishing or agrarian men have sought spouses from other Asian countries (Korean National Statistical Office, 2006). Arranged marriages through marriage brokers or by religion are common among internationally married couples in these rural areas. Most of the husbands are older than their wives. Many of these families struggle financially, and many of the immigrant mothers do not speak Korean and have difficulty adjusting to their new environment. The policy of the Ministry of Education indicated that these factors would directly affect the children's education (Korean Ministry of Education and Human Resources Development, 2007).

Educational Opportunities for Internationally Married Immigrant Women

Unlike the government policy's assumption that students from international marriage families would experience difficulties in language and school learning, Ms. Cha perceived that these children have no special problems and they should be treated as Koreans similar to other Koreans who had Korean parents. Rather, her school provided foreign mothers with multicultural education programs. Ms. Cha said teachers in her school believed that the most urgent problem was the immigrant mothers' adaptation to living in Korea, and they thought schools should provide these mothers with educational opportunities:

> The most important thing is that the mothers need to adapt here. We felt the need for our schools to provide the mothers with educational opportunities to help their adaptation, so we created and opened programs for the mothers although we have no programs for the children. If we educate them, it could help their children's education. Even though the education of elementary children mostly takes place in the school rather than in their homes, if mothers don't understand even an announcement or notice from school, this could influence their children's learning.

According to Ms. Cha, most international marriages in the area were arranged marriages, and most of these internationally married couples had married without an understanding of each other's cultural and language differences. In addition, these married couples, who had no shared language, were not even able to communicate with each other at the early stage of their marriage.

Ms. Cha's school was running a Korean language class and a computer class for married immigrant women after school. The time after regular classes was used for the Korean language class and the computer class. In practice, the mothers who took the computer class made good use of the computer to visit websites written in their native language and to hear news about their native lands by exchanging e-mails with their family members. The educational programs for married immigrant mothers in Ms. Cha's school developed to help foreign mothers adapt to Korea life included a culture field trip, in which foreign immigrant mothers went to a museum of historical artifacts or historical sites to understand Korean culture.

Immigrant Women's Heritage Culture

In Jeollabuk Elementary School, all internationally married immigrants were women who had come from other Asian countries, that is, China, Japan, and the Philippines. They entered South Korea bringing different cultural and linguistic backgrounds and lifestyles. How have their heritage culture and language continued to be used and taught to the children within their family? Ms. Cha said, "These mothers tended not to display their own culture; consequently, their children cannot learn their native languages". She also mentioned, "The Korean father's culture and language were emphasized, but those of the immigrant mother tended to be put aside within their family or in the local community". She continued that these immigrant mothers had difficulty having their voices heard at home and in the community because "their cultures are not naturally accepted". What is more, she said that parents from international marriage families seemed not to recognize the need to teach their children to use two languages and hold two cultures from both parents; rather, their concern was adaptation.

CONCLUSION

Through an examination of policies, school practices, and teachers' responses in South Korea, this chapter discussed educational issues related to migrant workers and international marriage minorities.

The most important educational issue of Ms. Hong for undocumented foreign students was the undocumented children's educational neglect resulting from their uncertain legal status. However, among teachers in schools that enroll children of documented foreign migrants, concern with foreign children's legal status was less evident. None of the teachers of children of international marriages in the rural school mentioned that legal status was a constraint. At Jeollabuk Elementary School, children whose fathers were Korean were able to register as Korean nationals at birth due to the personal nationality principle of South Korea. In addition, foreign wives of Korean men were qualified to seek Korean nationality after the couple had been married for two years (Oh, 2005).

Both Ms. Hong and Ms. Cha recognized that the most urgent educational problem they had to solve was the undocumented children's or the immigrant mothers' adaptation to life in Korea. Two schools implemented educational programs targeting foreign children and married immigrant mothers to help them in their adaptation to Korean life. The findings from this study indicated teachers stressed that minorities' maintaining and sharing their own heritage culture and language were not realistic for living in poor conditions, so the goal of these programs was focused on adaptation to Korean culture and life. Gay (1988) and Ladson-Billings (1994) emphasized culturally relevant pedagogy, which provides students from cultural minorities with teaching that is culturally compatible with their own home culture, in the hopes that this may promote genuine academic success and strong sense of self-esteem in cultural minority students. Some studies have explored the significance of this type of teaching (Ladson-Billings, 1994; Lee, 1991). Contrary to these studies and arguments, the teaching experiences and perspectives of the teachers, for practical reasons, emphasized adaptation as their multicultural education. However, adaptation may reinforce the assimilation of minority students into the dominant mainstream culture and values. It may marginalize the cultural values and experiences of these students. Critical multiculturalists have confronted such assimilation in the mainstream culture (Giroux, 2000; McLaren, 2000). Ethnic studies of multiculturalists have attempted to incorporate the voices of marginalized ethnic and cultural groups into the curriculum (Glazer, 1997).

The teachers argued that children of international marriages have no special problems and giving special attention to them may be considered discriminatory treatment, unlike the government policy's assumption that they would experience difficulties in language and school learning and in shaping their own interpersonal relationships.

In conclusion, this chapter contributes to an understanding of foreign migrant worker families and international marriage families with related population descriptions, policies, and school practices phenomena. Using narrative inquiry, this chapter contributes to theoretical literature, allowing readers to deeply penetrate the participants' perspectives and experiences.

NOTES

1. All names are pseudonyms.
2. This manuscript is based on a dissertation study (Lee, 2008).

REFERENCES

Cho, Y. (2006). *Damonhwa gajeongeui janey kyoyook siltae josa* [Investigation of education of children in multicultural families]. Seoul: Korean Ministry of Education and Human Resources Development.
Clandinin, D. J., & Connelly, F. M. (1994). Personal experience methods. In N. K. Denzin & Y. S. Lincoln (Eds.), *Handbook of qualitative research* (pp. 413–427). Thousand Oaks, CA: Sage.

Connelly, F. M., & Clandinin, D. J. (1990). Stories of experience and narrative inquiry. *Educational Researcher, 9*, 2–14.

Gay, G. (1988). Designing relevant curricula for diverse learners. *Education and Urban Society, 20*, 327–340.

Giroux, H. A. (2000). Insurgent multiculturalism and the promise of pedagogy. In E. M. Duarte & S. Smith (Eds.), *Foundational perspectives in multicultural education* (pp. 195–212). New York: Longman.

Glazer, N. (1997). *We are all multiculturalists now.* Cambridge, MA: Harvard University Press.

He, M. F. (2002). A narrative inquiry of cross-cultural lives: Lives in China. *Journal of Curriculum Studies, 34*, 301–321.

Korean Ministry of Education and Human Resources Development. (2006a). *Educational support for children from multicultural backgrounds.* Retrieved June 14, 2006, from http://www.mest.go.kr/

Korean Ministry of Education and Human Resources Development. (2006b). *Damonhwa gajeong gyoyook jiwon daechaek* [The educational supports for the children from multicultural families]. Retrieved May 1, 2006, from http://www.mest.go.kr/

Korean Ministry of Education and Human Resources Development. (2007). *Damonhwa gajeong gyoyook jiwon* [The support to multicultural families]. Seoul: Author.

Korean Ministry of Education and Human Resources Development. (2008). *Number of children from international marriage families enrolled in primary and secondary schools by region.* Retrieved July 1, 2008, from http://www.mest. go.kr

Korean Ministry of Gender Equality and Family. (2007). *Yeoseong gyeolhon iminja gajogui sahoe tonghap jiwon daechaek* [Support plan of social integration of families of female married immigrants]. Seoul: Korean Ministry of Gender Equality and Family.

Korean National Statistical Office. (2006). *Statistics on international marriages.* Retrieved July 20, 2006, from http://kosis.nso.go.kr

Ladson-Billings, G. (1994). *The dreamkeepers: Successful teachers of African American children.* San Francisco: Jossey-Bass.

Lee, C. D. (1991). Big picture talkers/words walking without masters: The instructional implications of ethnic voices for an expanded literacy. *Journal of Negro Education, 60*, 291–304.

Lee, J. (2008). *Multicultural education in South Korean public elementary schools: An analysis of teachers' experiences and perspectives and school curriculum.* Unpublished doctoral dissertation, Purdue University, West Lafayette.

McLaren, P. (2000). White terror and oppositional agency: Towards a critical multiculturalism. In E. M. Duarte & S. Smith (Eds.), *Foundational perspectives in multicultural education* (pp. 213–242). New York: Longman.

Oh, S. (2005). *Kosian adongui seongjanggwa hwangyeonge gwanhan sarye yeongu* [Case study on the growth and environment of Kosian children]. *Korean education, 32*, 61–83.

Phillion, J. (2008). Multicultural and cross-cultural narrative inquiry into understanding immigrant students' educational experience in Hong Kong. *Compare: A Journal of Comparative Education, 38*, 281–293.

Seol, D. (2005). *Estimated number of illegal foreigners.* Seoul: Korean Ministry of Justice.

14 From Assimilation to the Assertion of Subjectivity

Critiques of Indigenous Educational Policies in Taiwan

Dorothy I-ru Chen

INTRODUCTION

When powerful typhoon Morakot swept across Taiwan on August 8, 2009, many indigenous peoples (IPs) were trapped in the South, hundreds were buried alive, and houses were destroyed. This disaster exemplifies the dilemma faced by IPs in Taiwan. Due to the difficulty of finding jobs in cities, most of them remain in rural and mountainous areas, which are usually the worst-hit regions when natural disasters strike.

After decades of public policies promoting economic growth and development at all costs, the backlash from nature has finally taken its toll, and IPs have become the primary victims. Some argue that these people should go back to their native territories and start anew, or they should be relocated to more populated areas. The government has been proposing assistance for the relocation of these people to safer areas, but the offer has encountered strong resistance from IPs themselves.

This chapter reviews related Western IP literature, the history of IPs in Taiwan, indigenous educational policies in Taiwan, and policy critiques. For decades, the Taiwanese government has been paying much attention to underachieving indigenous students. As someone living in an IP-populated area, Nantou County, the author is particularly aware of the educational problems faced by IPs. Although more and more indigenous students are entering universities, their performance remains problematic. This chapter traces the theoretical underpinnings of Taiwan's indigenous educational policies and discusses how— due to changing political and social climates at the national and global levels—the focus of these policies has shifted over the years. Whether these policies have reached their intended goals or have created new problems is also examined.

ETHNICITY AND RELATED EDUCATIONAL REFORMS

To gain a better understanding of the development of indigenous policies in Taiwan, it is necessary to review discussions on various ideologies that affect the formation of indigenous policies. According to Banks (1994), although many educators agree that schools should not ignore ethnicity, there are no agreements on the kind of reforms that should be implemented or on the method of implementing reforms. He identifies two major ideological positions related to race and ethnic diversity in major Western societies: assimilationism and cultural pluralism.

According to Banks, the pluralist argues that ethnicity and ethnic identity are very important in pluralist Western societies. The cultural pluralist assumes that "ethnic minorities have unique learning styles and that school curricula and learning strategies should be revised to be more consistent with the cognitive and learning styles of ethnic group students" (Banks, 1994, p. 123).

Assimilationists see ethnicity and ethnic attachments as fleeting and temporary in an increasingly modernized world. They argue that ethnicity would wane or disappear under the forces of modernization, industrialization, and democratization. They believe that "the best way to promote the goals of society and to develop commitments to democratic ideals is to promote the full socialization of all individuals and groups into the shared culture" (Banks, 1994, p. 125). They assume that groups causing their members to function unsuccessfully in the common culture are deficient, deprived, and bereft of necessary functional characteristics. All citizens must learn to participate in a common culture, and this requires universal skills and competencies.

Banks (1994) believes that the two foregoing ideologies do not sufficiently guide educational reforms. He asserts that the pluralist fails to see that high levels of cultural assimilation have taken place in modern societies, such as the US. The assimilationist also fails to notice that certain educational assumptions and practices often hinder the academic success of indigenous students (i.e., those socialized within ethnic communities with cultural characteristics that are quite different from those of the school). Thus, according to Banks, the multicultural ideology can best guide educational reforms and school policies. In a multiethnic open society, individuals are free to maintain their ethnic identities within the common culture—and within and across other ethnic cultures (Table 14.1). However, even Banks (1994) admits that difficulties may emerge: "How does the individual function within two cultures that sometimes have contradictory and conflicting norms, values, and expectations?" (p. 131). Despite this question, Banks still posits that public institutions, such as schools, can and should allow ethnic groups to practice their culture-specific behaviors—as long as these are not in conflict with the major goals of the school.

Based on Banks' analysis of ethnicity-related ideologies and educational reforms, the development of indigenous educational policies in Taiwan is discussed.

Table 14.1 Ideologies Related to Ethnicity and Pluralism in Western Societies

Cultural pluralist Ideology ◄———	Multicultural Ideology ———►	Assimilationist Ideology
Separation	Open society Multiculturalism	Total integration
Primordial Particularistic	Universalized primordialism	Universalistic
Minority emphasis	Minorities and majorities have rights	Majoritarian emphasis
Curriculum Culture-specific materials and teaching styles should be used. The goal of the curriculum is to help students function more successfully within their own ethnic cultures and to help liberate their ethnic groups from oppression.	The curriculum should respect the ethnicity of the child and should use it in positive ways. The goal of the curriculum is to help students learn how to function effectively within the common culture, their ethnic culture, and other ethnic cultures.	CurriculumMaterials and teaching styles that are related to the common culture should be used. The goal of the curriculum is to help students develop commitment to the common civic culture and its ideals.
TeachersMinority students need skilled teachers who are of the same race and ethnicity to serve as their role models—for them to learn more effectively and to develop more positive self-concepts and identities.	TeachersStudents need skilled teachers who are very knowledgeable about and sensitive to their ethnic cultures and cognitive styles.	TeachersStudents need skilled teachers who are familiar with learning theories and who can implement these theories effectively for any group of students, regardless of these students' ethnicity, race, or social class. Good teachers must be trained.

Source: Banks, J. A., 1994, p. 129

OVERVIEW OF INDIGENOUS GROUPS IN TAIWAN

Indigenous groups in Taiwan are composed of Austronesians (Malayo-Polynesians) who have linguistic and genetic ties with other Austronesians, such as people from the Philippines, Malaysia, Indonesia, Madagascar, and Oceania (Hill et al., 2007). They have been colonized by the Dutch, Spaniards, Hans, Japanese, and Chinese (the Nationalist government). To varying degrees, these colonizers have influenced or transformed the language and culture of these indigenous groups.

During the Qing Dynasty (1644–1911), officials classified aboriginals into two categories: "sheng-fan" (raw, wild, or unripe savages) and "shou-fan" (cooked, tame, or ripe savages) to define whether these aboriginals have submitted to Qing rule and have been assimilated into the Han culture (Harrell, 1995, p. 19). In the late 19th century, the terms "plains tribes" (pingpuzu) and "high mountain tribes" (gaoshanzu) were also used (Teng, 2004, pp. 125–127). During the Japanese occupation, this binary classification was maintained. When the nationalist government came to Taiwan in 1949, the binary terms "mountain compatriots" (sandi tongbao) and "plains compatriots" (pingdi tongbao) were used.

The impacts of foreign colonization and Han culture are more obvious among the tribes in the plains. In the beginning of the 20th century, aboriginals were largely assimilated into the contemporary Taiwanese culture; the tribes in the plains were first assimilated, followed by the highland groups. This assimilation caused certain degrees of language decay and loss of indigenous cultural identity. Moreover, with centuries of intermarriages between Hans and IPs, many Taiwanese have indigenous ancestries. Hence, relatively pure-blooded IPs comprise roughly 2% of Taiwan's population. As of July 2009, their total population was estimated at 500,429 (Council of Indigenous Peoples, 2009a).

Today, the Taiwanese government officially recognizes distinct tribes based on the qualifications drawn by the Council of Indigenous Peoples (CIP). Presently, 14 tribes (Table 14.2) have been recognized, although there is no scholarly consensus on the demographic division of Taiwan's IPs. Among those who have applied for tribal status, only two indigenous groups in the plains have been officially recognized. The remaining 12 recognized tribes are traditionally regarded as mountain IPs.

Table 14.2   Population and Distribution of (Recognized) Indigenous Tribes in Taiwan

Tribes	Population	Location
Amis	180,978	Mainly in eastern valleys and coastal areas
Atayal	79,128	Scattered throughout the northern part of central Taiwan's mountainous region
Bunun	50, 823	In the central and southeastern mountainous regions
Kavalan (plains)	1, 201	In Taiwan's eastern counties
Paiwan	87, 166	In the southern Central Mountain Range, Hengchun Peninsula, and southeastern coastal region
Pinuyumayan	11, 654	Concentrated in Taitung County
Rukai	11, 800	In Pingtung, Kaohsiung, and Taitung counties
Saisiyat	5, 786	In northwestern Taiwan (Miaoli and Hsinchu counties)

Continued

Table 14.2   Continued

Tribes	Population	Location
Sakizaya (plains)	406	Mainly in eastern Taiwan (Hualien County)
Sediq (Seediq/Seejiq)	6, 052	In Nantou, Hualien, and Ilan counties
Thao	663	Once resided in Lalu Island in the middle of Sun Moon Lake, later moved to the lake's edge
Truku	25, 286	In the eastern coast (Hualien County) and the mountainous region of Nantou County
Tsou	6, 648	Once lived around Jade Mountain, now in Nantou, Chaiyi, and Kaohsiung counties
Yami	3, 606	In Orchid Island (off Taiwan's southeastern coast)

Source: Government Information Office, Republic of China, 2006; Council of Indigenous Peoples, 2009b

RECENT DEVELOPMENTS IN INDIGENOUS EDUCATIONAL POLICIES

To improve the living standards and work opportunities of IPs in Taiwan, the government has adopted a series of educational policies to raise the educational attainment of indigenous students. However, to date, IPs in Taiwan still face economic and social barriers to progress, including high unemployment rates and substandard education. Indigenous educational policies are largely affected by the broader social and political context (i.e., the lifting of Martial Law in 1987 and the Demonstration for Educational Reform in 1994); hence, it is necessary to trace the evolution of Taiwan's public policies.

Public Policies for IPs in Taiwan

Since the 1990s, there has been a growing awareness and appreciation of indigenous rights and cultures from both government and indigenous groups. Heber (2003) believes that the growing concern for IPs has much to do with global trends. The global recognition of indigenous rights, including the right to education, began in the late 1960s. In 1992, the UN published the Draft Declaration of Indigenous Peoples Rights. Five years thereafter, the UN Declaration on the Rights of Indigenous Peoples was finally approved by 143 votes, with only 4 negative votes (Canada, Australia, New Zealand, and the US) and 11 abstentions. The declaration spells out the individual and collective rights of IPs, particularly their rights to culture, identity, language, employment, health, education, and other concerns.

Andres (2006) divides Taiwan's recent public policy development into three periods. During the first period, low profile period (1949–1986), public policies were focused on infrastructure. These policies were adopted for state reasons, not because of the needs of cultural minorities. In 1962, policies were aimed at integrating aboriginal economies into Taiwan's economic structure. For example, the Shandi Pingdi Hua aimed to "make the mountains like the plains"; it resulted in the influx of people into the cities. Most of these city newcomers became low-waged laborers. During the second period, medium profile period (1987–1995), public policies focused on the needs of IPs, although the opinions of indigenous groups were not strongly considered. During the third period, high profile period (1996–present), public policies upgraded all issues connected with IPs, not only from the institutional point of view but also from the humanitarian perspective. As such, natives were appointed to serve in important IP-related offices.

In the 1990s, IPs witnessed three dramatic milestones in their struggle for recognition (Cheng & Jacob, 2002). First, in 1992, various indigenous rights were incorporated into the constitution. Second, in 1994, IPs were officially recognized as "yuachumin" (original inhabitants); "yuachumin" replaced the derogatory term "shanpao" (mountain people). Third, in 1996, the Council of Aboriginal Affairs (ministry level) was established to coordinate and plan IP-related activities. The Council was renamed Council of Indigenous Peoples (CIP) in 2002. Among the current minister and three vice ministers, only one of the vice ministers is a Han. The remaining three are all IPs. In 1998, the Society for Promoting Rights of Taiwanese Indigenous People (established in 1984) was renamed the Society for Promoting Rights of Taiwanese Indigenous Peoples. In the same year, the Developmental Programs for Taiwan Aborigines was launched by the Executive Yuan.

In the 21st century, major developments include the enactment of the Indigenous Peoples Basic Law in 2005. According to Article 4 of the law, the government shall guarantee the equal status of IPs with other members of the society, the development of their self-governance, and the implementation of IP autonomy in accordance with the will of IPs (Council of Indigenous Peoples, 2005).

Generally, these policies are closely related to the ongoing political liberalization and democratization initiated in the late 1980s. Major events, such as the amendment of the constitution in 1992, the establishment of the CIP, and the launching of the Developmental Programs for Taiwan Aborigines in 1998, made significant impacts on indigenous educational policies. However, challenges remain in promoting indigenous cultures, especially with the migration of IPs to the cities. Another current major dispute is the official recognition of other tribes in the plains. To date, the CIP is not willing to recognize more tribes in the plains besides the current two (i.e., Kavalan and Sakizaya). They argue that the tribes in the plains have been generally assimilated into the Han culture; thus, they have ceased to exist as tribes. Some claim that the CIP's rejection is economically motivated; with more recognized tribes, limited resources to be distributed to other indigenous groups would be affected. In May 2010 the United Nations accepted the request of some plains tribes' activists to launch an investigation into the Taiwanese government's refusal to grant them official aboriginal status.

Developments in Indigenous Education since 1945

The Ministry of Education (MOE) (2005) has divided the development of indigenous educational policies into the following four stages:

1. Equal treatment stage (from the Restoration to 1962): During this stage, IPs were treated equally with the rest of the population. Schools for aboriginal children during the Japanese occupation were converted into national schools, with indigenous students receiving the same preferential treatment as students in remote areas.
2. Fusion stage (1963–1987): The government encouraged IPs to mix with the Hans. The objective was for them to accept Han culture and to be protected from prejudice. Their assimilation into the rest of the nation was reinforced with Mandarin and skills learning.
3. Open development stage (1988–2000): It was during this stage when the Society for Promoting Rights of Taiwanese Indigenous Peoples announced the Declaration of Rights of Taiwanese Indigenous Peoples. The declaration asserts that IPs have the right to establish their own schools and to receive education through their native languages. Accordingly, the government should respect the equal status of indigenous languages with the mainstream language. Furthermore, the declaration maintains that in indigenous areas, indigenous languages should be taught (Bawnay, 2008).
4. Identity development stage (2001–present): In 2003, during the National Education Development Conference, "respecting indigenous identity and developing indigenous tribal education" was announced as an objective. In 2006, the Five-Year Medium-Term Program to Develop Indigenous Education was launched.

Not surprisingly, 1987 is also a key point in the development of indigenous educational policies. Before 1987, the Kumintang government worked to create a strong national Chinese cultural identity at the expense of local cultures. Textbook contents, such as the Wu Feng Legend, were considered offensive to IPs. Since the 1980s, the rights and social concerns of Taiwan's indigenous tribes have received increased political and public attention.

Indigenous educational reforms are initiated not only by political democratization but also by major educational reforms. On April 10, 1994, a mass demonstration demanding educational reforms took place. The movement,

Table 14.3 Development of Indigenous Educational Policies

1949	The Three-Year Plan to Improve the Educational Facilities of Aboriginals was drawn by Taiwan's Provincial Board of Education.
1951	The Program to Implement Improvement of Aboriginal Education was announced and enacted.
1952	The Essentials for Various Counties to Improve their Educational and Administrative Facilities for Aboriginals was enacted.
1963	The Program to Improve Aboriginal Administration was drawn.
1970	The Measures to Reinforce Aboriginal Education was announced. Teachers were encouraged to teach aboriginal students, while students enjoyed free textbooks and stationeries.
1988	The MOE established the Aboriginal (Shanpao) Education Committee. The committee aims to help aboriginals "adapt to modern life and maintain traditional culture."
1992	Indigenous education gained legal recognition when indigenous rights were incorporated into the constitution.
1993	The Five-Year Program to Develop and Improve Aboriginal Education (1994–1998) was drawn.
1994	The Aboriginal Education Committee was renamed the Indigenous (original inhabitants) Education Committee.
1996	The Council of Aboriginal Affairs was established in the Executive Yuan.
1998	The Education Act for Indigenous People was enacted. The Second Five-Year Program to Develop and Improve Aboriginal Education (1999–2003) was launched.
2000	The College of Indigenous Studies (CIS), National Dong Hwa University (NDHU), was established.
2006	The Five-Year Medium-Term Program to Develop Aboriginal Education was launched.

which was later called "the 410 Demonstration for Educational Reform," demanded the removal of all unreasonable governmental controls on education and the use of a student-centered approach in the educational system. Consequently, in 1994, the government published the Consultants' Concluding Report on Education Reform, which included several recommendations on indigenous education.

According to Heber (2003), aboriginal education gained legal recognition in Taiwan when, in 1992, aboriginal rights were incorporated into the constitution. In 1998, the Education Act for Indigenous Peoples was enacted. In the same year, the Five-Year Action Plan for Educational Reform was drawn, and indigenous education was one of its key areas. In 1998, the official curriculum in Taiwan schools was modified to contain more frequent and favorable allusions and references to IPs.

Two events are of particular significance. First, the Education Act for Indigenous Peoples was promulgated in 1998. The act covers many areas, such as school education, curriculum, faculty, social education and research, evaluation, and incentives. The act states that IPs are the center of indigenous education (Section 2); hence, every department of the government should provide active assistance to IPs, and the government should ensure equal educational opportunities for IPs and establish an education system suitable to the demands of IPs (Section 3). The act also requires that school curricula and textbooks employ multicultural perspectives and include the ethnic historical cultures of IPs, as well as their sense of values (Section 18). Furthermore, preschool and public educational programs should provide indigenous students an opportunity to learn their ethnic language, history, and culture (Section 19) (Council of Indigenous Peoples, 1998).

Second, the first major higher education institution related to ethnic studies, the College of Indigenous Studies (CIS), National Dong Hwa University (NDHU), was established. Currently, CIS has three undergraduate programs and three graduate institutes. In addition to the academic programs, there is also an Indigenous Research and Training Center. Since 1993, more and more teacher training colleges and universities, such as Hualien Teacher Training College, Taichung Teacher Training College, Pingtung Teacher Training College, Taitung Teacher Training College, and National Dong Hwa University, have established indigenous educational centers and postgraduate programs; however, these initiatives are small in scale and are generally limited to teacher training institutions. The establishment of the CIS shows that the concern for indigenous students has expanded from compulsory to higher educational levels. It also means that Taiwan is on its way toward establishing an educational system for IPs.

CONTEMPORARY IP EDUCATION

According to Mo and Chen (1996), due to assimilation-oriented policies, indigenous education faces several problems. First, the government does not pay attention to the different learning styles of indigenous students, and it only focuses on policies, such as tuition discounts, tuition-free measures, and preferential treatments in education. Indigenous students do not adjust well to their school lives, they experience identity problems, and they are even blamed for their failures. Second, academic gaps exist between indigenous and non-indigenous students. Third, conflicts exist between family education and school education. Fourth, teacher shortage is severe and teacher turnover is high. Most teachers do not belong to indigenous groups, and they are often frustrated by cultural gaps and communication problems with students. Fifth, most young and elite IPs migrate to the cities, leaving children and teenagers under the care of grandparents. Hence, schools have to exert more effort to support student learning. Sixth, indigenous pupils in cities also face adjustment difficulties. They have few opportunities to be exposed to their own cultures, and they are not used to the competitive culture of city schools. Thus, they are often less confident and have lower self-esteem.

It is necessary to assess whether the situation of indigenous education in Taiwan has improved. In the following section, related official statistics are reviewed to illuminate the current situation of indigenous students at all levels.

Current State of Indigenous Education

This section examines (a) the number of indigenous students at all levels, (b) the language courses offered to indigenous students, and (c) the ethnicities of staff in indigenous schools.

Table 14.4 shows the growing number of indigenous students at all levels from 1998 to 2007. Generally, the percentage of indigenous students in Taiwan schools seems to be reasonable because IPs only comprise 2% of the total population. Since the 1990s, the rapid expansion of higher educational institutions (HEIs) on the island has been reflected in the growing number of IP students at senior high school and higher educational levels. However, the percentage of indigenous students receiving higher education is much lower compared with indigenous students at other educational levels. In particular, the percentage of indigenous students at the doctorate level is only 0.1%.

Indigenous students at HEIs are concentrated in the areas of administration, education, politics, and police and military education (Tan, 2002). There are very few in the areas of engineering, medical studies, science, law, finance, and management, causing a serious shortage of indigenous professionals. Moreover, even if indigenous students are admitted to HEIs, they are often unable to afford tuition and living costs (Tan, 2002). The completion rate of indigenous students in higher education is still lower than that of their non-indigenous counterparts. Most of the resources (scholarships)

Table 14.4 Percentage of Indigenous Students at All Levels (1998–2007)

Academic Year	Total	PhD	MA	Under-Graduate	Senior high school	Vocational senior high school	Junior high school	Elementary school
1998	1.68	0.00	0.04	0.68	0.68	1.91	2.05	2.07
2000	1.76	0.02	0.09	0.81	0.98	1.78	2.16	2.29
2005	2.09	0.11	0.26	1.13	1.88	1.85	2.60	2.68
2007	2.29	0.10	0.32	1.30	2.32	2.50	2.82	2.81

Source: Council of Indigenous Peoples, 2008a

go to elite students from middle or upper-middle class families (T. T. Wu, 2007a). T. T. Wu argues that what these elite students need most are not grants or affirmative actions, but guidance toward success and respect for their culture.

Since the ratification of the Education Act for Indigenous Students in 1998, indigenous language teaching has been offered in most indigenous elementary and junior high schools. Table 14.5 shows that among 1,118 elementary and junior high schools that provide indigenous language courses, 879 are experiencing difficulties. Although most schools include the course in their formal school curriculum, there are few full-time language teachers. What is even more alarming is that the majority of these schools are experiencing difficulties in running these language courses.

Table 14.6 shows the high percentage of indigenous staff in Taiwan schools. Interestingly, the percentage of indigenous staff is the highest at the principalship level, which means that indigenous principals can be found in more than one-third of indigenous schools.

Current Key Indigenous Educational Policies: Practices and Critiques

Following the abolition of Martial Law in 1987 and the 410 Demonstration for Educational Reform in 1994, more attention was paid to indigenous education. Below are a few contentious policies related to indigenous education.

Educational Priority Area Plan (EPA) (1996–Present)

The EPA was launched in 1996, and it aims to offer more support for rural schools with (a) high proportions of indigenous students, (b) high proportions of students at a learning disadvantage, and (c) high proportions of students being taken care of by grandparents. These students come from low-income families and single families, and others have foreign-born or mainland Chinese mothers. The program has formulated suitable educational assistance strategies for schools that lack cultural resources and that are taking care of relatively disadvantaged students; it provides vigorous differential treatment compensation measures and invests adequate educational resources in an effort to raise the educational levels of students in such schools (Ministry of Education, 2006).

The implementation of EPA is not without problems. Research finds that EPA funds are mostly spent on equipment and facilities (Hsu, 2006; Lin, 2002). Other problems include the high turnover rate of teachers and their lack of professional development opportunities, the shortage of teachers who can teach traditional cultures and languages, and the lack of understanding of indigenous students among teachers (Hsu, 2006; Lin, 2002; J. F. Shih, 2008). Teachers do not change their teaching styles and their expectations toward these students. There is also a lack of effective and

Table 14.5 Indigenous Language Teaching in Elementary and Junior High Schools (2007)

Number of Schools / Education Level	With or without indigenous language course		Operations			Teachers				Difficulties		
	None	Yes	Student Clubs	Formal Curriculum	Other	Full-time	Part-time	Old-Timers & Priests	2688 Program[a]	Others	No	Yes
Total	2,299	1,118	305	635	305	46	695	99	306	13	239	879
Public	2,169	1,111	305	635	292	46	692	98	306	13	236	875
Private	130	7	0	0	13	0	3	1	0	0	3	4
Education Level												
Junior high	651	226	139	23	159	11	174	34	12	5	63	163
Indigenous Key Areas	9	70	34	18	22	9	45	23	5	2	24	46
Non-key areas	642	156	105	5	137	2	129	11	7	3	39	117
Elementary	1,648	892	166	612	146	35	521	65	294	8	176	716
Indigenous Key areas	6	273	21	252	15	25	115	49	102	5	72	201
Non-key areas	1,642	619	145	360	131	10	406	16	192	3	104	515

[a]Since 2001, to improve the student-teacher ratio, the government has allowed all the 2688 elementary schools to recruit hourly paid part-time teachers.

Source: Council of Indigenous Peoples, 2008b

Table 14.6   Indigenous Principals, Qualified Teachers, and Supply Teachers in
Indigenous Key Areas (2007)

	Schools reported	Indigenous principals		Indigenous qualified teachers		Indigenous supply teachers	
		Number	%	Number	%	Number	%
Total	358	129	36	1,035	13	61	6

Source: Council of Indigenous Peoples, 2008c

coherent teaching strategies among school teachers in improving the academic performance of these students (Hsu, 2006). J. F. Shih (2008) also
argues that the time arrangement of EPA's after-school lessons tends to be
in conflict with characteristic activities held by schools.

Preferential Treatment in Student Admission

Actions related to the admission of indigenous students have a long history
in Taiwan. The Education Act for Indigenous People in 1998 states that
educational establishments (senior high school or higher) should safeguard
the admission and schooling opportunities of indigenous students (Section
16). Since 2004, CIS, NDHU, has reserved half of the slots in the undergraduate program for indigenous students (T. T. Wu, 2007a).

Chuan (2006) evaluates admission policies for indigenous students and
finds that these policies are so far the most effective in terms of improving the educational conditions of indigenous students. However, Y. J. Wu's
(2002) research criticizes this policy, stating that it only benefits certain
elite indigenous students. Wu further argues that this kind of policy only
deals with the problem on a superficial level, and it ignores the fundamental
problem that the curriculum and teaching materials are strongly embedded
with mainstream Han culture and values. Consequently, with little prior
knowledge, indigenous students encounter more learning difficulties than
Han students when they enter universities. Finally, Wu sees that there is not
enough guidance and counseling in the academic work and life adjustment
of indigenous students.

In 2007, the MOE reviewed the preferential regulations in the admission of indigenous students to higher schools. The Ministry has confirmed that indigenous students should get extra points when taking
entrance examinations, and the original quota for indigenous students
should be expanded by 2%. After the MOE's review, indigenous students
were asked to obtain indigenous language proficiency certificates before
availing of the priority service. This new measure intends to end the long-
running controversy, which regards the earlier approach to indigenous
student admission as excluding excellent non-indigenous students. However, indigenous researchers, such as Bawnay (2008), assert that even if

students get the certificate, it does not mean that they can actually speak the language. Thus, whether indigenous languages can be preserved through this measure remains debatable. Furthermore, for students from lower socioeconomic backgrounds, the language requirement may mean an extra burden, given that their academic attainments are already lagging behind. Thus, T. T. Wu (2007b) argues that it is crucial to recognize that indigenous students from different social classes have different needs. There should not be a standardized approach. Moreover, other than the foregoing preferential treatments, the learning experiences and school adjustment of indigenous students are being highlighted by more and more scholars (e.g., T. T. Wu, 2007b).

Establishment of the CIS: An Indigenous Higher Education of Their Own?

Higher education is another key area that must be examined. The Education Act for Indigenous Peoples mandates the establishment of an educational system suitable for indigenous students. With key indigenous elementary and junior high public schools already in place, does the establishment of CIS, NDHU, mean that the aforementioned goal has been reached?

Evidence suggests that there are still many challenges ahead. The difficulties faced by CIS can be summed up in three aspects: staff recruitment, student admission, and students' career prospects. In terms of staff recruitment, the indigenous scholar Dadu (2008) argues that there is an insufficient number of indigenous academicians because of academic qualification and productivity requirements. He finds that only 6 (18%) of 33 full-time teachers at CIS are indigenous. He argues that this number cannot demonstrate the subjectivity of indigenous education in a multicultural environment—which is the reason why the college was established in the first place.

The limited number of indigenous staff at CIS is caused by numerous factors. First, the college is only a part of NDHU. Thus, its recruitment procedures must conform to NDHU's regulations, which means that recruitment must first pass through approval at the departmental, collegiate, and university levels. It is possible that CIS and the senior managers of NDHU have different priorities in staff recruitment. Second, a more serious problem is the availability of qualified individuals. According to the Council of Indigenous Affairs, 54 indigenous people were admitted to doctoral studies from 2005 to 2008, but only 9 were awarded their Ph.D. degrees during the same period. Thus, to start with, there are very few qualified (holding Ph.D. degrees) indigenous applicants for academic jobs. Dadu (2008) proposes that CIS secure a certain proportion (30–40%) of indigenous staff. However, in the era of globalization, competitiveness and productivity issues are more valued than equality and justice concerns. Today, indigenous academic staff may find that they are alienated by a highly individualistic and competitive culture, which is very different from the indigenous collectivist culture they are familiar with.

Furthermore, student admission at CIS, NDHU, still faces many difficulties. In 2008, only 19 students were admitted to the undergraduate program and 43 slots were not filled—the highest shortage among all undergraduate programs in public universities (Joint University Admission Committee, 2008). After much effort, the Dean of CIS announced that the total number of applicants dramatically increased in summer of 2009 (College of Indigenous Studies, NDHU, 2010).

To solve the problem of admission, policies must deal with the career prospects of students. Currently, CIS encourages its students to pursue civil service and teaching careers. However, in 2008, students at CIS found that under the new MOE regulations, they are not qualified to take the Secondary Teacher Training Program offered by the university. The MOE requires that the specialization of applicants matches the stipulated subjects for secondary teacher training at the university.[1] The courses offered by CIS are not seen as relevant to the stipulated secondary teacher training subjects at NDHU. At the moment, CIS is trying to negotiate with the Teacher Training Center and other colleges for them to offer subjects, such as citizenship and society, so that CIS students would be qualified to apply for the teaching program (College of Indigenous Studies, NDHU, 2009). Furthermore, Y. J. Wu's (2002) research criticizes the overemphasis on Han culture in Taiwan's teacher training programs. Indigenous students trained in these teacher training institutions are being alienated from their own cultures, and they may even experience confusion over their own cultural identities. Thus, they cannot play key roles in transmitting indigenous knowledge and cultures to indigenous pupils when they become school teachers.

CONCLUDING THOUGHTS: THE FUTURE OF INDIGENOUS EDUCATION IN TAIWAN

The development of indigenous educational policies has much to do with the democracy-inspired political reforms that started in 1987 and the educational reform in the early 1990s. Below, what has been achieved and the challenges that lie ahead are discussed.

Progress So Far

The Education Act for Indigenous People (1998) and the Indigenous Peoples Basic Law (2005) have paved the way for future reforms. Huang (2005) considers that related laws pay too much attention to the subjectivity of IPs. However, what has been achieved needs further investigation because she also finds that corresponding derived laws have not been formulated accordingly.

Furthermore, responding to the criticism that current policies benefit elite indigenous students more than others and the fact that most indigenous students are from lower socioeconomic backgrounds, the government has recently introduced a tuition-waiver program that will initially waive tuition for about 4,700 indigenous senior high school, college, and university students affected by Typhoon Morakot. Starting in 2010, the project will be expanded to cover all indigenous senior high school students in Taiwan. The MOE expects that the program will eventually benefit 18,000 indigenous students (H.C. Shih, 2009).

Challenges Ahead

In terms of the challenges ahead, more attention should be given to teaching strategies, curricula, and student learning experiences. It is argued that affirmative actions, such as EPA and preferential admission policies, tend to pay too much attention to certain issues and neglect dimensions such as teaching strategies, indigenous students' learning experiences in non-key indigenous schools, and a well-structured indigenous education for both indigenous and non-indigenous students. Due to the lack of job opportunities in rural areas, it is increasingly common for IPs to leave their children in the care of grandparents to find jobs in big cities. With little academic support from grandparents, these pupils have limited chances of succeeding academically. On the other hand, prior to the unprecedented expansion of higher education in the 1990s, the preferential admission policy mostly benefited elite indigenous students. In recent years, with more indigenous students entering higher education, it has become important to explore the learning experiences and future career prospects of these students, as well as the academic support and career guidance programs that are available to them.

Teacher recruitment and the professional development of teachers are keys to the success of indigenous education. At compulsory educational levels, the high turnover of teachers in key indigenous areas remains a problem. It is important to help Han teachers, who are working in indigenous schools, have a better understanding of indigenous languages and cultures so that proper teaching methods can be developed.

At higher educational levels, faculty recruitment is facing the dilemma of balancing the competitiveness and subjectivity of IPs. In the era of globalization, competitiveness and productivity issues are much more valued than equality and justice concerns. Moreover, most indigenous academicians are concentrated in the humanity and social science fields. It is necessary to encourage more indigenous students to develop interests in the fields of science, engineering, and technology; this way, they can contribute more to their cultures and their peoples.

From Assimilated-Oriented Policies to the Assertion of Indigenous Subjectivity

Indigenous educational policies in Taiwan have moved gradually from assimilation toward acculturation (Tan, 2002). In recent years, multiculturalism has become the trend in the development of indigenous educational policies (Huang, 2005). Huang considers that indigenous educational policies have taken a pluralist point of view, taking the mainstream culture as the center and recognizing the differences between Han and indigenous peoples.

However, although Taiwan is moving away from the assimilationist ideology, many current policies are still embedded with assimilationist elements. Thus, the prevalence of the multicultural ideology, which Banks envisions, still has a long way to go. Banks and Banks (1995) remind us one important goal of multicultural education:

> to help all students acquire the knowledge, attitudes, and skills needed to function effectively in a pluralistic democratic society and to interact, negotiate, and communicate with peoples from diverse groups in order to create a civic and moral community that works for the common good. (p. xi)

To date, the operation of indigenous education is mostly for indigenous students, instead of the general public. In multicultural societies, such as Taiwan, indigenous education should not be limited to indigenous students but to all future citizens. Moreover, because most policies are initiated either from the top or from elite IPs, the lack of subjectivity among IPs remains a problem. Therefore, it is necessary to include more IPs in related decision-making. If more reforms are initiated from the bottom rather than from the top, policies will be able to meet the needs of more IPs. Although Taiwan has made much progress in developing a better educational environment for indigenous students, fulfilling the ideals of multicultural education may still require time.

NOTES

1. Currently, the secondary teacher training program at NDHU only provides training in Chinese, English, history, physical education, and counseling for teachers in humanity and social science areas. There is no training for civic teachers. Citizenship study is considered more relevant for the College of Indigenous Studies.

REFERENCES

Andres, S. N. V. (2006). *Taiwan public policies for indigenous people* (Centro Argentino de Estudios Internacionales [CAEI] Working Paper No. 23). Retrieved January 10, 2011, from http://www.caei.com.ar/es/programas/di/23.pdf
Banks, J. A. (1994). *Multiethnic education: theory and practice.* Allyn & Bacon.
Banks, J. A., & Banks, C. A. M. (Eds.). (1995). *Handbook of research on multicultural education.* New York: Macmillan.
Bawnay, P. (2008). *The indigenous peoples' right to education: theories and practices.* Unpublished MA thesis, Graduate Institute of the Taiwanese Ethno-Development, National Dong Hwa University, Taiwan.

Cheng, S. Y., & Jacob, W. J. (2002). Marginality and aboriginal educational policy analysis in the United States and Taiwan. (ERIC Document Reproduction Service No. ED470504)

Chuan, C. W. (2006). *The study of the perquisite admission policy for aboriginal students in Taiwan*. Unpublished MA thesis, Department of Education Policy and Administration, Nation Chi Nan University, Taiwan.

College of Indigenous Studies, National Dong Hwa University. (2009). *Updated news*. Retrieved March 20, 2009, from http://www.cis.ndhu.edu.tw/zh/html/index.php

College of Indigenous Studies, National Dong Hwa University. (2010). Updated news. Retrieved Feb 9, 2011, from http://www.cis.ndhu.edu.tw/files/14-1016-9891,r21-1.php

Council of Indigenous Peoples. (1998). *Education Act for Indigenous Peoples*. Retrieved Feb 9, 2011, from http://www.apc.gov.tw/portal/docDetail.html?CID=7 4DD1F415708044A&DID=3E651750B40064679056ED1F4F06701A

Council of Indigenous Peoples. (2005). *The Indigenous Peoples Basic Law*. Retrieved Feb 9, 2011, from http://www.apc.gov.tw/portal/docDetail.html?CID=74DD1F41 5708044A&DID=3E651750B4006467D4B40DD3AC1D7378

Council of Indigenous Peoples. (2008a). *The current state of indigenous education*. Retrieved Feb 9, 2011, from http://cip.cpc.org.tw/index.aspx?DOC_SNO=WP02-39&Page_ID=WP02&Yearly=97&PageFrom=0

Council of Indigenous Peoples. (2008b). *Indigenous language teaching in elementary and junior high schools (2007)* Retrieved Feb 9, 2011, from http://cip.cpc.org.tw/ index.aspx?DOC_SNO=WP01-86&Page_ID=WP01&Yearly=97&PageFrom=0

Council of Indigenous Peoples. (2008c). *Indigenous principals, qualified teachers, and supply teachers in indigenous key areas (2007)*. Retrieved Feb, 9, 2011, from http://cip.cpc.org.tw/index.aspx?DOC_SNO=WP01-87&Page_ID=WP01& Yearly=97&PageFrom=0

CouncilofIndigenousPeoples.(2009a).*ThepopulationofindigenouspeopleinJuly,2009*. Retrieved from http://www.apc.gov.tw/main/docDetail /detail_TCA.jsp?isSearch =&docid=PA000000003350&cateID=A000297&linkSelf=161& linkRoot=4& linkParent=49&url= (original site no longer active).

CouncilofIndigenousPeoples.(2009b).*ThetribesinTaiwan*.Retrievedfromhttp://www. apc.gov.tw/main/docDetail/detail_ethnic.jsp?cateID=A000427&linkSelf=147 &linkRoot=101 (original site no longer active).

Dadu, M. Z. (2008, November). *Employment of indigenous higher personnel and indigenous groups' development as a whole: Take the College of Indigenous Studies, NDHU as an example*. Paper presented at Affirmative Action and University Teacher Employment Conference, National Dong Hwa University, Hualien. Retrieved March 20, 2009, from http://www.cis.ndhu.edu.tw/zh/html/research_1.php

Government Information Office, Republic of China. (2006). *An overview of Taiwan indigenous groups*. Retrieved from http://www.gio.gov.tw/taiwan-website/5-gp/ culture/indigenous

Harrell, S. (1995). Civilizing projects and the reaction to them. In S. Harrell (Ed), *Cultural encounters on China's ethnic frontiers*(pp 3–36). Seattle: University of Washington Press.

Heber, R. W. (2003). Comparisons in aboriginal education: Taiwan and Canada. In J. Gifford & G. Zezulka-Mailloux (Eds.), *Culture and the state: Alternative interventions* (pp. 188–196). Retrieved from http://www.arts.ualberta.ca/cms/v_fou.htm

Hill, C., Soares, P., Mormina, M., Macaulay V., Clarke, Blumbach, D. P. B., et al. (2007). A mitochondrial stratigraphy for Island Southeast Asia. *American Journal of Human Genetics, 80*(1), 29–43.

Hsu, T. M. (2006). Jiaoyuyouxianqu dui tisheng ruoshizuqun jiaoyu de shijichengxiao pipan [The critique on the actual effect of EPA in promoting education for disadvantaged groups]. Xiandai Jiaoyu Luntan [Forum on Modern Education], 15, 433–441. Retrieved from http://search.nioerar.edu.tw/edu_paper/ data_image/g0000305/0n15/20061100/p0000433.pdf

Huang, Y. P. (2005). *A study on the discourses and practice of indigenous education policy in Taiwan: Perspective from multiculturalism.* Unpublished master's thesis, Department of Public Administration and Public Policy, National Chi Nan University, Taiwan.

Joint University Admission Committee. (2008). *Undergraduate programs with unfilled places.* Retrieved from http://www.uac.edu.tw/downloads.htm

Lin, L. Y. (2002). *The research of implementation of the Educational Priority Area Policy in Taitung elementary and junior high schools.* Unpublished master's thesis, National Taitung Teacher College, Taiwan.

Loa, I. S. (2009, July 27).Aborigines condemn CIP's Pingpu snub. Taipei Times, p. 4. Retrieved from http://www.taipeitimes.com/News/taiwan/archives/2009/06/27/2003447222

Ministry of Education, Republic of China (Taiwan). (2005). *Aboriginal education.* Retrieved from http://english.moe.gov.tw/ct.asp?xItem=7157&ctNode=510&mp=11

Ministry of Education, Republic of China (Taiwan). (2006). *MOE subsidy guideline for areas of educational priority.* Retrieved from http://english.moe.gov.tw/ct.asp?xItem=7155&ctNode= 510&mp=1

Mo, C. Y., & Chen, B. C. (1996). Yuanzhumin jiaoyu [Indigenous education]. Jiaogai Tongxun [Educational Reform Newsletter], 21, 13–17. Retrieved from http://www.sinica. edu.tw/info/edu-reform/farea8/j21/

Shih, C. F. (2009). *Who can decide who is an aboriginal?* Retrieved from http://faculty.ndhu.edu.tw/~cfshih/politics%20observation/newspaper/20090629.html

Shih, H. C. (2009, August 29). Yuanzhumin shenfen sheilai jueding? [Who can decide who is an aboriginal?] Retrieved from http://faculty.ndhu.edu.tw/~cfshih/politics%20observation/newspaper/20090629.html

Shih, J. F. (2008). *The implementation of "Education Priority Area (EPA)–Student's learning counseling" in the key elementary schools of the indigenous people in Taiwan area.* Unpublished master's thesis, Department of Educational Policy and Administration, National Chi Nan University, Taiwan.

Tan, K. D. (2002). *Taiwan yuanzhumin jiaoyu—cong feixu dao chongjian* [Indigenous education in Taiwan—Rebuilding from ruins]. Taipei: Shida Bookstore.

Teng, E. J. (2004). *Taiwan's imagined geography: Chinese colonial travel writing and pictures, 1683–1895.* Cambridge, MA: Harvard University Press.

Wu, T. T. (2007a). Bulaxiaoyuan yu yuanzhumin minzuxiaoyuan bijiao yanjiu chulun [The comparative study of Tribal College and College of Indigenous Studies]. In T. T. Wu (Ed.), *Taiwan yuanzhu minzu daolun* [The introduction of Taiwan indigenous peoples: Cultures and education] (pp. 21–33). Taipei: Wu Nan.

Wu, T. T. (Ed.). (2007b). *Taiwan yuanzhu minzu daolun* [The introduction of Taiwan indigenous peoples: Cultures and education]. Taipei: Wu Nan.

Wu, Y. J. (2002). *The comparative study of indigenous educational policies in Taiwan and Canada: A post-colonial perspective.* Unpublished master's thesis, Department of Comparative Education, National Chi Nan University, Taiwan.

15 Conclusion
Where Does Multicultural Education in Asian Countries Lead?

Tak Cheung Chan

As explained by the editors, the purpose of this book is to highlight the key educational conditions of specific minority populations in specific regions of Asia. The authors focus on providing a contextualized understanding of the educational issues of minority students. The major themes for discussion include government policies on the education of minority students in terms of retaining their native language, learning of new languages, cultural adaptation, parental involvement, and preparation for higher education, among other concerns. The disparity between government policies and the experiences of students in schools and educational outcomes is described, based on the research conducted by the authors.

In this concluding chapter, I highlight the major concerns of multicultural education in Asian Pacific regions as expressed by the book authors. In reviewing the outstanding findings of the research papers, I conducted a brief synthesis of their emerging themes and learned many invaluable lessons from their professional multicultural experiences. In the following sections, I summarize the multicultural education issues by country or region, and then illustrate lessons I learned in government policy and instructional strategy.

MAINLAND CHINA

The People's Republic of China's Regional Autonomy Law for Minority Nationalities, which was enacted in 1984, clearly stipulates that the state protects the lawful rights and interests of the minorities and upholds and develops any concerted effort towards equality, unity, and mutual assistance among all of China's minorities. However, in the same legislation, it also specifies that any act that undermines the unity of the minorities or instigates their secession is prohibited. Clearly, the policy of the Chinese government is established to offer assistance to minority groups, but it also sets the limit of assistance to minorities when national unity is challenged. As a result, educators give their own interpretations of the law within its restrictive range (Wang & Zhou, 2003). Therefore, teaching Han culture and practices in schools where a substantial number of students are minorities is common. Certainly, a significant gap exists between China's minority policy and its implementation practices. As pointed out by Zhenzhou Zhao, one of the authors, public education in China is a process of reproducing mainstream Han ideology and repressing minority culture, knowledge, and identity (Hansen, 1999). Although the government can be blamed for not thoroughly standing behind its minority policy, some minority families prefer to send their children to Han schools to learn the Han culture and Mandarin for better job opportunities in the future (Wan & Jun, 2008). In most of the schools minorities attend, minority students learn everyday things that are not reflective of their own culture; thus, they struggle between an imposed national identity and their ethnic identity (Postiglione, 2009).

JAPAN

The Japanese educational plan of internationalization (1983) helped increase the number of international students to 100,000 by 2003. A subsequent policy enacted in 2008 aims to increase the number of international students to 300,000 by 2020. In this new policy, efforts are encouraged to promote the acceptance of international students and at the same time to adopt a mechanism toward their residency and employment after graduation. The intent of the policy is clearly to recruit and retain outstanding international professionals to join the Japanese workforce to help in the development of the country. Japanese language instruction is mandatory. However, recent studies have indicated that most international students have limited opportunities to be involved in social activities with the local communities. This has immensely hindered the Japanese language learning experiences of international students. If the ultimate goal of internationalization is to recruit and retain these experts in Japan, then strategies should be developed to eliminate the classroom experience in the language instruction program and allow international students to learn through their social activities. Many immigrant children in Japan go to international schools that emphasize the practices of their native languages and culture. Much has to be done in international schools to promote socialization activities that allow immigrant children to be immersed in Japanese society. Japan's education policy on internationalization can be well implemented by creating more channels for social access (Sharkey & Layzer, 2000).

TAIWAN

Multicultural education issues in Taiwan are concentrated on the 14 indigenous minority tribes whose people are mostly socioeconomically disadvantaged and academically underachieved. Since the abolishment of Martial

Law in 1987, much has been done to improve the living conditions of the indigenous people, including the educational development of the younger generation. The enactment of the Indigenous People's Education Act and the development of the Five-Year Educational Reform Action Plan in 1998 solidified the specific student-centered strategies toward the improvement of indigenous education. Since then, the official curriculum of Taiwan schools has been changed to contain more frequent and favorable mentions of indigenous people, and indigenous language learning has been offered in most indigenous elementary and junior high schools. In recent years, Taiwan's indigenous educational policies have moved gradually from assimilation toward acculturation (Huang, 2005). The mainstream culture is considered the center, while the differences between Han and the indigenous people are recognized. Despite these advancements, indigenous children in Taiwan schools face such challenges as the shortage of well-qualified indigenous teachers, lack of unique teaching strategies for indigenous children, little family support for learning, and shortage of opportunities for exposure to their own culture. In reviewing the history of educational development of the indigenous people, much has been done to offer basic education to the youngsters. The movement away from assimilation is healthy and constructive toward respecting the identity of the indigenous people. However, creating an environment of multiculturalism and achieving its long-term goals in Taiwan will take some time (Bawnay, 2008).

SOUTH KOREA

In recent years, an increasing number of poor Korean fishermen and farmers have chosen to seek their spouses from neighboring Asian countries. As a result of these international marriages, many children with a Korean father and a non-Korean mother are attending schools in rural areas. The Korean Ministry of Education has assumed that these children are likely to be left behind in their Korean language development and academic learning because their immigrant mothers are not fluent in Korean and do not know Korean culture and practices to help their children learn at home. Thus, in May 2006, the Ministry of Education implemented a policy in support of developing plans to assist children of international marriages in schools. The plans include an after-school program for Korean language learning, Korean culture classes for non-Korean mothers, designating special teachers to communicate with these children, and a peer mentoring program to work on their socialization (Korean Ministry of Education and Human Resources Development, 2006). Moreover, plans have been made to add multicultural education contents in textbooks, multiculturalism and minority issues in teacher training programs, and cultural experience programs of the cultures of the foreign mothers (Korean Ministry of Education and Human Resources Development, 2007). Clearly, the policy intends to promote ethnic homogeneity in Korean society while understanding the multicultural elements in the Korean society. This point of view is not shared by all the teachers who have experiences working with children of international marriages. Some teachers argue that children of international marriages do not have problems in learning the Korean language and other academic subjects in school and that the non-Korean background of their mothers does not have any negative effect on their learning. The teachers feel that these children do not need to be educated differently from other Korean children. Apparently, the South Korean Ministry of Education is doing its best to offer assistance to children of international marriages. The focus is on helping these children merge into the mainstream Korean culture and become successful in school. Understanding the language and culture of their mothers is only secondary.

HONG KONG

For years, minority issues were not the priority of the Hong Kong government because minorities represent less than 5% of the total population. However, after Hong Kong became a special administrative region of China, many mainland Chinese moved to Hong Kong. A Racial Discrimination Ordinance was initiated to protect minorities from exploitation in a majority-centered society. At the same time, the Education and Manpower Bureau started programs to help new immigrants in adopting the language. Various support schemes and resources were also offered to improve the learning opportunities for ethnic minority students. However, government officials have been reluctant to meet the full demands and needs of immigrant students (Hong Kong Education Bureau, 2008). The rapid increase in the number of students from mainland China took the unprepared teachers by surprise. The teachers tried their best to adjust their teaching strategies to facilitate the academic needs of immigrant students, establish partnerships with their parents, and help students raise their aspirations on their education and career. The results of their efforts show that, with close teacher–student relationships, students can achieve more (Lam, 2005). Many of them seem to adapt well with the new academic setting except for their continued struggle with the language. Their parents have not been active with regard to their educational involvement because of the parents' perception of social discriminating environments. Teachers, counselors, and school administrators need to be better prepared to work with families of minority students to ensure that schools and families are on the same page in terms of developing the talents of minority students (Yuen, 2004).

LESSONS LEARNED

The previous chapters of this resourceful book have presented the valuable experiences of educators from different Asian countries and regions in working with students with multicultural backgrounds. The authors have been open and honest in sharing what they thought and what they found in their academic studies on multicultural education. The success stories and challenging difficulties they encountered provide learning opportunities for scholars and practitioners in the field of multicultural education.

Lessons Learned from the Policy Perspective

First, multicultural education policies established with good intent may not necessarily reflect the wishes of the people. Retaining the identity, culture, and language of immigrants while they learn the culture and language of the host country has been believed to be the way to go. However, many immigrant families think differently. When they decide to make their permanent homes in the host country, they prefer their younger generation to receive an education that will not only help them adapt to the new society but also equip them with competencies to compete in the job market in the future. It is thus easy to understand why their first priority in their children's education is to make sure that they learn the culture and language of the host country. Learning their native culture and language is considered a secondary priority.

Second, the original assumptions on which the development of multicultural education policies is based may be wrong. Immigrant children are assumed to have problems in learning the language and culture of the host country and thus have difficulty in catching up with their schoolwork. The assumption does not always hold true. It all depends on the children and their family background in their home countries. Evidence shows that many immigrant children of Asian countries are among the top students in their class in their host countries.

Third, the multicultural education policies of a country are not always in tune with the ideologies of its educators nor are they supported by informed research. Many educational policies have been established by voting in the legislative bodies of the countries. In many cases, educators are not even involved in the policy development process. This creates problems in the implementation of the policies carried out by the teachers. In some cases reported in Asia, classroom instructional processes do not always reflect what the multicultural education policies dictate.

Fourth, for a multicultural education policy to be effective, it needs to be a solid mandatory piece of legislation with specific references to multiculturalism. Some Asian countries that face minority issues have created legislation to address anti-discrimination situations that could develop into serious social unrest. Policies like these have more political value than educational value. These policies are subject to interpretation by educators who are asked to implement the policies. Only multicultural education policies with a specific mandate and required support can be effectively implemented.

Fifth, multicultural education policies may be written differently to address different multicultural situations. As discussed in earlier chapters in this book, multicultural education issues in China and Taiwan center on working with minority groups within the country, whereas in Japan, the focus of the policy is on international students who have potential to seek permanent residency in Japan. The problems in South Korea and Hong Kong are unique. An educational policy to help Korean children whose mothers are non-Koreans is quite challenging. In Hong Kong, policymakers have to work on the best way to help children from mainland China who are Chinese but are brought up in a different culture. Policies have to be developed to address the specific needs of the types of ethnic minority or immigrant children.

Lessons Learned on Instructional Strategies

First, social activities play an important role in learning a new language. The cases cited in Japan and South Korea show that schools and learners need to work together to seek suitable social settings where language learners can feel comfortable in learning the new language through meaningful social functions. Learning a new language within the confines of the four walls of the classroom cannot match daily practice and application.

Second, effective language learning takes place among peer learners of the same cohort and the host country (Vygotsky, 1962). Learning a new language is similar to learning in other disciplines. No matter how well a teacher plans his or her instructional activities, there are always instances when peer learners can enlighten one another better than the teacher. New language learners enjoy the company of peer learners. They are also willing to accept the challenge of being in class with a majority of native speakers. Exposure to peer experiences contributes to effective language learning.

Third, the school and family connection bridges the gap for effective language learning. In learning the language of the host country, immigrant children receive instruction from teachers in school. Family support can enhance learning effectiveness. The family can reinforce learning in school by encouraging children's language practice, monitoring their training exercises, and creating fun situations for language exercises. In many cases, schools can initiate language games for the entire family to learn the new language together. Some parents of immigrant families are not proficient in the use of the host country's language. Although they may not be able to work with their children in some of the language exercises at home, parents should give encouragement to their children in mastering the language of their host country.

CONCLUSION

When young immigrants become permanent residents of a country, the host country has the responsibility of offering them opportunities for adequate education and of preparing them for their life-long stay in the country. A program to teach the language and culture of the host country should only be the minimum. A further step is to help the immigrant families adapt to the language and culture of the new country. A close relationship between the school and the family results in improved student achievement. Educators from elementary schools, secondary schools, and institutions of higher learning need to work together to develop multiple practical programs to help immigrant children in school. School teachers and administrators also need to be trained to be able to offer their best educational service to immigrant children. To substantiate these meaningful initiatives, relevant policies should be established with appropriate funding for implementation. Governments need to be clear in their mindset that immigrants are assets, not liabilities, to the country. Dollars spent in multicultural education are not expenditures but long-term investments for the future of the country. In the same vein, promoting the cultural identities of the home countries of the immigrants is a means of enriching the quality of life of the country in the future. As Banks (2001) stated, only through a healthy sense of cultural identity can a person have a strong desire to function effectively in two cultures. Due to the broadening of international cooperation, the number of immigrants in Asian countries will continue to increase. Governments of Asian countries should consider this as unique opportunity to absorb the best quality of human capital. Spending in multicultural education is the most rewarding investment for the growth of talents as represented by immigrant children.

REFERENCES

Banks, J. A. (2001). *Cultural diversity and education: Foundations, curriculum, and teaching.* Boston: Allyn & Bacon.

Bawnay, P. (2008). *The indigenous peoples' right to education: Theories and practices.* Unpublished master's thesis, Graduate Institute of the Taiwanese Ethnodevelopment, National Dong Hwa University, Taiwan.

Hansen, M. H. (1999). *Lessons in being Chinese: Minority education and ethnic identity in Southwest China.* Seattle: University of Washington Press.

Hong Kong Education Bureau. (2008). *Education and support services for newly arrived children.* Retrieved July 30, 2010, from http://www.edb.gov.hk/index. aspx?nodeid=636&langno=1

Huang, Y. P. (2005). *A study on the discourses and practice of indigenous education policy in Taiwan: Perspective from multiculturalism.* Unpublished master's thesis, Department of Public Administration and Public Policy, National Chi Nan University, Taiwan.

Korean Ministry of Education and Human Resources Development. (2006). *Educational support for children from multicultural backgrounds.* Retrieved July 20, 2010, from http://english.moe.go.kr/main.jsp?idx=030101&brd_mainno=253&mode=v

Korean Ministry of Education and Human Resources Development. (2007). *The support to multicultural families.* Seoul, South Korea: Author.

Lam, C. M. (2005). The situation and needs of cross-border students and families. In C. Y. M. Yuen (Ed.), *Border-crossing education and parent support services: A review* (pp. 9–13). Hong Kong: Christian Action.

Postiglione, G. A. (2009). The education of ethnic minority groups in China. In J. A. Banks (Ed.), *The Routledge international companion to multicultural education* (pp. 501–511). New York: Routledge.

Sharkey, J., & Layzer, C. (2000). Whose definition of success? Identifying factors that affect English language learners' access to academic success and resources. *TESOL Quarterly, 34*(2), 352–368.

Vygotsky, L. S. (1962). *Thought and language.* Cambridge, MA: MIT Press.

Wan, G., & Jun, Y. (2008). How China best educates its ethnic minority children: Strategies, experience and challenges. In G. Wan (Ed.), *The education of diverse student populations* (pp. 139–158). Athens, OH: Springer.

Wang, C., & Zhou, Q. (2003). Minority education in China: From state's preferential policies to dislocated Tibetan Schools. *Educational Studies, 29*(1), 85–104.

Yuen, C. Y. (2004). The early experience of intercultural teacher education in Hong Kong. *Intercultural Education, 15*(2), 151–166.

Contributors

Tak Cheung Chan, Professor of Education Leadership at Kennesaw State University, is a former school teacher and administrator in the Hong Kong School System, Greenville County School District in South Carolina, Cobb County Public Schools, and Gwennett County Public Schools in Georgia. He also served as an Assistant Professor of Educational Leadership at Valdosta State University and as an Associate Professor of Educational Leadership at Georgia Southern University. His areas of academic interest include educational planning, school facilities planning, school business management, and international education.

Dorothy I-ru Chen is an Associate Professor in the Department of Comparative Education at the National Chi Nan University, Taiwan. Her research interests are on gender education, higher education, and educational leadership. She has published a series of papers related to the work experiences of female academics in universities as well as in higher education reform both in Taiwan and the United Kingdom. Her recent research projects are related to undergraduates in science and technology and the experiences of research students in Taiwan. She has been a member of the Curriculum and Instruction Consulting Committee: Gender Equity Education, Ministry of Education in Taiwan since 2009.

Stella Chong is an Associate Professor at the Department of Educational Psychology, Counseling, and Learning Needs of the Hong Kong Institute of Education. Her research interests are multicultural education, special education, and teacher education. Her current research is on students with emotional and behavioral challenges in mainstream schools for the lower academic achievers. Her most recent publications include the following: "What Works for Teachers of Students with Emotional and Behavioral Difficulties in Hong Kong's Special Schools," *International Journal on School Disaffection* (2008); "The Influence of an Inclusive Education Course on the Attitude of Pre-service Secondary Teachers in Hong Kong," *Asia-Pacific Journal of Teacher Education* (2007); "Critical Issues in Diversity and Schooling within Asia," in S. Phillipson (Ed.), *Learning*

Diversity in the Chinese Classroom: Challenges and Practice (2007); and "The Logic of Hong Kong Teachers: An Exploratory Study of Their Teaching Culturally Diverse Students," *Teaching Education* (2005).

Betty C. Eng is an Assistant Professor in the Department of Applied Social Studies at the City University of Hong Kong. Previously, she was a teacher for over 10 years at the Hong Kong Institute of Education, a major education institute that provides pre-service and in-service training for teachers. Betty was a counselor at an international school in Hong Kong and in universities in the United States, where she focused on the diverse learning needs of students. Prior to living in Hong Kong, she was a faculty member at the University of California and California State University in the departments of Asian American Studies, Women's Studies, and Counseling and Education. Her research fields include teacher knowledge, narrative inquiry, counseling, cross-culture studies, and inclusive education. She obtained her Ed.D. from the Ontario Institute of Studies for Education at the University of Toronto. Her doctoral research explored teacher knowledge through personal narratives of identity, culture, and sense of belonging.

Ming Tak Hue obtained his M.Ed. from the University of Bristol and his Ph.D. from the Institute of Education, the University of London. He is currently an Associate Professor in the Department of Special Education and Counseling at the Hong Kong Institute of Education. He teaches graduate courses on self and personal growth, school guidance and counseling, classroom management, behavior management, and inclusive education. He research interests include pastoral care, liberal studies curriculum, whole-person growth of students, support of non-Chinese students, and development of school-based guidance and discipline programs. His recent publications include "Emergence of Confucianism: Narrative Study of Hong Kong Teachers' Experience of School Guidance" (2008); "Cross-Cultural Experience of Immigrant Students from Mainland China in Hong Kong's Secondary Schools" (2008); and "Independent Enquiry Study Skills for Liberal Studies" (2009).

Kerry J. Kennedy is Chair Professor of Curriculum Studies at the Hong Kong Institute of Education, where he also holds the positions of Dean, Faculty of Education Studies, and Associate Vice President (Quality Assurance). He is the author of *Changing Schools for Changing Times— New Directions for the School Curriculum in Hong Kong* (Chinese University Press, 2005). He co-authored *The Changing Role of Schools in Asian Societies—Schools for the Knowledge Society* (Routledge, 2008), *Curriculum Construction* (3rd ed.) (Pearson Education Australia, 2007), and *Celebrating Student Achievement—Assessment and Reporting* (3rd ed.) (Pearson Education, 2008).

Jungmin Lee is currently an Assistant Professor at Sangmyung University, Seoul, South Korea. She graduated from Purdue University, Indiana, with a Ph.D. in 2008. She was a Research Professor at Korea University, Seoul, South Korea, in 2009. She earned her B.A. from Korea University, with a major in Education and a minor in Sociology. She also has a secondary-level teaching license for Social Studies and Education in Korea. She received her master's degree in Education from Korea University. For her master's degree, she conducted research on the Korean national curriculum. Before she came to the US, she taught educational courses in colleges as a visiting lecturer and worked at the Korea Institute of Curriculum and Evaluation (KICE) as an assistant researcher. Her current research is on multicultural education in South Korea, specifically focusing on educational policy created by the recent increase in international marriages and foreign migrant workers that has resulted in diversity in Korean schools. She has examined school practices and teachers' experiences and perspectives in working with these diverse students.

JoAnn Phillion is a Professor in the Department of Curriculum and Instruction at Purdue University, Indiana. Her research interests are narrative inquiry in immigrant student education, multicultural education, and teacher education. She has published extensively on her long-term narrative inquiry into an inner-city Canadian school. Her recent research is on the experiences of minority students in Hong Kong schools and the understanding of pre-service teachers of diversity issues in an international field experience. She directs a study-abroad program in Honduras. She authored *Narrative Inquiry in a Multicultural Landscape: Multicultural Teaching and Learning* (Ablex, 2002). She co-edited *Narrative and Experience in Multicultural Education* (Sage, 2005) with Ming Fang He and Michael Connelly and *Research for Social Justice* (Information Age, 2008) with Ming Fang He. She is also the Associate Editor of the *Handbook of Curriculum and Instruction* (Sage, 2008) along with Michael Connelly and Ming Fang He.

Ying Sun is a Ph.D. candidate from Northeast Normal University in China. She was a visiting scholar in the Department of Curriculum and Instruction at Purdue University in the U.S. Her research interests are multicultural education, teacher's education, and comparative education. She published the article "Reflection on the Problems in Boarding School Education" (2007), co-published (with Wei Yu) the article "A Probe into the Implementation Puzzledom of *No Child Left Behind Act* and Its Reason" (2008), and co-published (with Haibin Niu) the article "A Report on the Education and Training for Farmers in Liaoning and Jilin Provinces" (2008).

Zhiyan Teng is an Associate Professor at the Research Center for the Educational Development of Minorities at the Northwest Normal University in China. Her research interests include comparative education and minority nationality education. She has written many articles in this field. She also studied the relationship between religion and education. She is currently participating in a program on the comparative research between Chinese minority nationality education and American multicultural education.

Tae Umino received her Ph.D. from the Institute of Education, University of London. She is an Associate Professor at the Department of Japanese Studies, Tokyo University of Foreign Studies, Japan. Her responsibilities include teaching Japanese (to international students), pre-service teacher training in language pedagogy, and supervision of Ph.D. dissertations in Japanese applied linguistics. She is currently a core member of the Global COE project "Corpus-Based Linguistics and Language Education." Her research interests include second language acquisition (of Japanese) from social-participatory learning perspectives and narrative inquiry in language learning and education. She recently published chapters in *Learners' Stories: Difference and Diversity in Language Learning* (Cambridge University Press, 2005), edited by Phil Benson and David Nunan, and in *Applied Linguistics and Language Teaching in Japan* (Hitsuji Shobo, 2008), edited by Kumiko Murata and Tetsuo Harada. She co-edited *Readings in Second Language Pedagogy and Second Language Acquisition: In Japanese Context* (John Benjamins, 2006) with Asako Yoshitomi and Masashi Negishi.

Yuxiang Wang received his Ph.D. from Purdue University, Indiana, in 2010. He is an International Student Experience Advisor in the School of Engineering Education at Purdue University. Prior to coming to the US, he was Associate Professor at Anhui University in China, where he conducted research and published articles in the area of language and culture. His research interests are multicultural education, teacher education, and curriculum theory. He uses narrative inquiry in exploring cultural recognition and identity construction of Hui minority students in eastern China. He has published articles in the *Journal of Educational Foundations* (2007), *Multicultural Education* (2009), *International Journal of Multicultural Education* (2009), and *Frontiers: The Interdisciplinary Journal of Study Abroad* (2009). He co-authored a chapter in *Global Issues in Education: Pedagogy, Policy, School Practices, and the Minority Experience*, edited by G. Wiggan and C. Hutchison, published by the University Press of America (2009).

Yuhua Ye studied at the School of Education Science in Northeast Normal University from 2005 to 2009. Her research interests are on the theory of education and rural education. As a minority, she especially focuses on education for minority girls.

Wei Yu is a Professor in the School of Education Science at Northeast Normal University, China. His research interests are the philosophy of education, rural education, and teacher education. He has published extensively in his field.

Celeste Y. M. Yuen is an Associate Professor in the Department of Educational Policy and Leadership, Hong Kong Institute of Education, Hong Kong, China. Her research interests include Chinese immigrants and cross-boundary students in Hong Kong, ethnic education, comparative education and intercultural teacher education, special and inclusive education, and curricular issues. For some years, she has been engaged in intercultural education research, especially on newly arrived students from mainland China. She also taught an optional module, *Educating Newly Arrived Students*. She is the principal investigator in several projects studying Chinese immigrants and cross-boundary students, and she has published several books in Chinese, as well as papers in both English and Chinese. Recently, she was awarded a research grant on a school-based support scheme for cross-boundary and immigrant children in Hong Kong, and a special grant for a comparative case study on immigrant and cross-boundary students in Hong Kong and Northern Ireland. She is also the principal investigator of a consultancy study on pedagogical strategies—a study commissioned by the Education Bureau to enhance learning effectiveness in small class settings.

Zhenzhou Zhao is currently a Post-Doctoral Fellow at the Centre for Governance and Citizenship, Hong Kong Institute of Education. She worked as an Assistant Professor of Education at Beijing Normal University before joining the institute. Her research interests include social development in education, civic and moral education, and ethnic and women's studies. She received her bachelor's degree from the Beijing Normal University (2002) and her Ph.D. from the University of Hong Kong (2006). She is the author of *China's Mongols at University: Contesting Cultural Recognition* (Lexington Press, 2010). Her articles have appeared in such journals as *Gender and Education*, *Cambridge Journal of Education*, *Discourse: Studies in the Cultural Politics of Education*, *Asian Ethnicity*, and *Chinese Education and Society*.

Zhiyong Zhu obtained his Ph.D. in Sociology of Education from the University of Hong Kong. He is now an Associate Professor in the College of Educational Administration at Beijing Normal University. He was awarded the prestigious Fulbright New Century Scholarship from the US Department of State (2007–2008). His research interests include the sociology of education in ethnic minority education, rural education, school management, and social development. He published *State Schooling and Ethnic Identity: The Politics of a Tibetan Neidi Secondary School* *in China* (Lexington Books, 2007) and co-edited *Social Development and Change: Theory and Practice* with Huifang Yu. He also translated Jeanne H. Ballantine's *The Sociology of Education: A Systematic Analysis* into Chinese in 2005 and is currently translating Patricia J. Gumport's *Sociology of Higher Education: Contributions and Contexts*. He is an advisory committee member of the journal *Chinese Education and Society*. He will be a visiting scholar at the School of Education at Stanford University in 2011–2012.

Index